TOUGH CALLS

AT&T and the Hard Lessons Learned
from the Telecom Wars

Dick Martin

AMACOM   AMERICAN MANAGEMENT ASSOCIATION
NEW YORK · ATLANTA · BRUSSELS · CHICAGO · MEXICO CITY
SAN FRANCISCO · SHANGHAI · TOKYO · TORONTO · WASHINGTON, D.C.

Special discounts on bulk quantities of AMACOM books are available to corporations, professional associations, and other organizations. For details, contact Special Sales Department, AMACOM, a division of American Management Association, 1601 Broadway, New York, NY 10019.
Tel.: 212-903-8316. Fax: 212-903-8083.
Web site: www.amacombooks.org

Library of Congress Cataloging-in-Publication Data

Martin, Dick, 1946–
    Tough calls : AT&T and the hard lessons learned from the telecom wars / Dick Martin.
        p. cm.
    Includes bibliographical references and index.
    ISBN 0-8144-7243-5
    1. AT & T—History. 2. Telecommunication—United States—History. I. Title.

HE8846.A55M37 2005
384'.06573—dc22

                                                                2004018451

Printing number

10 9 8 7 6 5 4 3 2 1

To my wife and partner, Ginny.
She makes liars of those
who say beauty is only skin deep.

Contents

Acknowledgments

Parts of this book have appeared in somewhat different form in the *Harvard Business Review*, *The Public Relations Strategist* of the Public Relations Society of America, and *The PR Encyclopedia*, scheduled to be released by Sage Publications in 2004.

Several of my former AT&T colleagues, especially Sue Fleming, Sheldon Hochheiser, and Bruce Brackett, searched their files and memories to help me keep dates, names, and events straight. Pat Pollino, who started at Western Electric with me several decades ago and today holds an impressive position at Mercer Management, provided the outside enthusiasm that I needed in order to get serious about this project. Most importantly, he introduced me to Paul Hemp at the *Harvard Business Review*, who convinced his colleagues that a PR guy from AT&T, of all places, might have something interesting to say— and then saw to it that I delivered the goods.

Paul and his colleague Andy O'Connell taught me the value of good editors. Ellen Kadin, at AMACOM, picked up where they left off, patiently helping me shape a book that would appeal to a broader audience than I first thought.

Several friends offered constructive comments and suggestions as I developed my manuscript. Ed Block provided the perspective of his own career directing public relations for AT&T. Gershon Kekst, one of the wisest PR counselors practicing today, helped me calculate the true meaning of my experience. Michele Tringali, who once handled public relations for AT&T's consumer long-distance business, helped me to better understand its intricacies and dynamics. Adele Ambrose and Burt Wolder helped me reinterpret several of the more significant experiences we shared.

Molly Dowd and Magda Guillen of Kekst and Company were particularly insightful "civilian" reviewers of the first draft and offered many helpful comments and suggestions. Jack Johnson gave me the benefit of his experience in both the legal and investment banking professions and proved to be a sharp-eyed editor in addition. Andy Black provided some of the financial analysis. Al Solecki, my attorney and friend, kept me on the right side of my responsibilities to my former employer as well as to my new readers. John Keller, who is no longer a working journalist, was generous with his time and thoughts, as were several current journalists and former colleagues who, for their own reasons, prefer to remain anonymous.

Mike Armstrong played no role in the writing of this book, although he saw a draft. He disagrees with my interpretation of some events and with many of my conclusions. But I must acknowledge his role in this story. I discuss his mistakes as well as my own in these pages. But no one should overlook the fact that he took on one of the greatest challenges in American business at a time in his life when he could have coasted into retirement in the glow of decades of achievement at IBM and Hughes Electronics.

Armstrong served his new company with integrity and courage. The same cannot be said of all the people upon whom he depended. I believe history will show that he had the right plan for AT&T and that, while some of the deals he approved were "fully priced," or badly structured, he might still have recovered if the company's biggest competitor had not engaged in three and a half years of fraud that distorted the markets and robbed him of the one thing he needed most: time.

Finally, I never would have finished this book were it not for the encouragement, patience, and prodding of my wife, Ginny, and my children, Christopher, Elizabeth, and Juli, as well as my daughter-in-law, Laura, and my cousin Marcel, all of whom gave me the courage to approach this story with candor and a degree of introspection that does not come naturally to me. My grandson, Sky, arrived around the same time as the first draft, so he has only had excerpts read to him. But I hope that someday this book will give him an idea of what "Gramps" was up to in the decade before he was born.

TOUGH CALLS

Introduction

*History is not what happened
but what is remembered of it.*

—ALVIN VON AUW, *Heritage and Destiny*[1]

Gilded and Gelded

A golden statue of a winged youth, brandishing lightning bolts and draped in telephone cables, once perched on the roof of the old AT&T headquarters at 195 Broadway in lower Manhattan.[2] When AT&T decided to move uptown in the early 1980s, it lowered the statue, popularly called "Golden Boy," in order to place it in the lobby of the company's new headquarters on Madison Avenue.

No one was surprised that after being exposed to the elements for sixty-four years, Golden Boy needed to be regilded. But AT&T's chairman at the time, a courtly southerner named John deButts, was shocked to discover that the twenty-four-foot-tall statue was also anatomically correct—and of heroic proportions. Concerned that the statue would scandalize genteel Madison Avenue shoppers, deButts was said to have decreed that it be not only gilded, but also gelded.

Apocryphal or not, Golden Boy's gilding and gelding became a metaphor for AT&T's embattled history in the last decades of the twentieth century and a cautionary symbol for all companies in an era in which perception has become the hyper-reality within which they do business. While a rah-rah brother- and sisterhood of stock boosters and image consultants work to gild a company's image, guerrilla bands of special-interest groups and the business media geld them with countless little cuts. No wonder corporate America feels that it is under siege. CEOs, boards, and their advisers vacillate between the instincts of fight and flight. They don't know whether to jump on a soapbox and fight back or to hunker down in the hope that they won't be noticed.

In recent years, AT&T has been buffeted by these opposing forces as were few other companies. A widely admired icon of American business for more than a century, the company made some strategic blunders and couldn't seem to get its management act together. All of this was reported in gory detail. AT&T looked like the gang that couldn't shoot straight—unless it was to take a bead on its own foot.

Perception matters. Just ask the New York Stock Exchange's former CEO, Dick Grasso. In a matter of months, he went from the personification of corporate courage and resilience, following the September 11 attacks on the World Trade Center, to Exhibit A of unbridled corporate greed.[3] Even retired GE chairman Jack Welch discovered how quickly public sentiment could turn—even though he increased his company's market value more than 3,600 percent.[4]

Imagine, however, that you were unlucky enough to take the most visible job in an industry that was inexorably melting away, your biggest competitor felt free to slash prices because it was making up its financial results as it went along, and you had to do whatever you were going to do in five years or less. That's the situation that my former boss, Mike Armstrong, parachuted into in 1997. In a sense, this book is his story. But it's also the story of his predecessor, Bob Allen, although neither man would tell the tale quite this way. And its roots go even deeper in the company's history, through a series of crossroads that, as it turned out, led only into swamps and dead ends.

AT&T at the Crossroads

For most of the twentieth century, AT&T was literally "the phone company." It provided telephone service to 90 percent of the country's population as a regulated monopoly. In 1982, AT&T agreed to divest its local telephone companies, breaking up what was known as the Bell System, to settle a federal antitrust suit and to pave the way to resolving a slew of suits filed by competitors. In a sign of the direction that life was taking, in that same week, the government dropped a similar antitrust suit against IBM, and *Time* magazine named the personal computer its "Man of the Year." Telephony was yesterday's business.

The breakup was predicated on the idea that local telephone service was a natural monopoly, like water utilities, but long-distance service and equipment sales operated in competitive markets. The local Bell monopolies would continue to provide a dial tone, serving all long-distance carriers equally; consumers and businesses could buy equipment from anybody they chose and plug it into the telephone network, just as they could plug a lamp into the electrical grid; and AT&T, MCI, Sprint, and a host of smaller players would knock themselves out competing for people's long-distance business.[5]

Of course, the idea that these so-called monopoly and competitive market segments would remain forever separate was seriously flawed, as was AT&T's belief that, having shed two-thirds of its assets, 70 percent of its employees, and more than half its revenue, regulators would leave it alone to compete on an equal footing. Both federal and state regulators, who had not been party to the settlement, continued to overestimate AT&T's capacity to absorb pain, subjecting it to unique filing requirements and subsidizing its competitors in the name of protecting "infant industries." The judge supervising the breakup, Harold Greene, had no sooner gaveled the case to a close than the Bell monopolies petitioned to enter the long-distance business.

When Greene proved less than enthusiastic about letting monopolists into a business that already counted more than 500 competitors, the Bell companies went over his head and took their case to Capitol Hill. Because the breakup had been wildly unpopular with the public—which, though it liked the lower prices and innovation that the breakup spurred, hated the confusion of dealing with multiple companies and the irritation of telemarketing calls during dinner—the Bell companies found sympathetic ears inside the Beltway. Besides, the only thing Congress loves more than a complicated issue with rich proponents on both sides is stringing such an issue out over several legislative sessions and, especially, elections.

By 1994, AT&T's general counsel, John Zeglis, decided that the Bells were gaining the upper hand. Zeglis, a magna cum laude graduate of Harvard Law who was still boyish-looking well into his thirties, had helped try the 1974 antitrust case as one of the youngest partners in the history of the venerable Sidley & Austin law firm, AT&T's outside litigation counsel.

Zeglis moved to AT&T after the suit was settled and swiftly became the company's general counsel, overseeing its law department and government affairs. Few outsiders understood the nuts and bolts of the telephone business better—he had literally studied engineering diagrams of the telephone network in his trial preparation. He absorbed the intricacies of arcane regulatory accounting with the relish of the champion Trivial Pursuit player he is. And he approached debate with all the enthusiasm of the brightest kid in the class. As the ultimate gamesman, he calculated that it was time for AT&T to stand *for* something and not simply be *against* anything that the Bell companies proposed. (No one knew how much longer Greene—then seventy years old—would be on the bench, and the company's opposition to any kind of telecom reform legislation had begun to sound shrill and whiny.) AT&T would be *for* getting back into the local phone business it had forced to leave when the Bell System was dissolved. And once it was in local telephone service, AT&T had no objection to letting the Bell companies into long distance. But not before.

AT&T's chairman at the time, Bob Allen, was decidedly skeptical about the whole idea of getting back into the local phone business. Among the top officers of AT&T in the mid-1990s, he alone had actually run a local telephone company. He knew how complicated it was, and he also knew that its profitability depended on cross-subsidies that would never survive in a competitive market. But as a tactic for postponing the inevitable, he was willing to argue for breaking the Bells' bottleneck on local service. So Zeglis and his lobbyists managed to turn the Bells' efforts to win permission to offer long-distance service into a legislated checklist of the conditions that they would first have to meet by opening their local markets to competition. The result was one of the most litigated laws ever passed by Congress—the Telecommunications Act of 1996.

AT&T in the Crosshairs

As those of us within AT&T understood only too well, the Telecom Act was a death sentence for stand-alone long distance, which accounted for 80 percent of AT&T's revenue and 100 percent of its profits (and then some, making up for losses in other areas). AT&T was living on borrowed time. While the Bells challenged the Telecom Act in court, effectively keeping AT&T out of their local markets, they pressed for further legislation to let them into long distance. And everyone knew that the Bells would eventually wear the regulators down and join the long-distance fray.

Thanks to Allen's 1996 divestiture of AT&T's equipment businesses, the company had the strongest balance sheet in the industry, with relatively little debt. Profits, for the moment, were at record levels.[6] But the crossroads through which the company had maneuvered put it in the crosshairs of competitors from the so-called New Economy, whose stock prices seemed untethered to anything as mundane as profits or even cash flow.

AT&T's serial efforts to diversify internationally and into new lines of business, on the other hand, were constrained by investors' fixation on growth in the company's earnings per share. New services, like the company's award-winning WorldNet Internet service, had their budgets cut so that the company could meet its earnings targets. One executive called it "the Grown Man Syndrome." We were like grown men in a sealed room with a dwindling air supply, he said. At some point, to save ourselves, we'd pinch a baby's nose.

Shaken by the storm clouds he saw forming, Allen's heir apparent, AT&T president Alex Mandl, jumped ship to join a start-up. The printing company executive hired to replace him, R. R. Donnelly's John Walter, was such an unlikely choice that he was dubbed "heir *un*apparent"[7] and was pushed out within nine months, costing AT&T about $25 million in severance payments. Embarrassed, the AT&T board of directors eased Allen aside and started looking for his successor. After a highly publicized three-month search, they settled on the man who many thought should have had the job the first time around.

C. Michael Armstrong arrived with sterling credentials, high-wattage energy, no entourage, and, at least initially, only the most basic play in the turnaround playbook—slash costs. Finding a longer-term fix for the company's broken business model would take more time. Implementing it would probably take longer than the five years on his contract.

All that we in public relations could hope to do was to give him time and space as he tried to reinvent the company and guide it toward a healthy future. We faced a classic public relations dilemma. We needed to convince employees, customers, the media, and Wall Street that the company, which was famous for being slow to change, was indeed changing—and fast. At the same time, in order to give the CEO a long enough runway to achieve strategic "lift," we needed to keep a low profile and avoid raising unrealistic short-term expectations. We managed the first task fairly well; unfortunately, it was at the expense of the second. And that was only one of our mistakes.

Why I Wrote This Book

Someone once said that experience comes from what you do; wisdom, from what you do badly. On that basis alone, I can share hard-won lessons in managing public relations for AT&T during one of the most tumultuous periods in its history. Even if I never made the same mistake twice, I still have enough mistakes to fill a book.

Daniel Kahneman, who won the 2002 Nobel Prize in Economics for path-breaking work in decision making, once said, "If I had one wish, it is to see organizations dedicating some effort to study their own decision processes and their own mistakes, and to keep track so as to learn from those mistakes."[8] I've tried hard in these pages to tell an unvarnished story without getting lost in the plumbing of an exceptionally complicated industry and company.

This book is titled *Tough Calls* because none of the choices that AT&T made during this period were obvious, except in hindsight. The same might be said of the calls made by the small army of AT&T watchers who kept track of the company's moves. The period following the passage of the Telecom Act of 1996 was exuberant, chaotic, and, in many ways, ineffable. Looking back, it's amazing how much we all got wrong, whether we were business leaders, professional investors, or the media.

This book focuses on mistakes, but it would be wrong to ignore what AT&T and its critics got right. AT&T's critics were correct in calling for more active board engagement in the company's succession planning. They were also correct in questioning some of the company's acquisitions (though not always for the right reason).

On the other hand, Bob Allen has seldom been credited with one of the most successful corporate acquisitions of the 1990s: AT&T's purchase of McCaw Cellular. Nor does he get much credit for restructuring the company at the precise moment when this would most benefit its equipment manufacturing business, putting that business under an exceptional CEO in the person of Henry Schacht and leaving AT&T with one of the strongest balance sheets in the industry.

Mike Armstrong, for his part, made a string of small acquisitions that expanded AT&T's wireless and data businesses. He built a $4 billion outsourcing business from scratch in less than four years. He cashed out of the wireless business at the precise top of the market. He reversed decades of revenue declines in his first two full years at AT&T, and, in fact, it was in the midst of his third year that MCI

WorldCom apparently resorted to accounting tricks to maintain the illusion of competitiveness. When Armstrong saw the industry turn, he was forthright in correcting his earlier forecast, while his competitors continued to trumpet financial results that they were manufacturing in their accounting departments. With all that, he delivered the earnings he projected in eighteen of the twenty quarters he led the company, even in the midst of an industry meltdown in 2001 and 2002.

Tough Calls

Of course, every CEO makes tough calls. As we shall see, Allen's and Armstrong's were made more difficult because the two men were sometimes caught in a web of outsized expectations, internal political games, and industry fraud. And the fog of war is not limited to the battlefield. Most major business decisions are made in a similar crucible of fast-changing, fragmentary, and conflicting data. Business decision makers are often just as torn between the success of their mission and the welfare of their troops. They suffer the same self-doubt, wishful thinking, and fear of failure. Their lieutenants are sometimes competent, sometimes conniving, and never completely transparent. If lives are seldom at stake in their decisions, the *quality* of lives certainly is, along with the prosperity of countless families and communities.

I've tried to capture how messy this period was for AT&T, lest anyone believe that the choices were obvious. But no one can adequately describe the unrelenting pressure to reverse a decline that had been gathering momentum for more than a decade.

I haven't told *all*, not only for reasons of space, but to honor personal confidences, protect the company's proprietary information, and also because some events, while perhaps titillating, were extraneous to my themes. During these years, I never made a secret of my plans to write about my experiences. All the quotes in this book are based on notes that I took at the time or in later interviews. When I quote people's thoughts, it is because at some point they told me what they were thinking.

This book is neither a pitch for sympathy nor an attempt at expiation. For all my mistakes, I am proud of my tenure at AT&T, and especially of the people with whom I worked. Nor is this an effort to shift blame. I was not a fly on the wall at meetings of AT&T's senior management; I had a seat at the table. I was a full participant in the decisions made between 1997 and 2002. For better or worse, I had my say, and if some of those decisions have proven less than brilliant, I can neither make excuses nor escape my share of blame.

Nor do I blame those who reported our misadventures for causing them, or even for aggravating them. With very few exceptions, the editors and reporters who covered AT&T in this period were honest and fair and gave us every opportunity to tell our story. A friend in the media reminded me that it's just as wrong to stereotype journalists as to stereotype businesspeople. You will find all kinds of reporters in these pages. If I seem to dwell on the few who were duplicitous or careless, it's because I learned more from them—just as I did from my own mistakes. Of course, I also realize that, while many journalists may agree with my observations about their profession, they will fight to the death my right to make them. After a career in public relations, my views will forever be suspect.

Public Relations

While I've tried to reexamine my corporate life with a clear eye and a nose for sour grapes, this is hardly the *Confessions of Saint Augustine*. It is a modest attempt to dispel a popular notion regarding public relations. If economics is the "dismal science," the practice of public relations in the 1990s came to be regarded as a kind of merry art, designed to incite sober people to spasms of irrational exuberance. Spin doctors became the high priests of the practice. Wordsmithing, glad-handing, and mud slinging became their sacraments.

AT&T's recent history demonstrates that public relations is not a tactic best left to specialists. It is a function of general management that a company's most senior leaders must embrace. Public relations, writ large, will be found not in a company's news releases or publicity stunts, but in its day-to-day operations and long-range strategic choices. There will be smaller PR lessons in these pages, if only because tactics can be informative in themselves. But the more significant lessons arose as we attempted to navigate the intersection of corporate and public interests, which is every executive's responsibility.

The business community now labors under a burden that historian

Daniel Boorstin first identified in American politics. Writing about the 1960 presidential elections, Boorstin noted that the communications media had put a higher premium on manufactured events—such as news conferences, photo ops, political debates, and such—than on the substance of public discourse. "Such 'pseudo-events,'" he wrote, "lead to emphasis on pseudo-qualifications."[9] Alas, that describes the focus of the business media in recent years almost perfectly. Meeting quarterly earnings expectations may be the ultimate "pseudo-event" in American business, conceived by sell-side analysts and propagated by media reaching for an easy headline.

And, as Boorstin observed in politics, reality eventually conformed to its manufactured version. The business scandals in the first three years of the millennium began as innocent-enough efforts to "manage earnings" and in some places escalated to wholesale fraud. Even companies that were scrupulous in their accounting practices sometimes mortgaged their future to meet short-term targets. And at least some of the productivity improvements of recent years came at the expense of real reductions in the quality of the extended product, as, for example, anyone who has tried to navigate his way through customer service telephone trees can attest.

Some in the business media have tortured themselves worrying about whether they should have been able to ferret through the phony accounting that was at the root of corporate scandals. (The answer is probably no.) But few have considered the second-order effects of the breathless coverage they gave the so-called New Economy. The Henry Blodgets and Jack Grubmans of the world are media creations on a par with the cast of *Queer Eye for the Straight Guy*.

Corporate Purpose

But a supple distortion behind the headline scandals is even more damaging in its ordinariness. Many business leaders, and their watchdogs, seem to have forgotten why public companies exist. Surely it is to create wealth, but not solely for companies' so-called owners. As business philosopher Charles Handy observed, there's a big difference between providing the financial backing for a company and "owning" it in the original meaning of the word. Further, he says that the idea that a company is a "piece of property" is an equally antiquated "hangover from earlier times." Rather, corporations are "communities, created with common purpose."[10]

That purpose, binds together not only a business's founders but also their successors; their employees, who contribute their energy and intellect; investors, who supply capital; the communities that provide a supportive environment within which the enterprise can prosper; and even their customers, who make purchases trusting that they will receive value in return.

Corporations exist to create wealth for all who provide their resources and bear the risks of their failure. Such wealth comes in the form of dividends, rising stock prices, jobs, careers, healthier communities, and valuable products and services. Sadly, many business leaders have myopically focused on one expression of wealth, an ever-rising stock price, and on a small subsegment whose fortunes rise and fall with the stock tables, professional money managers.

As in AT&T's case, such single-mindedness inevitably leads one to consider the company's shares as just one more form of "currency" to be used in the kind of financial engineering favored by investment bankers and deal lawyers. In time, even a hundred-plus-year-old company can lose sight of the broader publics who have a stake in it—its investors, customers, employees, and the communities in which they live and work. These "publics" are more demanding than ever because they have been ignored for so long, but their voices, if we will listen, are also clearer. We run into trouble when we concentrate on one voice to the exclusion of others or confuse their voices with the general clamor of the marketplace, with the gilding and gelding that passes for honest discourse.

1

Don't Dance to the
Music of Your Own Buzz

Public relations is not about polishing an image or creating buzz; it's about building a long-term relationship between an institution and its stakeholders. As in any relationship, image and buzz can be powerfully intoxicating pheromones, but they can also make at least one of the parties feel cheap and used the morning after. A company's clippings and the gyrations of its stock price are poor gauges of the relationship's strength.

Armstrong Arrives

Mike Armstrong boarded an AT&T corporate jet for the first time on Sunday, October 19, 1997. The crew had been told that they were shuttling an important customer from Los Angeles to a meeting in New Jersey, and they pretended to believe it, even though they all knew that they were carrying AT&T's new chairman and CEO.

When the plane landed in Morristown, New Jersey, and taxied to the AT&T hangar, the first person up the stairs and through the cabin door was the man widely believed to be Armstrong's most serious rival for the job: John Zeglis, the company's former general counsel and now its vice chairman. The two had never met, and Zeglis had volunteered to drive Armstrong in his own car to the Short Hills Hilton, where they would have a private dinner before the AT&T board of directors assembled on a 7:30 P.M. conference call.

Armstrong, who usually drives either a Porsche or a Harley, slid into Zeglis's Buick Roadster for the twenty-minute ride to the hotel.

Walter Elisha, the AT&T board member who had led the search, was already at the hotel, as was the man Armstrong would replace, Bob Allen. The board call had only two agenda items, electing Armstrong chairman and CEO and electing Zeglis president. Both decisions were foregone conclusions. So how the Armstrong-Zeglis dinner would go provided the only real suspense of the evening.

We had arranged for them to eat alone in a private room just down the hall from one of the conference rooms where we had gathered. Dinner was buffet-style, so there wouldn't even be a waiter hovering nearby. Zeglis had prepared by filling a yellow legal pad with lists of issues that Armstrong would have to address, people he would have to meet, and questions he would have to resolve. Zeglis later reported that the conversation flowed so naturally that he never got to his list.

When Allen, Elisha, and Zeglis went into another room for the board conference call that would end Allen's tenure as chairman and begin Armstrong's, I began briefing Armstrong on the announcement plan for the next day. It was scheduled from 7:30 A.M. to 8:00 P.M. in half-hour blocks that included a gathering of the company's senior management team, a conference call with financial analysts, a "town meeting" broadcast to AT&T employees around the world, a news conference, one-on-one media interviews, and live interviews on CNN, CNBC, and Bloomberg television.

It was a pretty standard AT&T PR plan, but as I ran through it, Armstrong looked at me with an intensity I hadn't felt since Sister Catherine of Siena caught me in the girls' coatroom. Armstrong is an imposing figure to begin with. He's six feet tall, and he still has the broad shoulders and barrel chest of the college football player he was more than forty years ago. He has the well-scrubbed, healthy complexion of an outdoorsman. His only concession to advancing years is male pattern baldness encroaching on carefully trimmed white hair. His default expression is a wide grin, and his voice is surprisingly soft, as if to compensate for a gaze that condenses from blue-eyed twinkle to laser intensity when he's really listening.

He was really listening as I ran through the schedule, and I couldn't tell whether he was thinking, "This guy's nuts" or "What the hell did I get myself into?"

My first question must have had him leaning toward the former:

"Before we get into anything else, let me ask you, who's your long-distance company?"

"Well, Hughes splits its traffic between . . ."

"No, no. I mean which company do *you* use . . . at home or when you're traveling. You know, *personally?*"

Now he *knew* I was nuts. He was about to risk his reputation by trying to turn around a $50 billion company that had been given up for dead by most serious investors, and his prospective PR guy was beginning a telemarketing pitch.

John Walter

What Armstrong didn't know—and what I could never forget—was that the last guy named AT&T's president and anointed as Allen's successor, R. R. Donnelly's John Walter, had been blindsided by a reporter who wanted to know who his long-distance company was. Flustered, Walter first tried to dodge the question. Pressed by reporters, who were already skeptical that a printing company executive could run—much less *save*—AT&T, he said that his wife made all those decisions and he had no idea. As reporters will, many of them used that bit of noninformation to demonstrate how little preparation he had for the job—why, he didn't even know the name of his own long-distance company. Run AT&T? He apparently couldn't even *spell* it. And so forth.

Armstrong, on the other hand, reached into the pocket of his sports coat, pulled out his wallet, and produced an AT&T calling card. "This is who I use," he said. "Is that the answer you were looking for?"

It was. And he answered the question exactly the same way the next day.

Armstrong would face more substantial questions, such as who had had the idea to make Zeglis president (he had), why he had taken the job (for the challenge), and what was he going to do first (listen). But most of the questions were predictable and, for perhaps the first and last time in his life at AT&T, whatever Armstrong said was taken at face value. He was not the "heir *unapparent*." He was, in fact, so anticipated that the latest issue of *Newsweek*, which came out before the announcement was made, had declared, "No one was confirming the reports. But by the time you read this, C. Michael Armstrong of

Hughes Electronics may well have been officially named the next head of AT&T."[1]

There were equally predictable questions for Allen and Elisha, some insubstantial but dangerous nevertheless.

When the AT&T board made the difficult decision to reverse course and tell John Walter that he was unlikely to become CEO of AT&T, it also decided to take complete control of the announcement. The board's attitude was "the less said the better," and to ensure that things were unsaid exactly as the board wanted them unsaid, it appointed one of its own, Walter Elisha, as its spokesman.

Walter Elisha

Elisha, a short man with a ring of longish white hair around his bald pate, was one of Bob Allen's oldest friends. They had both attended Wabash College in Indiana, though at different times. They shared the same practical midwestern values. And they had both worked their way up to prominent business positions without the benefit of family connections, lengthy pedigrees, or personal trust funds. Allen had spent his entire career within the bosom of AT&T and its subsidiaries; after acquiring a Harvard MBA, Elisha had moved through a succession of ever larger companies, winding up as chairman and CEO of Springs Industries, the textile and home furnishings manufacturer.

When Allen had come to the conclusion that John Walter had to go, Walter Elisha was the first board member he called on, flying to Elisha's summer home in Nantucket. The two old friends had struggled with the implications—Allen knew it meant that his AT&T career was over, and Elisha didn't try to persuade him otherwise. But he also reinforced Allen's determination to get it over with.

I was offended that the board apparently didn't trust me or my team to handle all aspects of the announcement, and I was dubious that Elisha was ready for what lay ahead, but I swallowed my pride and suggested that we might profitably spend a few minutes preparing for the conference call with reporters that would follow the news release. Elisha was game.

"The first question you're going to get is probably going to be something like, 'Why did you fire John Walter?'" I said.

"We *didn't* fire him."

"Uh-huh. Okay, then, why did you decide not to make him CEO as you had promised?"

"That's easy," he said brightly. "It's a private personnel matter, and I'm not going to get into it."

Trying to convince him that that wouldn't fly, I suggested that he fall back on the language in the news release that the board had approved—we felt John wasn't ready yet because the industry had gotten even more complicated since he was named president . . . Companies were merging, and so on. . . . John Walter disagreed, thought he was ready now, and decided to leave.

Nope. Elisha was going to stick to his guns and refuse to answer. "The problem with you AT&T guys," he said, "is that you think you have to answer every question. That's why you get so much press and why so much of it is bad."

I could see a new era of media relations dawning. And if it took that course, it would dawn without me. But as I would later decide, as antediluvian as Elisha's observation sounded, there was a germ of truth in it.

When the telephone news conference began, there were only three people in the room at our end: Elisha, me, and Dick Katcher, the Wachtell Lipton lawyer who was advising the board. After a few introductory remarks summarizing the news release we had issued an hour earlier, I opened the call for questions. The first was from CNN. As usual, it was a multipart question, but the gist of it was, "What happened in the last nine months to change your mind about John Walter's suitability to be CEO?"

True to his word, Elisha bobbed, weaved, and dodged and asked for the next question. It came from *USA Today*: "First of all, I'd like to repeat the last question. I don't think it was properly answered."

"No one is a chief executive officer until they are elected as a CEO. . . . [We] concluded it was not timely for him to move to that next position," Elisha said.

"Why? What was it about his performance that disqualified him?" *USA Today* wanted to know.

"I don't feel a need to get into all of the details . . . the directors unanimously felt it just wasn't timely."

I jumped in and asked for the next question. For a moment it seemed that the *New York Times* might be offering Elisha an out when its reporter asked whether one of Walter's problems might have been his lack of experience in telecommunications. "Are you today willing to say that you are focusing more narrowly on someone with telecom experience?"

Elisha said he wouldn't speculate on what the search for the new CEO might entail. Just when I thought the direction of the questions might be taking a safer turn, the *Nightly Business Report*'s reporter asked, "So what changed . . . in your evaluation of Walter's performance?" We were back in the same hole, and Elisha was using the same shovel. "I think the answer to that is we don't evaluate our executives in public or in press conferences."

And so it went until John Keller of the *Wall Street Journal* had his turn at bat. "With all the angst inside AT&T that has been well documented in the press over the last six months . . . with all that you said about John Walter when you brought him in, don't you think that the AT&T board owes the world and AT&T employees a better explanation than the one you have just given? He [John Walter] is getting an awfully expensive payout for having worked seven or eight months."

John Keller was the dean of reporters covering AT&T. He had followed the company for more than ten years, first at a trade magazine, then at *BusinessWeek*, and finally at the *Wall Street Journal*. He had impeccable sources inside the company at all levels and had broken more front-page stories about AT&T than all the other reporters working our beat combined. He was smart and knowledgeable, and he felt proprietary about the company. What he saw happening at AT&T angered him, and daily e-mails from employees in the trenches emboldened him to dig deeper. He was not going to settle for Elisha's bromides.

For his part, Elisha was not going to be pushed around by a reporter. He lectured Keller on the difference between "documentation" and "reporting." Keller countered that John Walter had been introduced as "the next CEO." Elisha shot back that we never said that. Keller persisted: "What made you lose confidence in him?"

Exasperated, Elisha fell back on Mark Twain. "When asked if there was a difference between being president and being vice president, [Twain said,] 'Yes, it is like the difference between lightning and lightning bugs.'"

Katcher, who had been quietly doodling on his legal pad, suddenly looked up. Had Walter Elisha just compared John Walter to a lightning bug?

But Elisha pressed on. "We became increasingly concerned about whether [John Walter] could provide the intellectual leadership for this company."[2] Katcher scribbled something on his pad, tore the page off, and slid it across to me. What it said was, "There's their headline."

I knew I couldn't take it back, but I could avoid helping it spread, so I stepped out of the conference call very briefly to cancel Elisha's subsequent interviews. That's when I discovered that CNBC was carrying the conference call live. Within seconds, John Walter's representative was on my phone, so angry that he was literally sputtering. I could hear Walter in the background, shouting at the television set. I gamely said that he was being an alarmist. Elisha's offhand comments wouldn't outweigh all the nice things we had said about Walter in the official news release. But we both knew I was wrong.

"Lacks intellectual leadership" became the board's reason for passing over John Walter in the *New York Times*, the *Wall Street Journal*, *USA Today*, the *Financial Times*, the *Washington Post*, *BusinessWeek*, *Time*, *Newsweek*, *US News & World Report*, and all points between. Even newspapers that seldom comment on business issues took the AT&T board to task in editorials. A week later, the influential *Wall Street Journal* columnist Roger Lowenstein used the quote to suggest that AT&T's board had been "reading Kierkegaard and Wittgenstein and passing around old term papers" while the company's reputation was "going down the tubes."[3] It was bad enough that he called Elisha "stunningly ungracious and lacking in class," but he went on to attack Elisha's performance at Springs Industries, which, he said, "while not the worst textile operator, has notably lower margins than its arch-rival."

The directors, management, and employees of Springs Industries could be forgiven for wondering how they became part of this circus. A little more than three months later, as we gathered in the Short Hills Hilton to prepare for yet another news conference, Walter Elisha needed to be ready for the obvious question: "So does Mike Armstrong have the intellectual capacity to lead AT&T? Have you seen his SAT scores?"

Similarly, Bob Allen needed to be prepared to deal with a question he had sown in a previous interview. During the original search for a chief operating officer to replace Alex Mandl, Allen, who was then nearly sixty, was asked whether he would resign if he found a candidate who was perfect but wouldn't take any job but the CEO's. Allen, who had no intention of retiring, said he was looking for a number two, but obviously if he found "god," he'd step aside to make room for him. So had he now found "god"? Why was this search different from the first one?

The media ask questions for three reasons: to elicit information and understanding; to needle a candid, colorful reaction out of someone they know is programmed for blandness; and to fish for quotes that fit into a preconceived story idea. We knew that the questions for Elisha and Allen would come almost exclusively from the latter two categories.

This time, I was dealing with a chastened Walter Elisha. The best way to handle the question of intellectual leadership, I suggested, is simply to admit that you used exceedingly poor language once before and you aren't going to repeat it. Mike Armstrong is a seasoned executive with a clear track record of success in the computing and communications industries. He understands the telecommunications industry. He has global experience in both consumer and business-to-business markets. Focus on Mike, not on the past.

As to Bob Allen, we decided to preempt the question as honestly as we could. "Some may feel they've seen this movie before," he would say in his prepared news conference remarks. "They may ask why we didn't pick Mike Armstrong the first time around. The answer is simple. That was then; this is now." If Allen was asked whether Armstrong had the "god-like" qualifications that would allow him to retire (as he would), he would simply say that he had been exasperated by persistent questioning on the same subject when he said that (as he had been), and that he was very comfortable leaving AT&T in Mike Armstrong's hands (which was mostly true).

Announcement Day

Announcement day got off to a rocky start with a particularly nasty front-page story in the *Wall Street Journal* by John Keller.[4] The story purported to reveal "how AT&T's directors decided it was time for a change at the top." No one was surprised that the news of Armstrong's selection had not held—AT&T's annual board retreat at the Greenbrier Resort had been just two weeks before, and the company had long been scheduled to release its third-quarter earnings on October 20. Most reporters expected the announcement to be combined with the quarterly earnings. When Keller discovered that neither I nor the company's media relations vice president were home on a Sunday evening, he assumed that something was up.

Knowing that everyone else would be writing about Armstrong, Keller decided to tell the background story that no one else had, piecing together details from multiple sources as he had done so successfully in the past. This time, however, his sources failed him. Keller reported that the Greenbrier meeting had been a "showdown" in which Allen had opposed Armstrong's selection. He said that the board had "forced [Allen] out" and had conditioned Armstrong's appointment on his acceptance of John Zeglis as president. He said that Allen had been so upset that he had commandeered a van that was waiting to shuttle the board members to the airport, leaving them without transportation.

I was stunned. I knew that Keller was writing for that morning's edition, but he had never hinted at the tone of his story and he had never asked for comment on the anecdotes. Since I had not been at the Greenbrier, I had no firsthand knowledge of how the meeting ended. I had heard about one incident so bizarre that it would certainly have been related to Keller by anyone who was actually there. When the AT&T executives in attendance left Allen and the directors alone to discuss the CEO search, a small plane buzzed the resort, trailing a banner that read, "Vote for Zeglis." John Zeglis, who was one of the first to see the banner, was apoplectic. "Can there be another Zeglis running for something in rural West Virginia?" he wondered. "Or is this someone's idea of a joke?" Either way, he was not amused, and he hoped the plane returned to crop dusting before the directors emerged. AT&T Security called the FAA and descended on every airport and farm runway in the region the next day, but the mystery was never solved.

I also knew that the idea of appointing Zeglis president had come up in a long telephone conversation that Allen had had with Armstrong after Elisha told him of the board's decision. Allen had told Armstrong that he wouldn't be surprised if Zeglis were to leave, since he was already being courted by other companies that were looking for a CEO. It was Armstrong's idea to offer the presidency to Zeglis, and if Allen had had any doubts about Armstrong, that dissipated them. He told several of us what a great conversation he had had with Armstrong and how encouraged he was by Armstrong's grasp of the issues that AT&T faced and his openness to a variety of options.

Keller uncharacteristically also had some of the other details wrong. Allen had not opposed the purchase of McCaw Cellular. The board had never considered buying Hughes to get Armstrong. The sale of our own satellite services business earlier in the year included a noncompete clause that would have made it impossible for AT&T to buy Hughes, which owned DirecTV. In fact, during the CEO search, we were actively negotiating with Hughes to get *out* of a marketing agreement that gave us warrants for a minority position in DirecTV. And knowing how board members were coddled (especially when their wives were around, as they were at the Greenbrier), I found it very hard to believe there was only *one* van to shuttle them to their corporate jets at the three airports serving the resort.

Announcing Mike Armstrong as his successor should have made for a satisfying, if not happy, day for Bob Allen. He had made a hiring mistake; he had admitted it, at great cost to his reputation; and now he was helping to fix it even though it meant leaving the company that had been his life for more than forty years. But Keller's front-page, right-hand-column story in the *Wall Street Journal* all but guaranteed that the photo op for the day would be of a tired, downcast, defeated Bob Allen.

For Mike Armstrong, the day was a blur of flashbulbs and microphones. Setting aside the homogenized remarks we had drafted for him, Armstrong spoke from a single sheet of paper with five or six lines of his left-hand scrawl, demonstrating the kind of confidence, optimism, and pent-up energy seen only in super salespeople and great racehorses. It was a *tour de force*, and it was on display all day. But after thirteen hours of employee meetings, investor calls, and media interviews, Armstrong slumped exhausted into the back seat of a company car to go back to his hotel. The driver, wanting to impress his new boss, peeled away from the curb . . . and promptly rear-ended a taxi.

We missed the symbolism at the time.

After a year-long honeymoon, the media would criticize Armstrong for moving too fast and acting too boldly—the same qualities for which they had lauded him just months before. Ultimately, they would excoriate him for reversing direction, demonstrating that business today is as much about managing expectations as it is about managing labor, finances, and hard assets.

Understand the Media's Mindset

Realizing that the reporters who now are at your feet may one day be at your throat, one might counsel a low profile. Unfortunately, that's seldom possible anymore. After his appointment, John Walter thought he could live quietly in the Short Hills Hilton until his family moved east to join him in the house he was building in the New Jersey countryside. His first night there, the guy running the newsstand complimented him on his picture in the latest issue of *Newsweek*.

Armstrong liked the media's attention as much as anyone—arguably more, since the camera loved his broad-shouldered, broadly grinning mien and young reporters were captivated by his Harley-riding reputation. But except for one profile in *BusinessWeek* during his first days on the job, he consciously avoided on-the-record interviews entirely for ninety days after being named CEO. He didn't know what he was going to do yet, and he didn't need the media's help in raising expectations or narrowing his options.

As it turns out, he may have slipped out of his self-imposed gag 1,735 days too soon. One-on-one interviews feed both a CEO's ego and one of the most dangerous tendencies in modern business writing: personality journalism. Armstrong gives great interviews—candid, colorful, and full of energy. While most executives go into an interview the way mediocre tennis players walk onto the court—focused on returning whatever is lobbed at them—the better players have a clear strategy for making points, no matter what comes over the net. Armstrong never went into an interview without understanding why he was doing it (and that was never simply because someone had asked him to). He always had two or three points that he wanted to make scribbled on a sheet of loose-leaf paper. He wasn't as obvious as Henry Kissinger, who once asked a group of reporters if they had any questions for his answers. But he never let an interview end if the points on the pad in front of him hadn't yet been crossed off.

Reporters and editors are never a blank slate. They can't afford to be—if they were, they would be in a constant state of discovery and evaluation and would never know for sure which stories to pursue. As far back as 1922, columnist Walter Lippmann, in his book *Public Opinion*, pointed out that "for the most part, we do not first see and then define, we define and then see."[5] The world is simply too complicated to do otherwise. Good reporters and editors make swift but complicated judgments, within the context of conclusions they have already reached, to capture what Carl Bernstein has called "the best available version of the truth."[6] The best journalists are always prepared to be surprised and to adjust their worldview. But one reporter who covered us for the *New York Times* once expressed great frustration that his story's angle had often been predetermined by an editor who had, at best, a passing acquaintance with our industry. The reporter's job was to do the legwork and flesh it out.

On major stories, reporters invariably want to speak to the top guy, if only because doing so sells magazines and newspapers. CEOs on the covers of business magazines are the equivalent of Britney Spears on the tabloids at the supermarket checkout counter. As improbable as it may sound, evolutionary psychologists say that our obsession with celebrities is hard-wired, a vestige of tribal gossip in the mating rituals of the savanna. The gossip-worthy are no longer just the buxom and fertile, but also the socially prominent. Just as bosomy starlets appear to have been bred to nurse a brood, and muscular hunks to drag meals back to the campfire, business celebrities are good prospective mates because they're successful and usually rich. As science writer William Allman once pointed out, our modern skulls house a Stone Age mind.[7] And that mind is connected to a wallet that buys newspapers and magazines.

Furthermore, as business has become more complicated, investors have turned their attention to something they think they *ought* to be able to understand: the people running the company, especially the CEO. According to a 2001 study by public relations agency Burson-Marsteller,[8] more than 90 percent of professional investors say that they are more likely to recommend or buy a stock based on the CEO's reputation, up from 70 percent five years before. In fact, when AT&T appointed John Walter its next CEO, AT&T's market cap went down by about $4 billion in a matter of hours. Conversely, on the day Armstrong's appointment was announced, confirming weeks of speculation, AT&T added about $4 billion to its market cap.

Finally, it's easier to tell stories by focusing on the actors rather than on the complicated backstage mechanics. And make no mistake, the business media trade in stories. Part of this is old-fashioned salesmanship. As *Forbes* managing editor, Dennis Kneale, told me, "In this day and age, no one wants to read anything. So you have to trick them into reading. For example, if you want to do a story about derivatives, you find someone who claims to be the king of derivatives based on some algorithm he invented. You do the story about him, explain the algorithm and fool people into reading it."[9] Like any good storyteller, Kneale and his counterparts at the other business magazines look for what he calls "conflict, drama, and setbacks." "Business news does not have to be negative," he says, "but there has to be conflict. Business is rife with conflict and struggle; we don't have to manufacture it."

The media also have help finding it. "Many times," Kneale says, "our best source is someone's competitor. We get them to tell us something about you, then we go to you to deny or confirm it and tell us something about them. It's a twofer."

"Very occasionally," he says, "we're spoon-fed a scoop, but that's not the point—the real goal is to unearth the conflict or drama that is inherently interesting." And Kneale may have revealed the schadenfreude in the media's soul when he told a group of PR people—with a sly wink—that he especially appreciates "mean-spirited ideas about your rival."

Kneale says there's room for "a silver lining" in some stories, but "if your client can be in *Forbes* and survive, then you've done a great job." Anyone who thinks he can beat those odds is too reckless to run a major corporation. That may, in fact, be why today's CEOs seem to metamorphose from prophet to pariah at an apparently accelerating rate. It's not that CEOs have enemies; it's that they make such great copy.

Breaking the Code

We thought we were being selective in the interviews Armstrong granted, but we didn't really break the code until late in the game. In 2001, when the controversy around AT&T was at a fever pitch, we wanted to present our story as forcefully and as broadly as we could. We knew that Armstrong was our strongest spokesperson, but we had long passed the point when reporters interviewed him in a search for understanding. He had become a fishing ground for quotes, and his quotes could not be too complex or nuanced because there was no space for it. We didn't want him entirely held hostage to the reporting and editing process. So we quietly let it be known that Armstrong wouldn't do exclusive interviews without a promise that big chunks would run as verbatim questions and answers.

At first, the major business magazines resisted the idea. We weren't asking for editorial rights (although we did ask for an opportunity to review the Q&A to ensure that the context wasn't changed and that Armstrong's off-the-cuff statistics were accurate). Nor did we try to specify how much space was to be dedicated to the Q&A; we simply asked that it be "substantial" and left it to them to decide what that meant. But our ground rule made them uncomfortable, and they claimed that there was no precedent for it. Besides, as the then editor of *Fortune*, John Huey, told me, "You need us more than we need you."

Huey was right, of course, but when I told him that my next call was to *BusinessWeek*, his candor surprised me: "You said the magic words," he said. "We'll do it." With that agreement in place, getting *BusinessWeek* to buy in was easy. The *New York Times* and the *Wall Street Journal* followed. Huey, now editorial director for all Time Warner publications, later told me: "If I think a competitor is going to get something and I can get it first, I'll go after it even if I don't want it."[10] Competition between publications is nothing new. No one likes to get scooped, and even a paper of record like the *Wall Street Journal* will often ignore or bury a good story if a competing publication has beaten it to that story.

However, our self-control was not always so resolute. When AT&T announced the spin-off of its equipment businesses in 1996, *Fortune* magazine was looking for an angle that no one else had explored. It decided to profile the executive who was in the lead to succeed Bob Allen as CEO of AT&T: Alex Mandl, who had joined the company just five years earlier as CFO and was then running the long-distance business. We wished *Fortune* well, but told them that their angle was premature. Bob Allen wasn't going anywhere. *Fortune*'s editor, though, knew someone who knew Mandl. "All they want to do is take your picture," she said. "They're going to run the story whether you help or not."

When you hear those words, take them as your cue to be unavailable. I have never seen a story change direction because its subject cooperated. The occasional modest improvement—usually a defensive quote that is promptly rebutted later in the story—seldom compensates for the greater credibility and prominence that you give the story by cooperating. It's far better to entrust a knowledgeable lieutenant with providing factual information and keeping tabs on the reporter's progress. Save yourself for stories you want to tell; don't spend your time rebutting someone else's.

In Mandl's case, *Fortune* did more than take his picture. While he was under the lights, *Fortune*'s editor engaged him in small talk about where he went to school, what it's like for an outsider to work at AT&T, and general Wall Street gossip. Big chunks of their conversation ended up in the story. Worse, the article contrasted Mandl's "flamboyant" style with that of his low-key boss. The story made it look like he was not only running for CEO, but also essentially running the company. AT&T headquarters reverberated to the sound of noses going out of joint. The board never formally named Mandl Allen's successor. And that contributed to his decision less than a year later to leave the company to become CEO of Teligent, a now-defunct wireless start-up, setting the stage for the subsequent hiring of John Walter.

The Media Noose

Many CEOs put themselves in an ever-tightening noose by tying themselves to news cycles. Armstrong calculated that he had only ninety days to outline his strategy. Because he didn't take over until November 1, 1997, that gave him until the end of January. Despite the holidays, he met his deadline and staged an analyst conference on January 26, 1998, to announce an impressive set of cost reduction targets, to be achieved largely through an early retirement offer that was wildly popular among employees. A series of quick acquisitions followed, including the largest collection of cable TV systems in the country. AT&T's revenue growth rate doubled in both 1998 and 1999. It looked as if Armstrong would succeed in rebuilding the venerable long-distance company around a promise of "one-stop shopping" for wired and wireless, voice and data communications, plus cable TV. Then the bottom fell out.

We now know that the problems of late 2000 and 2001 were not perpetrated by any of the suspects we had identified three years earlier. The Bell monopolies were still not in the long-distance business in any significant way. People were still not making many phone calls over the Internet. But wireless calling plans, which essentially made long distance "free," were putting a big dent in the business. Since we owned the wireless company that introduced the first of those plans, and since our major competitor, MCI WorldCom, had no wireless capability of its own, one would have thought that we were in a relatively better position. What no one knew until recently was that, in a desperate effort to maintain the growth rates on which its stock price depended, MCI WorldCom had engaged in the biggest accounting fraud in U.S. history—an $11 billion sleight of hand that allowed it to price below its real costs over a three-and-a-half-year period.[11]

AT&T was like a greyhound chasing a mechanical rabbit—it made us run faster and get in better shape, but the race was fundamentally rigged and took billions of dollars of cash flow out of the industry. Falling for the scam like everyone else, the same writers who had declared Armstrong "the new operator with a plan to save AT&T" didn't hesitate to hang up on him and the company.

None of that should have come as a surprise. The hallway outside my office at AT&T was hung with two sets of framed magazine covers and stories. Along one wall representative headlines read: "Could AT&T Rule the World" (*Fortune*) and "1 800-GUTS: AT&T's Bob Allen Has Transformed His Company Into a World-Class Risk Taker" (*BusinessWeek*). Along the other wall were "Why AT&T's Latest Plan Won't Work" (*Fortune*) and "AT&T: When Will the Bad News End?" (*BusinessWeek*).[12] The dates of the exhibits on the two sides of the gallery were only a few years apart.

The media, it turns out, have the same short-term focus as the markets they cover, and this expresses itself as journalistic avarice— getting scoops, finding new angles to grease rolling bandwagons, and unearthing conflict, preferably between powerful personalities. "Unnamed sources" have become the wellspring from which the juiciest stories flow. And, being at the wrong end of a twenty-four-hour news cycle, the print media have turned to interpretation and analysis as their competitive niche. As Felicity Barringer, the *New York Times* reporter who used to cover the media, once wrote, "Newspapers get pulled into the gravitational pull of the stock market. Invariably, highfliers get good coverage; laggards get criticized."[13] All this makes business news more entertaining, but it also explains why CEOs should no more depend on the media to be their primary means of communicating with stakeholders than depend on the media to run their board meetings.

Go Direct

One of the most common mistakes executives make is to confuse intermediaries such as the media, nongovernmental organizations (NGOs), financial analysts, and other luminaries with people who have a real stake in a company. They are not the same.

The media, for example, are interested in a given company as long as it is making news, and they are not immune from the strains of hysteria infecting the markets. Nongovernmental organizations' interest ebbs and flows with issues that may not even be central to a company's operations. Financial analysts put everything about a company through their own proprietary mathematical model, which may or may not reflect the real drivers of the company's success.

Such intermediaries can sometimes provide insight into the thinking of a company's primary stakeholders—its customers, employees, and investors and the communities in which they live and work—but they often skew stakeholders' views toward their own agenda. They can also be convenient channels for reaching primary stakeholders, but they will almost always add their own spin to your message, and occasionally they will ignore your message entirely. This is not an argument for dissing the media, analysts, and NGOs. You ignore them at your peril. They set the agenda for public discourse and define the environment within which you live. But a CEO's goal should be credibility, not celebrity. This often means being more boring, less newsworthy, and even less available than the media would sometimes like.

Companies are better served by communicating directly with their primary stakeholders. In AT&T's case, this was a challenge. We had more than four million shareowners. Just sending them a letter cost several million dollars. Early in Armstrong's tenure, we eliminated our quarterly shareowner reports to cut costs. This was penny-wise and pound-foolish. If anything, we should have spent even more to make the report as compelling to read as possible. It would have been worth it to deliver our message to individual investors free of third-party commentary. And our research showed that the most effective way to win community leaders' support was to meet with them individually. People who had met an AT&T representative at a social or civic event were far more likely to support the company than those who knew us only through the media or our own advertising. Person-to-person communication is the medium of choice for crucial matters at critical moments. You can't detect the currents of society unless you're in the pool up to your neck. We managed to beat back the Bells' efforts to keep AT&T out of their local markets largely by cultivating grassroots relationships with like-minded individuals and organizations.

CEOs need direct lines of communication with the four groups who are most critical to their success: their employees and their employees' families, their customers, their investors, and the leaders of the communities in which all these people live and work. That means writing a lot of letters, holding a lot of meetings, and giving a lot of speeches. In the first five months of 1998, when Armstrong came out of his self-imposed period of silence, he gave almost twice as many speeches as Bob Allen had in the same period—forty-four in all. He averaged six and a half days a month speaking to employees, customers, public officials, and investors. And while he was hitting the speaking platform, we were also identifying and cultivating allies who could help spread Armstrong's message.

Of course, it is impossible to avoid the media entirely. Nor would this be a particularly good idea if you could. You just need to be careful not to fall in love with the melody of your own buzz. Armstrong, who had spent much of his career in sales at IBM, had the salesperson's natural inclination to leave his audiences with something new. He seldom gave an interview or made a speech without first considering how he could use it to make news. For a while, that created a drumbeat of positive press. But hidden in those glowing clippings was an air of expectation—and the expectation, as it turns out, got out of hand. As Armstrong and I learned to our regret, if you dance with the media, you don't get to sit down until they get tired.

Lower Expectations

In retrospect, we would have been better served by making less news and focusing the media—and every other stakeholder—on the challenges we faced. We should have lowered expectations, saying over and over again that the company's transformation would take more than five years, more than the time on Armstrong's contract. We should have cut the dividend and lowered earnings projections (as we ultimately had to do anyway) and explained that we would plow the money we had thus freed up into the company's transformation. (I say this only with the benefit of hindsight. When the idea was finally proposed in late 2000, I argued against it, fearing that it would be interpreted as a last desperate attempt to right the ship. It was, and it was. I should have known better—reality always wins out.) We should have laid out the milestones by which we expected to be judged (and selected them with an eye toward exceeding them). And we should have repeated this litany over and over, no matter how familiar it seemed.

We should have tried a lot harder to be boring. Initially, our stock price would have taken a hit, but it would have happened at a time when most investors were willing to give us the benefit of the doubt, rather than two and a half years later, when the skeptics appeared to have been prescient. Eventually, we would have found the investors who would be with us for the long term. And we would have been less likely to disappoint them.

Armstrong's successor as AT&T's chairman and CEO, Dave Dorman, appears to have learned from his predecessor's tenure. While not invisible, he studiously avoided the public limelight in his first year as CEO. But one of his first acts when he was appointed was to hold a rededication ceremony for Golden Boy, which is now firmly planted outside AT&T's headquarters in New Jersey. He invited Armstrong's predecessor, Bob Allen, to the ceremonies as a special guest and pointedly read from a values statement that Allen had personally drafted seven years before on his kitchen table. Although Armstrong also participated in the ceremonies, employees took note that Allen—and the company's heritage—was back in style.

But Dorman does not suffer from terminal nostalgia. He never misses an opportunity to warn that the communication services industry is in nuclear winter and to worry out loud about whether the company has enough parkas.

That was the theme of his get-acquainted breakfast with Jim Cramer, hedge fund manager turned media machine, almost five years to the day after Armstrong's appointment. Cramer had been on Armstrong's back ever since he had been forced to unload "T" at a fat loss. As Dorman and Cramer shook hands outside the hotel where they had met, a pigeon left the flagpole overhead . . . and relieved itself on Cramer's shoulder.

Even the doorman caught the symbolism.

2

Understand the Power of Symbols

One of the biggest mistakes CEOs make is to neglect the emotional impact of their words and actions. The feelings that people attach to their opinions endure long after the rational arguments on which those opinions were based have been forgotten. Individuals or companies that evoke those feelings acquire symbolic power that can be displaced only by other, more powerful symbols. The most dangerous place to be is between clashing symbols.

Trivestiture

In September of 1995, Bob Allen and his wife, Betty, were guests of honor at the New Castle, Indiana, high school homecoming. Allen, whose father owned and operated a children's clothing store in New Castle, was the local boy made good. After graduating from Wabash College, where he met and married his wife, he went off to work for the telephone company as a manager for Indiana Bell. Now he was chairman and CEO of AT&T, traveling by corporate jet and golfing on national television with stars of stage, screen, and Wall Street. But he had never lost touch with his old friends in New Castle, and, as he waved to them from the football stands while Chrysler Newport High School played Kokomo, few would have guessed that he had a care in the world.

Actually, Allen harbored a secret that would make the financial markets swoon, and before leaving for New Castle, he had instructed his trusted lieutenants back in New Jersey to prepare to announce it in just two days.

Allen's plan had evolved in unprecedented secrecy over the spring and summer. At first, he had confided his intentions only to the company's chief counsel, John Zeglis, and its chief financial officer, Rick Miller. They, in turn, had engaged one of the company's outside law firms, Wachtell Lipton, and its long-time investment banker, J. P. Morgan, to run the numbers, do the research, and draft the necessary legal documents. The AT&T executives didn't even use their secretaries to prepare their memos; they wrote them out in longhand. Allen went so far as to carry documents home to burn in his kitchen sink.

By Labor Day, only about forty of the company's most senior officers had been briefed on the plan. Allen was going to ask the board of directors to split the company into three parts: an equipment manufacturer built around the venerable Western Electric company, which AT&T had controlled since 1881; a computer company built around the NCR Corporation, which AT&T had acquired in a hostile takeover just three years earlier; and a communication services company, which would carry the AT&T name.

In one stroke, Allen would extricate himself from a computer company acquisition that had never really worked out, free his manufacturing division from the increasingly contentious conflict of trying to sell equipment to local phone companies that considered AT&T their biggest potential competitor, and position the largest part of the company to focus on communication services. Resolving these last two issues had taken on greater urgency, as Congress seemed increasingly likely to pass a telecommunications reform bill.

The news release announcing what would come to be known as "Trivestiture" was issued on the morning of September 20, 1995. Shortly after the news hit the wires, Miller briefed a small group of financial analysts in a conference room at AT&T's official headquarters at 32 Avenue of the Americas in downtown Manhattan. It was clear that they liked the plan. Whether because they coveted the investment banking fees that would inevitably flow from the restructuring or because they honestly believed that it would unlock shareowner value, or both, they had difficulty containing their enthusiasm. The markets would confirm this, increasing AT&T's stock market value by $6 billion in two days. The analysts' questions quickly passed from "what" and "why" to "when." As agreed, Miller told them that we anticipated making an initial public offering of shares in the equipment manufacturer "sometime in the first half of 1996."

"Why so long?" they asked.

Separating the books of the three companies and giving each of them its own balance sheet was a monumental task. Together, the companies had revenue of $80 billion, debt of $20 billion, 300,000 employees, and facilities in all fifty states and around the world. They had contracts with each other, shared intercompany debt, and used each other's intellectual property. Miller, the proverbial "numbers man" who had made his reputation by helping Penn Central come out of bankruptcy and leading Wang Laboratories into it, did not normally find enthusiasm contagious. Thin, angular, and gray in hair and pallor, he was all edges and seemed too ascetic to get excited about anything but a checkbook that balanced to the penny on the first try.

But when he came to lunch in the executive dining room, just before a scheduled news conference, he told Allen that the meeting with analysts had gone very well. "They just thought we should move faster," he said. Then, in an almost offhand way, as he reached for the pickles, he added, "Why don't we say we'll do the IPO by the end of the first quarter?"

Thus were sown the seeds of a public relations crisis that would ignite a national debate on corporate responsibility and make AT&T and its chairman symbols of corporate greed.

A Matter of Numbers

Setting up three new companies was a once-in-a-lifetime opportunity to clean their books of obsolete equipment and facilities. Low-performing divisions could be sold off. Each company's workforce could be resized to its new competitive environment, and the separation charges could be wrapped into one magnificent write-off that would give all three companies as close to a clean slate as the accounting rules would allow. And if an extraordinary write-off was in the offing, why wait to do it in the middle of the next year and complicate continuing results? Why not do it on the last business day of the current year so it would all be charged to 1995? Wouldn't that give everyone the cleanest possible jumping-off point?

So on January 2, the first business day of 1996, AT&T greeted the New Year by announcing a restructuring charge against 1995 results of about $4 billion after taxes, about half of it to pay for the elimina-tion of 40,000 jobs.

Miller had hoped that the job reduction would be the biggest in history and had us do the research to prove it. He was disappointed when we discovered that General Motors, IBM, and Sears had already copped that distinction. We were in fourth place. Bummer. Neverthe-less, as designed, the announcement suitably impressed Wall Street. But those of us on the softer side of the executive table—in Human Resources and Public Relations—were more than a little uneasy. A downsizing of this size was unprecedented even for AT&T, which had developed a reputation as the incredible shrinking company ever since divesting its telephone company subsidiaries twelve years before.

Much of the previous downsizing had been accomplished through voluntary programs, but, although AT&T's separation benefits were among the best in industry, fewer people were raising their hands to be let go. An early retirement offer several months earlier had at-tracted only 3.6 percent of eligible managers. Furthermore, while in prior downsizings as many as 30 percent of the people whose jobs were eliminated were able to find other positions within the company, this time Human Resources estimated that a far smaller percentage would find such a safe haven. The current estimate was that as many as 30,000 people would be let go.

We took pains to ensure that the news release and the accompany-ing internal communications were as straightforward as possible. We made a clear distinction between the *positions* being eliminated and the number of *people* who were likely to be affected. We spelled out the reasons for the downsizing as best we could, division by division. And we detailed the separation benefits being given to everyone af-fected in an effort to demonstrate how compassionately it was all being done.[1]

The first day's news coverage was relatively straightforward and neutral, although most newspapers led with the 40,000 figure. The *New York Times*'s headline was typical: "Job Cuts at AT&T Will Total 40,000, 13% of Its Staff." And as if taking its cue from our own CFO, the story's opening lines continued, "The AT&T Corporation an-nounced the biggest single job cut in the history of the telephone busi-ness yesterday, and one of the largest corporate work-force reductions ever."[2]

If AT&T's bean counters were cheered by the prominence given the raw numbers on the downsizing, its public relations and human resources staffs were ecstatic that most of the coverage also included their messages. While conceding that "the AT&T downsizing still has far to go," the *Washington Post* continued that "thus far it is unfolding as what outplacement expert [Chuck] Albrecht [president of the nation's largest outplacement firm] called a 'textbook example' of how to do a layoff in today's economic climate. 'It's an excellent process,' he said."[3] The *New York Times* used an Allen quote from the news release acknowledging "how wrenching it will be for employees and their families," and then its reporter added that the company really had little choice but to slim down "in response to changes that are expected to rock the communications industry over the next few years—in particular as AT&T and other long-distance carriers prepare for the regional Bell telephone companies to attack the $80 billion long-distance market."[4]

The *Wall Street Journal* said that "the magnitude of the cuts stunned even some veteran AT&T-watchers," then went out of its way to give Allen an opportunity to explain himself in the third paragraph of a 1,777-word story. "'This is not one of my favorite days, but then I'm not one who is in so much pain as some of our workers,' AT&T Chairman Robert E. Allen acknowledged yesterday. 'But to the extent we can get in trim, we'll produce better margins, more flexibility and more cash flow . . . to defend our markets and attack others.'"[5]

A Bullet Dodged

As we shut off our PCs that night in the PR department, we felt we had dodged a potentially fatal bullet. But as it turned out, we had focused too much on the newspapers that were tucked into the seat pockets of the limousines that ferried AT&T executives between home and office. We took too much comfort in the fact that most of our "messages" made it into print, albeit at the end of long stories. We should have paid more attention to the evening news broadcasts, which were how most people heard about our downsizing.

For example, after reporting that AT&T had announced a cut of 40,000 jobs, CNN's *World News* went on to say that "The latest rounds of corporate cutbacks have left many people fearing that they may be the next to be fired."[6] NBC's Tom Brokaw predicted that "if what happened today to 40,000 workers at AT&T is any kind of barometer of what's ahead, it will be another long, anxious year for the American middle class."[7] The television news anchors tied AT&T's downsizing to the feelings of insecurity and fear that were rattling working people in every community.

On one level, objective economic data suggested that everything was fine—inflation was at historically low rates (2.7 percent), and unemployment, which had declined in the last four years, was at relatively low levels (5.8 percent). But what the statistics could not show was that many Americans were feeling increasingly worried, frustrated, and angry. In the previous ten years, more than one-third of Americans (35 percent) either had lost their own job or had an immediate family member who lost a job. Almost one-quarter (22 percent) of Americans worried that they would lose their job in the next twelve months. Despite low inflation, real incomes were being squeezed; all but the top 10 percent of wage earners had seen their real income decline. Optimism about the national economic outlook had taken a negative turn in December of 1995, and only three out of ten Americans believed that their children would be better off then they were.[8]

In addition to coming on the first business day of a new year, the AT&T downsizing touched a nerve. As then Secretary of Labor Robert Reich put it in a *New York Times* op-ed just two days after the announcement, AT&T "is but one in a long list of companies that have delivered large numbers of pink slips in recent years, *despite record profits.*"[9] (Emphasis added.) People could understand why companies in trouble had to let people go. But AT&T was recording its most profitable year in history. What was going on here?

Pat Buchanan, news commentator turned populist presidential candidate, thought he knew. "I was not discomfited by the shutdown of the government," he told an Iowa Republican caucus, "but I was discomfited when I read that AT&T is laying off forty thousand workers just like that, and the fellow that did it makes $5 million a year, and AT&T stock soared as a consequence, and his stock went up $5 million."[10]

As he moved his campaign to New Hampshire, Buchanan turned Bob Allen into a symbol of corporate greed that tapped into working people's very real fear and anger. In the process, he gave us all a mini-lesson in mob politics: Remind people they're scared and/or angry and blame it on an enemy they don't like in the first place. It doesn't even have to be the enemy you're running against, although it's helpful if you can tie the two together somehow.

Media coverage of AT&T's downsizing increased and became increasingly critical, with negative stories outnumbering positive two to one. For example, *Newsweek*'s Allan Sloan wrote that, while AT&T's downsizing made sense, AT&T's executives should share the pain. In reporting the story, Sloan even schlepped out to New Jersey so that he could look Allen in the eye when he asked if he thought it was "fair" for Allen to draw a million-dollar paycheck when workers were losing their jobs. Allen just glared at him and said it wasn't his job to decide what was fair.

Symbolic Meaning

Ironically, Allen genuinely worried about the people who were affected by his decisions. He expressed his feelings to Sloan, as he had to others. "I feel bad about it," he said, "but I don't know what to do. I wouldn't see any value of going on TV and crying and showing my sorrow for the world to see." [11] Sloan wrote that Allen seemed "like a decent and moral man," but also seemed to be totally out of touch with the "unfairness" of continuing to draw a fat salary while he laid people off. "Symbolism is terribly important," wrote Sloan, "and so is a sense of shared sacrifice. If Allen had announced that AT&T's top execs and members of its board of directors were donating some of their salaries and fees to a fund for the fired employees, it wouldn't make much financial difference. But it would make a huge symbolic difference." [12]

He was right—it would have made a difference. But because we didn't do it, the *New York Times* could dub AT&T's chairman a symbol of "corporate avarice." [13] Our carefully crafted messages had focused on demonstrating that our separation benefits were among the best in industry. That, of course, was beside the point.

We were trapped in a period of piling on, with the media competing with one another to tell the same story from different angles and to tie all their stories to the same theme: corporations' lack of social responsibility and the shocking disparity between the compensation of senior executives and that of rank-and-file workers. AT&T now suffered from a presumption of guilt that not only made recovery more difficult but magnified the impact of any missteps.

The next hit came in late February 1996, when the company issued its proxy for 1995 and tacitly confirmed Buchanan's hypothesis. Buried in the section on executive compensation was a paragraph revealing that, months before the downsizing had been decided (much less announced), the board of directors had given AT&T's most senior officers significant option grants as an incentive to complete the restructuring successfully. Although they couldn't be exercised for four years, the options were potentially worth millions. For example, by the arcane formulas of the Black-Scholes method of valuing options, the company's proxy said that Allen's special 1995 grant was worth about $9.7 million.[14]

That stimulated a new round of stories, and this time there were six negative stories for every neutral one. The Council of Institutional Investors, which represents over 100 public and private pension funds, prepared a report on the AT&T layoffs that concluded that Allen's compensation was at best insensitive and at worst undeserved, considering the merely average performance of AT&T stock in recent years. The council's report came against the backdrop of an article in *Fortune* by one of the most respected business writers of all, Carol Loomis. Titling her piece "AT&T Has No Clothes," Loomis documented how, since divesting its local telephone companies, AT&T had "lurched from one strategy to another . . . and specialized in huge write-offs tied to downsizings."[15] But the worst of the lot was *Newsweek*'s second bite at the apple—a February 26, 1996, cover story that proclaimed Allen a "Corporate Killer."[16]

Corporate Killer

We first heard that *Newsweek* was working on another story about corporate downsizing because a woman who worked in our Washington, D.C., office was married to Evan Thomas, one of the magazine's assistant managing editors. She carried their pillow talk into the office and tipped us off. Since we had already had our say with *Newsweek*'s Allan Sloan—in an encounter that neither he nor Allen had found particularly satisfactory—we decided to maintain a low profile and hope we would be mentioned only in passing.

By Friday morning, we learned that the story was going to be worse than we feared—it had become a cover story, and we were prominently featured. In mid-afternoon, as our Basking Ridge, New Jersey, offices emptied in advance of a full-blown blizzard, *Newsweek* called. One of the more senior editors had asked Sloan, the story's principal writer, if he had tried to contact AT&T's Allen. He hadn't because he still had his notes from an earlier story on the same subject and he doubted that we were going to make our boss available a second time. But he also realized that this was a tactical error—he didn't want to give us the opportunity to complain that we had never even been called. So he went one better. He offered us the chance to write 500 words defending the downsizings and promised to publish it with minimal editing.

As Sloan made the offer, my mind raced. Bob Allen was in Florida. The piece was supposed to run under his byline. Could we even reach him, and, if we did, would he approve it? *Newsweek* needed it by Saturday morning. Besides, wouldn't writing this put us right back in the middle of the downsizing debate? What was the advantage of that? Plus the snow was piling up outside my window. I passed and headed out into the storm.

Newsweek's cover on Monday was a nightmare. At first, I thought it was a parody put out by some slightly addled college kids. Mug-shot-quality photos of four CEOs—IBM's Lou Gerstner, Digital Equipment's Robert Palmer, Scott Paper's Al Dunlap, and AT&T's Robert Allen—appeared on a black cover between the words "Corporate Killers." The story inside was actually not as bad; it repeated much of Sloan's prior story, including the previous Allen quotes, and added about eight people to its list of "hit men." I noted that *Newsweek* had succeeded in getting only one CEO to present the opposing point of view: "Chainsaw Al" Dunlap. And I was amused to learn in later years that Dunlap's submission had been so disjointed that Sloan, a master of arguing both sides of any issue, had been forced to edit it heavily.

But the cover was over the top. When he saw it, Allen called the *Washington Post*'s CEO, Don Graham, who counted *Newsweek* as part of his media empire. Graham did what any CEO in his position would do: He sympathized and passed the buck. By the end of the week, Allen had received a fax from Richard Smith, *Newsweek*'s chairman and editor-in-chief:

Dear Mr. Allen:

Don Graham has told me of his conversation with you and of your deep concerns about our cover on this week's issue. First, let me say that I take those concerns very, very seriously. While the subject matter of the story is obviously a major topic of national debate, I sincerely regret any misunderstanding of our intentions caused by the cover itself. Immediately after seeing the magazine, I spoke with the editors of the issue about the tone conveyed by the image and the language. I say that not to avoid personal responsibility. Although I was traveling, I saw a fax of the cover shortly before press time. I could have changed it. I didn't. Had we been more sensitive to the possibility that the cover choice would distract readers from the seriousness of the story, we would have chosen a different approach.

As the person responsible for the magazine's operations, I wanted to let you know just how I felt. Beyond that, I genuinely hope that you will consider writing a piece for the magazine about the painful and difficult issues involved in corporate restructuring. I can appreciate that you might be uncomfortable writing a "response" to the cover, but I think your personal observations about these issues would be an important contribution to the current debate. We would welcome your thoughts at any time. If you would like to discuss these matters further, I am obviously more than willing to talk.

Yours sincerely,
Richard M. Smith

Allen passed the fax along with the notation "I got his attention, anyway!"

We took up Smith's invitation, and six weeks later Allen's essay ran in *Newsweek*'s "My Turn" column. Entitled "The Anxiety Epidemic," it said that "downsizing is a necessary evil, but business needs to do more to ease the pain."[17]

Newsweek's Sloan was incensed. He felt that by giving Allen a turn in the magazine's pages, his editors had implicitly distanced themselves from the story. The cover had not even been his idea. Like me, he had been fighting a blizzard at the time, and he remembers thinking that the cover was a little harsh when he saw it. But he felt that if Allen had a bone to pick, he should do it in the letters to the editor like everyone else.

At least partly to mollify Sloan, *Newsweek* ran four letters in its next issue, all taking issue with the Allen piece. Our own research was more positive: We found that over 60 percent of *Newsweek* readers had read at least some of Allen's "My Turn" column, which is one of the magazine's most popular features, and positive reactions outnumbered negative by two to one. In fact, 20 percent said that it made them feel more favorable toward Bob Allen. We mailed copies of the column to 5,400 business and community leaders. But we were fighting an uphill battle.

In March, the *New York Times* ran an unprecedented seven-part series on "The Downsizing of America." Not to be outdone, *Business-Week* followed with its own cover story on "Economic Anxiety."[18] Knowing that the easiest way to lead a parade is to jump in front when it passes, President Clinton announced a presidential summit on "corporate citizenship." He invited 100 top business executives (including AT&T's Bob Allen) to the White House and exhorted them to "do well" by their employees while "making money for their shareholders." Then he told *USA Today* that the CEOs made too much money.[19] It was going to be a long road back.

Backlash

Consumer attitudes toward AT&T had declined precipitously. The proportion who thought that AT&T was "well managed" fell from 65 percent prior to the downsizing announcement to just 47 percent in March. Not surprisingly, only 24 percent thought that the company "treats employees well." Nearly half of consumers said that the layoffs had negatively affected their feelings about AT&T. Most troubling, nearly a third (32 percent) said that the layoffs would decrease the quality and reliability of the company's long-distance service.

Of course, the company also had its defenders—some of them organized and equipped by us, and others who jumped in on their own simply because they saw larger issues in play. Columnists such as William Safire at the *New York Times*, George Will and James Glassman at the *Washington Post*, Robert Samuelson in *Newsweek*, and Michael Prowse in the *Financial Times* wrote contrarian stories that defended the company. Economist Herb Stein, reengineering guru Michael Hammer, his coauthor James Champy, and ethicist Marjorie Kelly wrote supportive op-eds. Even Ed Koch, ex-mayor turned columnist for the *New York Post*, weighed in with a surprisingly nuanced survey of think tanks.[20] The National Association of Manufacturers placed an op-ed in the *Washington Post*, rebutting "corporate bashing" and declaring, "We aren't 'corporate killers'; we're the envy of every country."[21] The chairman of Chrysler Corporation, on whose board Bob Allen served, gave a high-profile speech at the Detroit Economic Club, promising in the opening line "to complain about the ongoing demonization of corporate America by some of our prominent politicians and news organization[s]."[22]

While welcome, all the to-and-fro of supportive stories and rebuttals in the letters to the editor columns tended to reinforce AT&T's symbolic role in the downsizing story. And not all of the "help" was an unalloyed delight. After lighting into critics who were demonizing American business, *BusinessWeek* offered a suggestion: "Fire the CEOs whose strategic backfires lead to layoffs, as was the case at AT&T."[23]

Don't Miss the Symbolism in the Facts

The hardest part of counseling CEOs is getting them to look beyond rational arguments to stakeholders' emotional concerns. This isn't touchy-feely New Age mumbo jumbo. Walter Lippmann pinpointed its importance in the 1920s. "Opinions," he wrote, "are not in continual and pungent contact with the facts they profess to treat. But the feelings attached to those opinions can be even more intense than the original ideas that provoked them."[24] Over time, people come to know what they feel without being entirely certain why they feel it. And those feelings can be provoked by stimuli far removed from the ideas that aroused them in the first place.

No one at AT&T's executive table understood the full emotional impact of our downsizing announcement on people beyond those who were directly affected. Incredibly, in hindsight, none of us had connected the downsizing announcement to Allen's compensation, which had been largely decided months earlier. By the time we realized that public disclosure of the option grants would come on the heels of the downsizing announcement, those grants had already been given to Allen (and the other top officers). Allen was in no mood to buckle under media criticism by giving the award back. But we should have seen a hint of what was to come as far back as the September 1995 news conference we held to explain the Trivestiture restructuring.

The very first question at that news conference was about layoffs, and we were frankly not prepared for it. In a remarkable example of focusing on the wrong issue, we had spent much more time worrying about how people would react to our spinning off Bell Labs with the new equipment company. All the news release said about layoffs was, "It is likely that the combined new companies will have fewer employees than the present AT&T." In retrospect, we should have pressed for more information. Certainly one of our investment bankers had run "what-if" calculations.

In fact, within days after the announcement, the *Wall Street Journal* was speculating that 20,000 people would be laid off.[25] When Adele Ambrose, my media relations vice president, was quoted as saying that that number was probably too high, a very senior officer called and quietly warned her not to go so far out on a limb. Meanwhile, the official word she was getting from Finance and Human Resources was that we still didn't know.

The other big piece of the puzzle that we missed was that our negative press was not about ideas, it was about feelings. No rational arguments, no matter how persuasively arrayed, could dislodge those feelings. They could not even be countered with emotional arguments of our own. As Walter Lippmann wrote in *Public Opinion*, symbols "do not stand for specific ideas but for a sort of truce or junction between ideas" in which "feeling flows to conformity rather than toward critical scrutiny."[26]

Once Pat Buchanan had portrayed Bob Allen as the symbol of the corporate greed responsible for so much downsizing, it didn't matter how much emotion Allen invested in his defense. It would even have been futile for Allen to "go on television and cry," as he derisively told *Newsweek* his critics wanted.[27] His tears would have been met only with cynicism.

Political and social symbols do more than signify something; they actually evoke the strong feelings involved in their creation. Allen was a symbol, not simply in the sense that he stood for "downsizing" or "corporate greed," the way a barber pole signals haircuts, but in the sense that he actually evoked all the feelings of pent-up fear and anger that working people were experiencing. And no rational argument could change that. Again, once formed, symbols persist until they are replaced by other, more powerful symbols.[28] The window of opportunity to create positive symbolism around AT&T's downsizing had closed in the days following the Trivestiture announcement.

Ironically, we eventually did some of the right things, but by the time we did them, it was too late. For example, we ran ads to help displaced workers find jobs. Had the ads appeared in the first days following our downsizing announcement, they would have demonstrated some degree of social responsibility. Ninety days later, they appeared to be a reaction to the public backlash rather than a sincere effort to help our employees. And we never took what would have been the most significant step we could have taken: freezing executives' salaries and deferring their stock option grants. That not only would have denied our critics a potent argument, but would have symbolized a spirit of shared sacrifice.

At bottom, a fixation on the company's stock price blinded AT&T's top management to larger issues. It caused us to rush the process of breaking up the company, which led to a series of missteps. If we had kept to our original schedule, we would not have announced a writedown at the beginning of 1996, in the midst of the presidential primaries. And there would have been a good chance that when the writedown was announced, it would have been in the name of two companies, AT&T and Lucent Technologies, as the equipment company came to be known in February of 1996; in fact, Lucent accounted for more than half the jobs eliminated.

Because we failed to appreciate the symbolism behind the facts, one of the most decent men I know, Bob Allen, was unfairly portrayed as the symbol of corporate greed. But we learned.

Whereas Allen was suspicious of anything that looked like grandstanding, Armstrong was a master of the symbolic gesture. One of his first acts as CEO was to ban chauffeur-driven commutation for top executives. It was a popular move with rank-and-file employees, and it even made the business pages as a sign of how serious he was about cutting costs and changing the culture. In fact, exactly one executive commuted to work by company car at the time. Already slated to retire, she was driven to and from the office until her last day.

Recalling Allen's lambasting, Armstrong froze executive salaries when he announced the elimination of 18,000 jobs in January 1998. Even more important, though, this would be the last time we aggregated downsizing information for the media. From then on, we did our downsizing by department, providing the companywide numbers only to a very few executives who needed them to ensure that we were complying with SEC requirements for documenting accounting charges. And we tried to express downsizing targets in financial terms rather than as changes in workforce (reductions in overhead costs or increases in sales per employee, for example).

This Too Shall Pass

During this period, Bob Allen received direct encouragement from other CEOs as their "club" rallied around a beleaguered member. Jack

Welch wrote a note telling Allen to "hang in there" and reminding him that Welch himself had been known as "Neutron Jack" before GE started producing the predictable earnings growth that his downsizings made possible.

Chris Galvin of Motorola wrote to express his support (and to apologize for a Motorola executive who was quoted in the *Wall Street Journal* as saying, "The only thing Bob Allen and his managers know how to do is turn out the lights"). Betty Beene, the president of the United Way of Tri-State, sent a handwritten note with her favorite saying: "Don't take it seriously. And don't take it personally!" But it was *very* personal, even before AT&T's largest union marched on Allen's home in Short Hills, New Jersey, and dropped an empty casket on his front lawn, representing all the workers he had "executed."

Allen, an only child, is soft-spoken and a little stiff except on the golf course, which is where he truly relaxes. The game suits his personality—he's quiet, focused and deliberate. He keeps his own counsel and seldom dominates the conversation in business meetings, preferring to ask questions and listen to the give-and-take of a debate. Unassuming and low-key, he has even been described as "stoic." He is the kind of CEO who pulls the big levers and leaves the details to others.

He certainly doesn't torture himself over big decisions—he set the wheels in motion to buy McCaw Cellular at the end of a single twenty-minute phone call with his chief negotiator, in which Allen said less than five sentences. It ultimately cost AT&T $12.6 billion. The company would later spend about another $8 billion expanding its wireless footprint through acquisitions, but in 2000 and 2001 AT&T monetized its investment in AT&T Wireless to the tune of almost $30 billion before spinning off the remainder to its shareholders in July 2001 at a value of about $20 billion, which would increase to $41 billion under the terms of its 2004 merger with Cingular Wireless—not bad for a CEO who has been criticized for his acquisitions.

But Allen also does not dodge responsibility for mistakes. When the *Wall Street Journal* asked him to defend the ill-fated acquisition of NCR, his answer was crisp and unequivocal: "I studied it. The board believed in it. I thought we could make it work. We didn't execute."[29]

His natural reserve made him appear aloof and even cold to people he met individually or in small groups, especially compared to his predecessor as AT&T chairman and CEO, Jim Olson. Olson was garrulous, outgoing, impatient, and always on the move. When one of his meetings ended early, Olson famously asked his lieutenants who among them had conflicts so that he could resolve them in the time left. Allen could spend long hours in his office, rolling a cigar around in his mouth, just thinking. But those of us who saw Allen in those days did not question for an instant that he was in pain. He was hurt, embarrassed, and deeply sad—not only for his own reputation, which clearly weighed on him, but for all the people whose lives he had disrupted. He once even worried out loud what his mother, who died of leukemia when he was twenty-seven years old, would have thought of him. But there didn't appear to be a thing he could do about it—and, at least initially, the unofficial CEO club told him to accept that it was AT&T's turn in the barrel; he should tough it out and wait for the furor to subside.

That's not how Marilyn Laurie saw it. Olson had made her the highest-ranking woman in the company at least partly because she shared his impatience and activism. Her route to the top of what was then probably the largest corporate public relations organization in the world was as unconventional as she was.

Marilyn Laurie

In 1969, Marilyn Laurie was a stay-at-home mom, caring for two young daughters while her husband earned a living as a commercial artist. One Saturday, paging through the *Village Voice* classifieds for an ad her husband had placed for help in his art studio, she saw a tiny notice that a group was coming together to plan New York City's participation in the first Earth Day celebrations. The first meeting was scheduled to take place that afternoon at Barnard College, from which she had graduated ten years before. She hadn't been back since, and the coincidence of seeing an ad for a meeting taking place at her college almost ten years to the day after she had left made it seem somehow like a calling. She told her husband, "Watch the kids," and trotted off to the subway.

The meeting in the Barnard College Auditorium was a madhouse, with 500 people talking at once. Fewer people came to the second meeting and fewer still to the third and subsequent meetings, teaching Laurie the first rule of social activism, which, as Woody Allen might put it, is "just showing up." After two months, there were only five people left; everyone else had fallen by the wayside. When the small group discovered that Laurie had a degree in English, they named her to handle all their communications.

That's how, on April 22, 1970, she found herself sharing a microphone with New York City Mayor John Lindsay, whom she had somehow convinced to close off Fifth Avenue for two hours so that 100,000 people could stroll in the sun, listen to guitar players, and attend an ecology fair in Central Park. That led to a freelance assignment editing an environmental supplement for the *New York Times* and, in 1971, to a job offer from AT&T, which was trying to organize employee environmental activities.

Eventually she moved to the company's public relations department. Short, blond, and speaking with the no-nonsense cadences of a New York City traffic cop, she was put in charge of training AT&T executives for press interviews. She was so aggressive in putting the executives (most of them old enough to be her father) through their paces that AT&T's chairman, Charlie Brown, recommended her for an assignment that no one else wanted by saying, "Give it to Marilyn; she's not afraid of anything." By the end of the decade, she was the highest-ranking woman in the department, and by 1987, she headed it.

All this is by way of explaining that Marilyn Laurie was not of the "this too shall pass" school of public relations. But as I would later learn, being the top public relations officer at a major corporation is very lonely. Your colleagues in the executive suite either don't know what you're getting so worked up about or can't understand why you can't fix whatever is wrong. They measure the depth of public relations problems in column-inches of the newspapers they read, especially the *Wall Street Journal*, the *New York Times*, and *USA Today*, and they're incredulous that you can't schmooze those newspapers' reporters into line. When things get really bad, solicitous colleagues at other companies ask, "How are you holding up?" in a tone that suggests that they hope they never catch what you've got.

Outside Advice

When things are just about at their worst, your phone rings off the hook with experts of all stripes offering to solve the problem for you. One high-profile PR counselor offered to host dinners for Bob Allen with the "people who run the New York media." Doubting that that would accomplish much even if he could pull it off, we passed. Another advised, in all earnestness, that what we needed was "to put a stop to all these negative stories." Hello?

One outfit came in through our Washington, D.C., lobbying office and, after subtly criticizing what we had done to date (which admittedly wasn't working very well), proposed doing a "gap analysis" between current public perceptions and what we would like those perceptions to be. This group's method for articulating the gap was fascinating—it hired the U.S. editor of the *Sunday Times* of London to write two *Fortune*-like profiles of AT&T, based on everything that had already been published about us since the downsizing announcement.

The *Sunday Times* editor produced two pieces—titled "AT&T: Poised to Compete" and "AT&T: A Company at Sea"—that were remarkable examples of using the same material to make diametrically opposed cases. In one, Bob Allen was "a corporate hate figure not seen in America since the robber barons stalked across the nation, despoiling the country and abusing the workers." In the other, he "agonized over the hard decisions that he has had to make in recent months . . . for the long-term security of the majority of employees." That was the gap, all right. Filling it was another matter.

The best advice we got came from Tom Bell, who was then the president of the public relations firm Burson-Marsteller. Tall and phlegmatic, Bell looks as if he has recently lost a tremendous amount of weight but hasn't yet had time to have his suit retailored. He walks with a slight slouch, suggesting that he doesn't want to draw a lot of attention to himself. He'll sit through long meetings, resting his chin on one hand while scribbling with the other. Then, when there's a pause in the discussion, he'll cough and ask if he can say something. Inevitably, he'll not only summarize the situation with insight and precision, but also tick off steps we "might consider" to address it.

Boiled down, Bell's recommendation was concise: Change the subject. He reasoned that we were suffering from a "gang mentality" among the media, who were portraying the company as uncaring, unfocused, and poorly managed. AT&T and its chairman had become symbols of irresponsible downsizing. Attacking those issues head-on was a suicide mission that would only cement our position as the principal villain in the national soap opera. As it was, we had been forced onto "the slippery slope of reactive communications." The only way off that slope was through "extreme message focus," using the "new AT&T" as our platform. What had been lost in the blizzard of negative press was the concept that we were indeed building a new company.

"Changing these perceptions needs to be founded in reality," Bell said. "Allen needs to take charge of this—not the PR department—and he needs to create a sense of urgency by doing things that are different. Call a weekend session; cancel a trip; whatever it takes to bring 'command focus' to the task of defining and shaping perceptions of the new AT&T."

Bell wasn't talking about a PR campaign as popularly understood; he was talking about redefining the *company*—its mission, its goals, and the criteria by which it should be judged. Unfortunately, while Allen was willing to do whatever "PR stuff" we asked of him, as far as he was concerned, the Trivestiture planning was on a separate track.

The PR Plan

Our PR plan came down to a three-part strategy: Change the debate from defending the need to downsize to demonstrating the responsible way to do it, restore employees' badly shaken confidence, and rebuild the company's tarnished reputation for social responsibility.

To demonstrate that we were going the extra mile to help laid-off employees, in the late spring of 1996, we ran full-page ads in thirty newspapers across the country. Headlined "Wanted—Good Jobs for Good People," it reminded readers why we were downsizing and what we were already doing for the people affected, and it gave an 800 number for anyone "with job openings looking for skilled people." The ad was signed by Allen. I felt that, since we had already generated more than 115,000 job leads without advertising (182 per employee participating in the Job Bank program), we should be thanking the business community for responding to our prior requests, rather than asking for more leads. I was overruled on the grounds that a "thank you" ad would look too self-serving. I suspected that that was how any ad would look at this point. At any rate, the ad generated 1,406 leads.

To reconnect with employees, who were traumatized by media reports even more than by anything they saw happening inside the company, we organized an aggressive program of internal meetings. In a ninety-day period in the spring following the downsizing announcement, Allen and other senior officers met with more than 10,000 employees in seventy meetings across the country. After these meetings,

94 percent of the employees said that they found the meetings informative, and 75 percent said that the meetings increased their confidence and trust in the company's senior leaders.

To give employees a concrete stake in this "new company" we were creating, Allen announced that he would ask shareowners to approve the granting of 100 stock options to every employee. We had conducted focus group sessions with employees to see what would get them excited about the company again. To our surprise, of all the possibilities we reviewed, ranging from cash bonuses to stock options, the majority settled on options. They told us that they didn't really know what options were or how they worked, but senior managers got them, so they must be pretty good.[30]

To demonstrate AT&T's corporate responsibility, which had obviously taken a real beating, we called a news conference to announce that AT&T would donate $150 million to education over the next five years, not only from the company foundation, but in services from its businesses. AT&T Wireless, for example, would equip schools with cell phones that could be used in an emergency or to improve communications on field trips. AT&T's consumer long-distance business would provide schools with free Internet service. And the unit providing long-distance services to businesses would host a Web site that teachers could access to develop online lesson plans. The AT&T Foundation would fund the development of new course curricula and bring the best teachers from every state to AT&T Labs for summer workshops. By the time AT&T met its commitment, in 2001, it had been recognized and honored by most of the country's most significant educational organizations.

This all positioned Bob Allen to play a major role in an education summit in May 1996 that would bring together most of the country's governors and CEOs from forty-four major companies. Normally, Allen had little patience with politicians, whom he generally considered "grandstanders." He also didn't consider it particularly productive to spend a day listening to speeches that he could just as easily read in a fraction of the time. But he was genuinely interested in the subject (one of his daughters was studying to be a teacher, and his own mother had taught school), so he took the company helicopter to the education summit, which was being held at IBM's Executive Conference Center in Palisades, New York.

As he came out of a workshop on educational standards, he saw a familiar face coming quickly around the corner. Leslie Stahl, who was a correspondent for the *60 Minutes* television news magazine, was a casual acquaintance who had sat next to him at several dinners when Tom Wyman, an AT&T director, had been CEO of CBS. Assuming that she must be doing a report on the crisis in American education, Allen gave her a big smile and stopped to shake her hand. Then he saw the camera over her shoulder and the microphone in her hand.

"Mr. Allen," Stahl said, "I wonder if you would respond to the charge that you got a big pay package for millions and millions of dollars when you're laying off thousands and thousands of people?"

Like a deer in the headlights, Allen mumbled something about it not being the right time or place to get into such a discussion.

Stahl whispered, "I know, I know," sympathetically and plowed ahead with her questions in a louder, more insistent voice.[31]

When Allen finally got away and found a quiet corner, he called in. "I'm dead," he said.

He wasn't dead yet. There was still more pain to endure. The AT&T annual meeting would follow within weeks, just in time for the media and pundits of every stripe to take a few more swings at him.

3

Take Control

*What separates PR counselors from wordsmiths and spin doc-
tors is an ability to connect seemingly random signals in order to
anticipate and prepare for threats that may still be on the other
side of the horizon. Such counselors can often inoculate their
clients in advance. But not every threat can be anticipated, and
sometimes no vaccine is powerful enough. In those cases, your
only defense is to embrace the inevitable by making the best of a
bad situation. The most important thing is to take control of the
situation so that you can set the agenda of public discourse rather
than be put on the defensive.*

Annual Slugfest

AT&T's 1996 annual meeting was held in the Miami Convention Center amid the usual executive griping that the SEC-imposed ritual was
increasingly anachronistic and irrelevant.

Every year, the company would spend several hundred thousand
dollars swathing a convention hall in blue drapes and constructing a
multilevel platform reminiscent of the reviewing stand outside Lenin's
Tomb in Red Square. In the days of Bell System's monopoly, these
annual events served as traveling pep rallies for the company's small
investors, complete with World's Fair–quality exhibits in the lobby, a
free box lunch on every seat, and a heart-warming video at the end.

But in the leaner, meaner world of competition, there wasn't much
room for pep rallies that didn't deliver anything to the bottom line.

The first thing to go was the box lunches, replaced by coffee and do-nuts. The donuts were dropped the same year we did away with most of the exhibits, which incredibly was not until this 1996 meeting. By then, AT&T's annual meetings had become platforms from which the company's unions could decry the perpetual downsizing. Union lead-ers would fly in from Washington to lead groups of their red-T-shirted members, bused in from the nearest AT&T facilities, in a refrain of embarrassing questions and heckling.

If previous annual meetings had been pep rallies, the 1996 meet-ing was a public lynching. First, Allen was pelted with questions about his compensation at an early morning news conference, then he had to face an auditorium filled with militant union members and angry shareowners, most of them retirees, who applauded wildly whenever anyone said anything critical about him and laughed derisively when he tried to defend himself. In a year when the company had already endured four months of media coverage that Allen described as more "unfavorable and relentless [than] I can remember," the union mem-bers actually had to vie with other hecklers for time at the microphone.

By contrast, Evelyn Y. Davis, the septuagenarian annual meeting gadfly, provided comic relief. Proud of her multiple facelifts, but too vain to admit that she had become hard of hearing, she delivered her remarks in a shrill voice still accented by her native Dutch. At one point, when Allen tried to refer one of her questions to the company's president, Alex Mandl, she screamed, "I vill not deal vith vun of your flunkies!"

Mandl smiled gamely, shifted in his chair a level below the po-dium, and probably thought to himself that if all went well, he would not be anyone's "flunky" for much longer.

Mandl's the Man

Alex Mandl was born in postwar Austria and was brought up there until he was a teenager, when his parents divorced and he followed his father to the United States. He attended the Happy Valley School in Ojai, California, where his father was headmaster. Then, when it was time for college, he went to Willamette University, where his father took a job teaching literature. He got his M.B.A. at the Univer-sity of California during the antiwar turmoil of the late 1960s and can still remember walking through lingering tear gas on his way to classes. He had worked at only two companies before AT&T, spending eleven years at Boise Cascade right after college and then moving to a strategic planning job at CSX Corporation, where he worked on its 1987 acquisition of Sea-Land and eventually ran the subsidiary.

It has always been hard to pinpoint the secret of Mandl's success. He speaks with a Schwarzenegger-like accent and is not a particularly charismatic figure, being somewhat on the short side and fighting a slight paunch. He is obviously smart and quick-witted, but, more importantly, he has the gift of focus—not in the sense that his powers of concentration are particularly strong, but that he has an unusual ability to sort through the minutiae flying at him every day and pick out the one or two most important issues that deserve his extended attention. In addition, he has an unerring eye for finding the particular talent necessary to attack his chosen issue, and he follows up on these issues relentlessly. If you were to visit Sea-Land even at this late date, you would probably find an old-timer who could rattle off two or three Mandl initiatives that made a difference, whether it was putting everyone on e-mail or installing computerized tracking systems and charging customers a premium for their use.

Mandl joined AT&T in 1991 as chief financial officer and in short order cut $1 billion from the company's cost structure—not a particularly surprising move for a new CFO. Nor did it turn many heads when he revived negotiations with McCaw Cellular by devising a $400 million minority investment that demonstrated the seriousness of AT&T's intentions, while simultaneously getting McCaw through a cash crunch that was diverting its attention from the negotiations. Scrapping earlier plans to buy only a piece of the wireless company in favor of a full merger was audacious, but not unexpected from a top-flight CFO. But insiders knew that he was destined to be more than the chief financial officer when he began to preach the gospel of "promiscuous, fat minutes and bits."

By then, AT&T had spent millions investing in a mixed bag of proprietary technologies ranging from yet another generation of videophones to handheld tablets that were supposed to turn handwriting into computer text. Reasoning that AT&T would never be able to outdesign Apple or outprogram Microsoft, Mandl declared, "It's the network, stupid!" in so many words. He pushed for multiple nonexclusive relationships with companies that could put digital bits on the AT&T network. Let MCI and Sprint fight over the calls to

Grandma; he would replace them with new multimedia services, and he would tap all those kids working out of their parents' garage in Silicon Valley to help develop them.

In mid-1994, only about three years after arriving as CFO, Mandl was named head of the company's largest division, communication services, and in January of 1996, he was named president. But Allen remained coy about naming Mandl his likely successor, even when all the other obvious candidates had left, and when he named Mandl president, he also created a "Chairman's Office" that included the new CFO, Rick Miller, and the chief counsel, John Zeglis.

Publicly, Allen always said that he thought Mandl had a shot at someday succeeding him. Privately, he told board members that they needed to see how Mandl performed through a couple of business cycles. Mandl himself was worried that the long-distance business would get its clock cleaned when the Bells entered the market and he would be blamed for it long before Allen ever stepped down.

As it happened, Mandl and I were taking one of the corporate jets to a sales meeting in Maui immediately after the company's annual meeting in April of 1996. We talked about the meeting over drinks, and I said something like, "I'll bet Bob's glad he has only four or five of these to go." "What do you mean?" Mandl asked. "Well, Bob's made it clear that he doesn't plan to retire anytime soon and he's just turning sixty, so I guess he'll be around . . ." "Four or five years?" Mandl blurted. His apparent shock and disbelief surprised me, and I tried to back off: "Well, maybe once things are moving smoothly . . ." "Nah. He likes his corporate jets too much. You're right. He won't leave early." I quickly changed the subject.

What I didn't know—and Bob Allen wouldn't find out until mid-summer—was that Mandl had already begun thinking about leaving the company.

Less than a month earlier, Mandl had received a call from a young headhunter named David Beirne, who just the year before had lured McCaw CEO Jim Barksdale to a then little-known company called Net-scape Communications. When Barksdale signed on, he received a 12 percent interest in the company, which was worth more than $100 million when it went public. Beirne promised Mandl something simi-lar in a brief meeting at the Westchester County airport in early April. Mandl had never heard of Beirne's client, the Associated Companies, but he agreed to meet in out-of-the-way hotel rooms and at his home outside Washington with its principals, Myles Berkman and Raj Singh.

Berkman was an entrepreneur who had made a fortune buying and selling cellular systems in the industry's infancy. Since then, he had amassed licenses in thirty-one cities for wireless frequencies so far up in the nosebleed section of the radio spectrum that they were useless for cellular phone networks. Singh was a technical wizard who had figured out how to use the spectrum for point-to-point broadband communications in an end run around the local telephone companies' fiber-optic networks. All they needed was someone with the kind of business reputation that would make their new service seem real and the kind of operating experience to make it so.

Mandl was their man, and they spared no effort to attract him. They offered to put the new company's headquarters in Washington, D.C., eliminating Mandl's weekly commute to his AT&T job in New Jersey. Berkman promised to stay in his Pittsburgh office, leaving Mandl to run his own show as CEO of Associated's wireless subsidiary. They offered to pay him $1 million a year, a $313,000 cut from his AT&T salary, but cushioned by a $20 million signing bonus and 18 percent of the company when it went public. On hearing the details of his compensation package, a headhunter who was not involved in the deal said, "Alex Mandl will be the highest-paid American under seven feet tall."

For his part, Mandl kicked their tires by asking the chief technologist of AT&T's wireless business to give him a tutorial on the frequencies that Associated planned to use, without, of course, telling him why he was suddenly interested in the arcana of radio communications. McCaw had its own fixed wireless system, which it had kept under wraps from all but the most senior AT&T executives, and Mandl quizzed him on that, too. In late June 1997, when Mandl was convinced that the technology could work and was satisfied with the compensation package, he called me.

"A friend of mine has a kid who wants to work in PR," he said. "What agencies do we use?"

"Well, I'd be happy to put him in touch with the right people," I offered. "Why don't you have him send me his résumé?"

"Nah. I don't want to encourage him too much. Does Bob Dillenschneider, at Hill & Knowlton, work for us?"

I was mildly surprised that Mandl knew who Dillenschneider was, but not surprised that his information was out of date. "Dillenschneider left Hill & Knowlton some time ago. He has his own shop now, but he doesn't work for us. In fact, I think they've done work for MCI, so it would be a conflict," I said.

"Okay. Thanks. That's all I need."

"But, Alex, don't you want . . ." He had already hung up. And I would not put this conversation together with our chat on the corporate jet for another month.

Olympic Moments

The opening ceremonies of the 1996 Olympics in Atlanta were held on July 16 in warm, but not oppressive weather. The AT&T executives and their guests were protected from the crowds and the humidity in a three-story tent constructed in the middle of Centennial Park around the main entertainment stage. Bob Allen was noshing on hors d'oeuvres when I brought him word that the papers in France were reporting that the head of our European operations was leaving the company. I wanted to know if it was true and, if so, what I should say.

"If he wants to leave, let him leave," he said. That wasn't exactly what I was asking, but I took it as an answer. What I didn't know until much later was that Allen had earlier received a phone call from Hal Burlingame, the head of Human Resources, reporting on a meeting he had just finished with Alex Mandl.

When we reached the stadium for the opening ceremonies, Allen told his security people that his wife was not feeling well and the crowds were making her claustrophobic. He expressed his regrets to the business customers we had invited and asked to be taken back to his hotel. He flew back to New Jersey that night. What had actually happened was that Allen, who suffered from a congenital narrowing of the aortic valve, was experiencing what his doctor called "an episode." He couldn't catch his breath, and he felt dizzy. He would undergo an operation to replace the valve the following February. Meanwhile, he kept the symptoms from everyone except his wife.

The Spider at the Center of the Web

In the history of AT&T from the breakup of the Bell System to the arrival of Mike Armstrong, Harold "Hal" Burlingame is the spider at the center of the web. As head of Human Resources, he naturally managed executive compensation, including bonus and option awards. Few officers other than the CEO spent more time with the board of directors, especially with the powerful compensation committee. In mergers and acquisitions, he sorted out reporting relationships, compensation, and benefits. His approval was required for all executive promotions, and he was also responsible for all executive recruiting—by 1996, many of the company's top officers, including Mandl, owed their jobs to him. And when it was time to let someone go, it was usually Hal who wielded the axe, smoothing the path out with generous separation payments and even helping people find jobs elsewhere.

So Burlingame was not only a close confidant of Bob Allen, for whom he had worked since the mid-1980s, but a sort of coach, counselor, and chaplain to most of AT&T's executives.

Over the years, Burlingame had learned to be an extremely sympathetic listener. And he has the two qualities most valuable in a chief human resources officer, beyond native intelligence: He's frugal, and he's discreet. Mandl was counting on both when he called Burlingame into his office in mid-July and closed the door behind him. "Hal," he said, "I've been thinking a lot. I can't sleep at night."

Thinking that this was the beginning of another "why doesn't Bob like me?" discussion, Burlingame leaned forward. "What is it?" he asked.

"I'm leaving the company. I have a chance to run a small start-up and build something from the ground up. It doesn't compete with AT&T, and it's too good an opportunity to pass up," he said.

Burlingame had heard this story before, not from Mandl, but from others. It was usually a ploy to renegotiate compensation. "Alex, we just made you president a few months ago. You have a real shot at succeeding Bob as chairman. If it's money . . ."

"Hal, they're offering me a $20 million signing bonus and 18 percent of the equity."

Burlingame was impressed. No public corporation could match that. He knew it was similar to Barksdale's package at Netscape, so it was probably true. This was no negotiating ploy. But coming on the heels of the previous six months' misadventures, Burlingame, who had spent much of his earlier career in public relations, knew that this would be big trouble for his boss and for the company.

"Alex," he said, "you know that you can't tell me something like this without my doing something with it." Mandl said he understood, and Burlingame asked his secretary to find Allen.

Brain Drain

Years after he left AT&T, Allen said that his biggest mistake as CEO was not preparing adequately for his own succession. Considering that he had come to the job after the untimely death of his predecessor, this is a curious admission. But like most CEOs, particularly those who have held the role for five to ten years, Bob Allen had a hard time imagining one of the executives who reported to him in his job. There is a hierarchy even among CEOs, and the CEO of AT&T at that time was arguably in its upper reaches. The old Bell System had had farm teams in the form of its twenty-one local telephone companies and Western Electric, each of which had its own CEO and board of directors. Allen was the last AT&T CEO to emerge from that training ground, and he thought it had served the company well. That was one of the reasons he had hired Mandl and Miller, who had both been CEOs at smaller companies.

Allen seemed to consider CEOs different in kind, not just in quality, from other senior businesspeople. In a sense, he saw CEOs as the ultimate hyphenates—player-coaches, salesmen-statesmen, servant-leaders, practical-visionaries. He believed that CEOs had to have the gravitas to represent the company to multiple stakeholders, but also had to have the down-to-earth operating skills to produce consistent financial results in changing business environments. Most of all, he believed that CEOs had to take a longer view than anyone else, be immune to fads and fashion, and, when the chips are down, do the right thing for the institution, even at high personal cost. Allen had reservations about Mandl on many of those counts, so he did not try to convince him to stay. Nor did he try to hide his irritation at the fact that Mandl had entertained outside offers just four months after being named the company's president.

Most of their discussion was about how and when to make the announcement. Although they never admitted it to each other, Allen's and Mandl's goals for the announcement were diametrically opposed.

Mandl wanted to use the announcement to help launch his new venture, attracting potential investors and eventually customers. Allen wanted to keep the announcement low-key. While he knew that it could not be positioned as "business as usual," he didn't want anyone doubting the company's ability to meet its financial goals or complete its restructuring. We told him that there was one more issue he needed to address—although he had never officially anointed Mandl as his successor, most reporters and financial analysts assumed that he was. Whoever Allen selected to replace Mandl also had to have sufficient standing to be seen as Allen's eventual successor.

That, of course, complicated matters for Allen. Selecting a CEO is the board's prerogative. Allen himself had been tapped to be CEO in a remarkably informal process when Jim Olson succumbed to colon cancer just days after it was diagnosed. The senior director at the time, Rawleigh Warner of Mobil Oil, had simply taken it upon himself to assemble a conference call the night before the company's annual meeting and recommend that Allen, the company's president at the time, succeed Olson. Of course, the whole process had been made easier because Olson, long before he knew he had cancer, had told Allen not to worry, Olson didn't plan to work until he was sixty-five and Allen would succeed him. Plus, he had shared his recommendation with the board. As a result, when Olson died on a Monday morning, Allen was elected to succeed him the evening of the next day, just in time to chair the company's annual meeting on Wednesday morning in Denver, Colorado.

But Allen had not made any such arrangements. On the contrary, he had resisted naming a president at all until Trivestiture forced him to do something with Mandl, who was running the company's most significant operating division. That reluctance, combined with leaving Mandl out of the planning loop for Trivestiture until the final hours and Mandl's increasingly obvious restlessness, created the impression that Allen was one of the small group of men who consider themselves "CEOs for life." True or not, the announcement of Mandl's resignation would reinforce that impression.

Many executives assume that a news release is the foundation document for all the stories that are written about a particular announcement. They sweat over it, tweaking the language and worrying about the order of paragraphs. Or they sprinkle adjectives and jargon around it in the hope of making the news seem more exciting or current. Magic words like *state-of-the-art, seamless, robust,* and *multitasking* are meant to lift the announcement of a new widget to the front page of the *Wall Street Journal.* But except for the wire services, which base their first reports almost entirely on news releases, few journalists use them as more than a starting point. Many don't even read them all the way through. And given a choice between using a quote from a news release or the same quote from an interview, a speech, or a letter, most reporters would choose the latter almost as a matter of pride.

So I knew that the Q&A (questions and answers) that we prepared as guidance for all the AT&T media relations people who would be fielding reporters' calls was the most critical element of our communications plan. Next in importance was getting our release out at the same time as Mandl's new employers released their's so that we would have an equal shot at positioning the story with reporters. The fly in the ointment, from my perspective, was Dillenschneider's involvement.

Mandl had hired his firm, and I knew that the temptation to leak the story to a favored reporter in advance of the official release time was going to be almost irresistible. We agreed to release the news early Monday morning, but I warned everyone to be ready to go on Sunday evening at the first hint that the story had leaked. Much to my surprise, no reporters called on Sunday evening and there was nothing in Monday morning's papers about Mandl's resignation. Dillenschneider had kept his word, something that is not always the case in dealing with outside agencies.

Allen began a regularly scheduled 8 A.M. meeting of the senior officers in the so-called anteroom outside the boardroom of AT&T's Basking Ridge facility by announcing that Mandl had decided to resign to take a "once in a lifetime" position at another company. He said that Mandl's responsibilities would be split between Miller and Zeglis while he conducted an outside search for a new president and chief operating officer. Then he asked Mandl if he wanted to say anything. About half the people in the room already knew of Mandl's decision. The others looked around the oversized round table for a hint of what this really meant. From the curt way Allen had announced the news, they could tell that he found the whole episode a little distasteful. Even Mandl, normally confident and a little brash, seemed uncomfortable as he expressed the customary words of mixed feelings. When he finished, Allen thanked him and said he was sure he had other things he had to take care of. Mandl left the room, and Allen moved on to other subjects.

The News Breaks

At 9:02 A.M., twenty-eight minutes before the news release was to be issued and even before the meeting in the anteroom broke up, a Salomon Brothers research analyst named Jack Grubman broke the news in what the *New York Times* called "a harshly negative note to his clients."[1] The note was picked up by the Bloomberg newswire, and the games began.

Our strategy had been to emphasize three points: Mandl was leaving for an outrageous amount of money, his resignation would not affect the company in any way, and we would begin an external search to replace him as chief operating officer. Grubman, whom *Institutional Investor* magazine perennially ranked as the number one or two telecom analyst, wrote that Mandl's resignation could cause "major management disruption" and "may be an indication of deeper issues within AT&T." He concluded, "Needless to say, we remain cautious on the stock." AT&T stock dropped like a stone as soon as the opening bell rang on the New York Stock Exchange.

Mandl had already left the building to begin a media tour with his new PR representatives. By the time we caught up with him by phone, he swore that he had not told Grubman about his decision to leave. Considering how close the two were, that was hard to believe. As CFO, Mandl had entertained Grubman at his homes in New Jersey and outside Washington, D.C. They regularly traded industry gossip, and we suspected that Mandl had fed Grubman backdoor information about AT&T. In any case, by early afternoon, Grubman issued a second note, suggesting that his initial assessment might have been overly negative.

But the damage had been done. We were successful in focusing the media's attention on Mandl's new compensation package. That was like pushing through an open door—the media love to write about what people make. But we were not able to defuse the impact of the Grubman-incited stock decline, which became a big part of the story. Our protests that "nothing will change" were rebutted by a 2.5 percent drop in our share price on extremely heavy volume. The combination of the surprise announcement, Grubman's negative analysis of its significance, and especially the absence of any moderating comments caused investors who were on the fence to put in sell orders before the markets opened for trading. The selling then fed on itself, and it was days before the stock recovered.

By then, the media had set the storyline explaining the first day's decline in the stock: Mandl was the apparent successor to Allen, he had been frustrated at playing second fiddle to a CEO who showed no inclination to leave the stage, and the company was unlikely to find a capable player who was also willing to sit quietly in the wings. Sadly,

Bob Allen once again became the story. *Fortune* magazine perhaps characterized it best as more "salt in [Allen's] wounds."[2]

Keep Control of the Story

It's always nice to have the last word in a debate, but in the real world, where first impressions are often the basis for hair-trigger decisions that tend to reinforce themselves through repetition, getting the first word is critical. We lost control of the announcement of Mandl's resignation at the precise moment that someone leaked it to Jack Grubman. At that point, we were not just dealing with Mandl and Allen's competing interests, we were pawns in Grubman's drama.

Jack Grubman had once held a relatively low-level management position within AT&T's Finance Department. He probably had not even met the company's CFO, much less its chairman, in all the time he was with the company. But over the years, he had leveraged his status as a "former AT&T executive" to position himself as an expert on the company and the telecommunications industry. His gift for trenchant comments led him to be quoted on a semiregular basis in the *Wall Street Journal* and, eventually, elsewhere. As he became better known, he forged relationships with key executives within the company, many of whom spoke candidly about the company's problems and challenges.

This access made Grubman a regular source for the preeminent AT&T-watcher, the *Journal*'s John Keller. For much of the 1980s and into the early 1990s, Grubman was positive, if not overly enthusiastic, about AT&T. But then his allegiance changed, and by the time Mandl resigned, Grubman was touting the stock of AT&T's archrival, MCI. He saw Mandl's resignation as an opportunity to drive one more nail into the company's coffin, on the theory that anything that was bad for AT&T was probably good for MCI.

Ironically, the news had probably been leaked to Grubman in the hope that he would throw his support behind Mandl's new venture. Grubman eventually did so (in fact, about a year later, Salomon Smith Barney co-managed the initial public offering of Mandl's new company, now known as Teligent), but not before tending to his own parochial concerns.

Sadly, there are only two ways to control the timing of a news release: either severely limit the number of people involved, keeping anyone with a separate agenda in the dark about your actual plan, or leak it yourself to selected reporters. For obvious reasons, we had only the second option in Mandl's case, and we chose not to exercise it. If I had it to do over again, I would probably make the same decision, but I would also try to find a way to better align Mandl's goals and our own, making him less likely to leak the information (as he probably did in this case, despite his later protestations). For example, in later years, I went so far as to prepare two releases announcing an executive's departure. In one, the executive was leaving to take advantage of other opportunities; in the other, he was being replaced. Not one of those stories leaked.

Unfortunately, it is not always possible to make the penalty for early disclosure so evident. Nor is it always possible to align goals in other ways. And the legal penalties for selective disclosure—though murky when working journalists are involved—are severe. One alternative is to pre-brief selected reporters who agree not to publish the information until a set hour. This allows you to put your announcement in perspective for the journalists. It gives them time to think about its implications, and even to do some discreet research, but it preserves the release date. Few, if any, journalists will sign a formal agreement not to disclose information, but in decades of dealing with the media, I can remember only one instance in which a reporter violated such a verbal agreement, and even then it was through a misunderstanding.

To be sure, this will work only with journalists who have an ongoing relationship with you. Buttressing their own integrity is the knowledge that they will have to continue to deal with you when today's newspapers are lining the floor of birdcages. Of course, many journalists don't like background briefings, particularly if they are sharing the information with others. They know that they are being used and, to some extent, manipulated. And although they want to get the story right, their primary goal is to break news.

Background briefings are as interesting to many reporters as foreplay that leads to a kiss on the forehead and a hearty handshake. For that reason, the briefing should be scheduled as close to the release date as practical. It should involve all the principals. And it is absolutely critical that you do not embellish your story or hold back negative information. If you can't give all the details, say so and explain why. It also helps if you can explain why you are conducting the background briefing in advance of the official release. For example, if the story is particularly complex or subject to misinterpretation, most reporters will understand the need for an advance briefing. They will also understand if the final decision depends on factors beyond your control, such as government approval or a shareowner vote, although they will expect you to be forthright in assessing all the contingencies affecting your decision.

But all this is tactical. The bigger challenge in situations like the Mandl resignation is to see around the next corner, understanding the larger issues that are at play and anticipating their ultimate impact. This requires a level of strategic analysis that is often difficult to accomplish under fire.

Embrace the Inevitable

With 20/20 hindsight, it is easy to see the sequence of events that would make Mandl's resignation more than the typical executive passage. Coming just as criticism of AT&T's layoffs and its CEO's compensation was beginning to die down, it stimulated new questions about CEO succession. We should have seen then that it would inevitably subject the company's board to increased scrutiny, particularly if the search for Mandl's successor faltered. Few, if any, boards are comfortable when the media's lens focuses on them. Inevitably, they do whatever is necessary to shift the focus of attention back to management, even if it means installing a new set of managers. Of course, it's easy to predict this outcome years after the fact, but Burson-Marsteller's Tom Bell had, in fact, forecast this possibility as far back as the previous February, when we were trying to work our way through the media storm surrounding our layoff announcement.

AT&T has always had a blue-chip board, and its members at that time included *Fortune* 50 CEOs, the president *emeritus* of an Ivy League university, a renowned economist, and a former ambassador to the U.N. To a person, they were stalwartly loyal to Bob Allen, whom they considered a thoughtful, principled, and strong leader. They were naturally concerned about the negative publicity that the company had received over the past few months, but it was not an unfamiliar phenomenon to any of them. They considered it all a failure of perception (and therefore a PR problem) rather than a failure of strategy or execution, and certainly not a failure of integrity. Besides, throughout the media firestorm, no one had seriously questioned the board's role or suggested that it was accountable for any of the company's perceived failings. We should have seen that Mandl's resignation was the leading edge of a wave that would change all that.

In fact, in drafting the release about Mandl's resignation, I had hypothesized a board-level search committee to select Mandl's successor as president. That was quickly struck from the release, and I was reminded that we were searching for a chief operating officer, not a CEO.

When Allen installed the leadership team at Lucent Technologies prior to its spin-off from AT&T, he felt that he had broken the code on planning for CEO succession. The Lucent team consisted of an experienced CEO, the former chairman of Cummins Engine, Henry Schacht, acting as mentor to a younger but promising president, Rich McGuinn. Since he was only sixty-one, Allen believed that the same model was appropriate for AT&T, which, while not a new company, was navigating uncharted technological and regulatory waters. What he didn't appreciate was that McGuinn, who had spent most of his career at AT&T, was more amenable to a period of apprenticeship than most qualified outside executives would be. Anyone who would be ready to take the helm at AT&T in three or four years was unlikely to believe that he or she needed to wait three or four years to do it.

In retrospect, we should have anticipated this and embraced it. For example, we could have used Mandl's resignation as an opportunity to describe the kind of leadership that would be required for the next phase of AT&T's transformation. Allen could have announced a definitive plan to adopt the Schacht/McGuinn model that he had devised for Lucent in preparing to step aside as CEO of AT&T. And we could have made the search much more of a board responsibility rather than something the board was briefed on but didn't really control. Had we taken this approach, we might have avoided the painful disruptions that lay ahead of us. As we shall see, we ended up in the same place, but at a much higher cost to both the company and its CEO.

4

Complete the CEO

CEOs, like the rich, are different from you and me principally because they think they are. What makes them dangerous is the ways in which they're the same. For example, they suffer from the same selective hearing and wishful thinking as you and me. They have the same frustrating combination of strengths and weaknesses. A PR counselor's job is to provide peripheral vision and some grounding in reality. The board of directors' job is to ensure that the team surrounding the CEO compensates for, and doesn't exacerbate, his or her weaknesses.

John Walter

The afternoon of October 17, 1996, was unseasonably warm, and Marilyn Laurie was sitting on the patio outside her Basking Ridge, New Jersey, office when I showed up in response to her phone call.

"I just spent three hours with our new president," she said.

I had been expecting her call. The media were full of speculation about the search for Mandl's successor. The latest two names that had been added to the list of potential candidates were Mike Armstrong, a former IBM executive and the current CEO of Hughes Electronics, and William Esrey, the CEO of Sprint. The others included George Fisher, the CEO of Kodak, and James McInerney, the head of General Electric's lighting division, who was on everyone's list of potential CEOs while he waited for Jack Welch to pick his eventual successor. One favorite, James Barksdale, the CEO of Netscape, had publicly taken himself out of the running (although he had reportedly suggested that he would take the job if AT&T bought his fledgling Internet browser company).

Such was the caliber of the talent that Allen and his two search firms, Spencer Stuart and Korn Ferry, were reportedly considering. My own money was on Fisher, who had begun his career as a Bell Labs scientist before moving to Motorola, where he ultimately became CEO before leaving for Kodak. His record at the giant photography company had been mixed, and I thought he would be more comfortable, and more successful, at the helm of a communication services company.

The search itself had taken on a new urgency ever since AT&T had announced in September that it expected third- and fourth-quarter earnings to be as much as 10 percent below analysts' expectations because of intense price competition in communication services. Coming on the heels of Mandl's resignation, the change in earnings guidance underlined the importance of identifying and installing effective operating management. For the first time, Allen had even said that he would step aside if that was what it would take to find the right person for the job.

So whom had we chosen? "I don't think you'll know his name, but you know his company," Marilyn said. "What is it?" I asked, not really understanding why we were suddenly playing Twenty Questions.

"R. R. Donnelly," she said in the flattest tone I had ever heard from her.

"The Yellow Pages advertising people?"

"You're thinking of R. *H*. Donnelly," she said. "This is R. *R*." As if that cleared everything up. Seeing that I was still drawing a blank, she helped me out: "The Chicago-based printing company. I think R. H. and R. R. were brothers or something."

I gave up. "So who is it?"

"John R. Walter. He's the president of R. R. Donnelly. He just led them through a major transformation from paper and ink to digital media. Bob's betting he can do the same kind of thing here."

She then told me that the board members had met individually with Walter two nights before, followed by a group dinner at the Pierre Hotel in Manhattan. She, Rick Miller (AT&T's CFO), and Zeglis had met individually with Walter the next morning. Her meeting, she said, had been the longest, and she had come away impressed with his energy, self-confidence, and engaging personality. However, he was the darkest of dark horses. And Marilyn was smart enough to know that his appointment would not be received enthusiastically by the media, investors, or even employees, all of whom were expecting someone with more marquee value.

Furthermore, his appointment could still fall through. He had been offered the job informally, but he hadn't accepted yet. He and Allen were still dancing around the issue of when he would take over as CEO. Allen wanted to leave it open; Walter wanted a specified date. Of course, neither of them would broach the subject with the other; they were negotiating through Burlingame.

Nevertheless, Laurie wanted me to take a swing at preparing the communications plan for an announcement, assuming that everything could be resolved by the following week. She gave me a slim folder, which she told me contained all the background information she had on Walter.

When I got back to my office, I was surprised to discover that the folder contained exactly three documents: Walter's official Donnelly biography, listing an impressive number of board memberships (three corporate and seven nonprofit); a copy of a very favorable January 15, 1996, *Business Week* article about Walter; and what appeared to be a report by author and educator Warren Bennis on Walter's "leadership style."

I was sure that the executive recruiting firms had prepared fat dossiers on Walter, which I could get from Burlingame when he returned to the office. Meanwhile, I went onto the Internet to see what I could find. At Donnelly's Web site, I downloaded the last eleven years of the company's financial results. Now, I am not a numbers person. I gave up balancing my checkbook years ago because I find it too tedious and ultimately frustrating. Presented with columns of numbers, my eyes have difficulty focusing. But even allowing for my innumeracy and the fact that, at about $6.5 billion in revenue, Donnelly was much smaller than AT&T, its financial results looked very familiar—revenue in the latest quarter was down 6 percent; in the first nine months of the year, the company had incurred pretax restructuring charges of $560 million as it closed printing plants and wrote off part of a software venture touted in the *Business Week* article; and excluding those charges and one-time gains, net income had declined 26 percent.

Not trusting myself to interpret these results, I returned to Laurie's office. "Marilyn," I said, "unless I'm missing something, Donnelly's financial results look an awful lot like ours, with declining revenue, lower earnings, and lots of write-offs, layoffs, and bad investments."

She looked at the material I thrust into her hands and said, "Let's go find Zeglis."

Public Relations had begun reporting to Zeglis when Mandl left and Allen had split operational responsibility between him and the CFO, Rick Miller. As it happened, they were both behind closed doors in Zeglis's office when we arrived. I briefly outlined my concerns. Miller glanced at the spreadsheet I had downloaded from the Donnelly Web site, said "Well, this isn't my problem," and left. Zeglis called Burlingame and put him on the speakerphone. "Hal, Martin and Marilyn are war-gaming the Walter announcement and want to know how to handle questions about Donnelly's financial results. How did you cover this with the board?"

There was a long pause. "We didn't get into that level of detail with the board." Another pause. "How bad is it?"

"Well, I'm not sure," Zeglis said, "but I want to be sure the board considers it before they formally vote. I'll call Bob."

Instead of calling Allen, who was traveling, Zeglis called the company's treasurer, who had one of the sharpest financial minds around. "I'm going to have some financial data faxed over to you," he said. "It's for a company whose chairman is being considered for our board. Could you do a quick analysis of its results, compare them to the S&P or whatever other benchmark you think appropriate, and let me know what you think? I need it by the end of the day."

I never saw that analysis, but Zeglis said that he would be sure the board did. Nevertheless, at 7:30 P.M. on the evening of October 22, 1996, the board unanimously voted to offer the position to John Walter, as recommended by Allen. Walter, whose name had been on long lists prepared by both search firms at the beginning of the search, had been the only candidate the board interviewed.

Meeting Walter

I met Walter for the first time on the evening he was selected. I was struck by his resemblance to a local New York City news anchorman, Chuck Scarborough. They both had the same chiseled good looks, blond hair graying slightly at the temples, crinkly eyes, and sparkling smile. He was also quite young—just forty-nine, about a year younger than I was at the time. Walter was seated at the long conference table in the office across from Bob Allen's, sorting through all the material we had prepared in the past few days, including a detailed timeline, news release, letter to employees, and Q&A.

Walter could be forgiven for finding it all a little confusing. He also had a similar pile of material that Donnelly planned to issue the next day. But he seemed fixated on the fourth question in our Q&A: "Isn't R. R. Donnelly having serious problems of its own? Their third-quarter earnings declined 26 percent. They recently had to take $560 million in restructuring charges because of a failed strategy. If Walter couldn't solve Donnelly's problems, why do you think he can solve AT&T's?"

The answer to that question had come from eleven pages of material faxed to us by Donnelly's corporate communications department. But Walter seemed less concerned with the answer than with the question.

"Who asked this?"

I explained that we tried to think of the rudest questions that reporters might throw at us to be sure we were equipped to answer them.

"Well, it's wrong," he said. "Did this come from Donnelly's Investor Relations department? If it did, it's only because the head of that department knows that I wanted to fire her. She's totally incompetent."

I tried to change the subject, drawing his attention to the other questions he might be asked.

"Let's change this question," he said as he started scribbling on the Q&A in front of him.

When the meeting broke up at around 10 P.M., Walter was still obsessing about how his record at Donnelly would be perceived. Indeed, it was still on his mind at lunch the next day, when he asked to be briefed on the news conference. Marilyn looked at me, and, between bites of my sandwich, I ran through the agenda again, describing the setup for the news conference and reiterating our key messages: Walter's experience and leadership qualities would supplement our senior team; he had already proven himself by transforming a traditional business into a thriving, global high-tech company; Walter and Allen will partner closely, and so on.

Out of the corner of my eye, I could see Allen getting restless. He could feel a full-fledged rehearsal coming on, and he hated to be "handled." He wanted no part of it, preferring to read his remarks and the Q&A we had prepared in the quiet of his office. Walter apparently was used to having his staff stage-manage every appearance.

We would later learn that he had a very short attention span; he seldom read anything that was longer than a page, and he preferred to work from highly graphic "mind maps" that outlined the major ideas of his speeches, with lines and arrows connecting boxes of memory-jogging bulleted items like "snake story, off-line, acronyms, Carpet-land."

(The snake story was Ross Perot's oft-repeated remark that if a snake showed up in General Motors's boardroom, the board would form a committee to study it rather than simply kill it. "Off-line" referred to a frequent habit within AT&T of taking contentious issues "off-line," or dealing with them outside a meeting rather than confronting them when they came up. Acronyms referred to telecommunications people's love of reducing everything to initials, then turning them into words and using them as if everyone knew what they stood for. "Carpetland" referred to the executive floors at Basking Ridge, where the offices were arrayed around the perimeter of the building so that each could have a terrace, leaving a broad expanse of thickly carpeted, empty floor in the middle. Most of Walter's speeches criticized what he considered AT&T's hidebound culture.)

The Media Reacts

Even mind maps, however, could not have prepared Walter for the news conference that followed. The media arrived with chips on their shoulders. Allen was reminded that he had said he would step aside only if he had found "god." "Is John Walter god?" someone from the national media actually thought to ask. And then, of course, Walter was asked the most challenging question of all: "Who's your long-distance company?" His answer: "I don't know."

No one was thrilled with the news conference. When we returned to our offices for one-on-one interviews, we discovered that "Chainsaw Al" Dunlap was on CNBC blasting Walter's appointment and asking why AT&T's board had not sought someone "with a proven record of wealth creation, which is what suffering shareholders are looking for." Furthermore, AT&T's stock price was down half a point on volume of 4.8 million shares, about twice the normal volume. By the end of the day, it would be down nearly $2 on volume of 9 million shares in primarily institutional trading.

I didn't realize how upset Walter himself was until dinner. We had arranged to meet at the restaurant in the Olde Mill Inn, just across the highway from AT&T's Basking Ridge headquarters, at the end of the day. It was supposed to be a celebratory dinner, but Walter understandably was not in a joyful mood. He was convinced that his inability to name his long-distance company had torpedoed any chance he had of establishing himself as the visionary kind of CEO that AT&T needed. And he blamed us for not preparing him for the question. "The prep you guys gave me for that news conference was just awful," he said. "More than awful, it was appalling."

I stared at my menu while Marilyn gamely declared that we would work harder to get into sync with his expectations. "Just appalling," he continued. "I thought AT&T would have a real professional operation. All you guys did was point me to the elevator and warn me that there'd be a lot of photographers."

In fact, we *had* spent an inordinate amount of time warning him that the moment he stepped off the elevator to walk the ten yards or so to our auditorium, he would be confronted with a phalanx of about a dozen photographers, each flashing strobe lights in his face. We had experienced the scene before, and we knew it could be unnerving. On the other hand, we had also given him five pages of questions that were likely to come up. Admittedly, where he got his long-distance service was not one of them.

Thankfully, at about that point, the waiter brought the wine list. The Olde Mill Inn's dining room appeared nowhere in *Wine Spectator*'s list of fine wine cellars. But Walter fancied himself an oenophile, and he discovered a vintage that was to his liking. When the bottle was brought to him and uncorked, he swirled a sample in his wine glass, expertly took in its bouquet, sipped, and ran it over his palate.

"That's really exceptional," he said. Then he told the waiter—a kid who was just trying to work his way through college—"You really ought to try it."

The waiter demurred, but Walter insisted, pouring some into an empty glass. "Go on. Feel empowered," he said.

Again, the waiter—now becoming embarrassed—said he really couldn't. It was against house policy to drink on the job.

"Your only policy should be to please the customer," Walter said.

Then, while the poor waiter tried to pour the rest of the wine so that he could escape, Walter began a lecture on customer relations, employee empowerment, and winning organizations.

While all this was going on, Adele Ambrose, AT&T's media relations vice president, was working her cell phone to get a handle on the tone of the next day's stories. Ambrose had been the steady, reassuring voice of AT&T through the turmoil of the previous year.

Bringing a dogged intensity to representing the company, Ambrose took the negative media personally. A slight woman, just a little over five feet tall, she has a full-throated horselaugh that can erupt unexpectedly, then be quickly brushed away with a flutter of hands. The reporters she dealt with trusted her as they would a colleague. They knew that she would never mislead them and would always be accessible, even if it meant carrying cell phone, pager, and laptop to the beach.

Although Ambrose brought icy skepticism to the company's position on almost any subject, asking tougher questions than most reporters would, by the time she faced the media, her steely conviction had wound itself tightly around the issue until it sprung free and uncoiled in a rat-a-tat-tat volley of punctuation-free argument.

The issue this evening was John Walter's appointment, and she was not optimistic. The *Wall Street Journal*, she reported, would carry three stories, including one on the impact on Donnelly. The *New York Times* would carry three, all on Walter. The *New York Post*, always a wild card, would probably be the most negative, focusing on the decline in the company's stock price on the day of the announcement. Most of the third parties we had lined up for interviews had been called by at least one reporter. Following our recommendation, they had stressed Walter's transformational leadership qualities.

The search firms had worked their contacts at the various news outlets, providing enough background information on the search process to demonstrate that it had been thorough and that the board of directors had been deeply engaged. In fact, two directors—Walter Elisha, chair of the board governance committee, and Tom Wyman, chair of the compensation committee—had met with Walter several times and reported their findings to the other board members. In summary, Ambrose felt that the coverage would be prominent, with a range of perspectives from critical to skeptical and wait and see. Everyone would play up the surprise of Walter's appointment.

"Well, that positions me to exceed their expectations, doesn't it?"

Walter said. "Let's go around the table. What's your advice? If you were me, what would you do?"

I don't remember if I went first, but I do remember what I said, both because of Walter's reaction and because it unfortunately proved prescient. "Don't underestimate the complexity of the company," I said. "It's big, but, worse, it's highly complex. Everything depends on everything else. At GE, the jet engine people don't particularly care what the lighting people do. But here, if you change pricing by a quarter of a penny in a data service that only multinational companies buy, it inevitably has repercussions in our consumer long-distance business." I was exaggerating, but not by much.

"I disagree," Walter said. "I don't need to get into the nuts and bolts of the business. In fact, what I need to do is stay naïve and push for simple solutions. AT&T needs leadership, not more management."

In fact, we needed both.

Vying to outdo each other in archness, the next day's papers variously described Walter as "a bolt from the blue," "a distinct letdown" (*New York Times*), "a Telecom Novice," "a curveball," "found in the Yellow Pages," "John Walter Who?" (*Wall Street Journal*), and "heir un-apparent" (*New York Daily News*). Morgan Stanley's research analyst headlined her investor note "AT&T: My Mother Warned Me There Would Be Days Like This," but reiterated her strong buy on the stock. Most analysts expressed surprise at Walter's selection, particularly in view of his relative youth and his lack of industry experience, but they generally adopted a wait-and-see attitude.

We also surveyed employees following the announcement. Most rank-and-file AT&T employees either didn't have an opinion about his appointment (27 percent) or thought it was a good idea (38 percent). But among AT&T executives, 53 percent were unfavorable, citing especially his lack of industry experience. However, a whopping 69 percent of those same executives said that, now that Walter had the job, he should make changes, and he should make them quickly.

Personality Matters

One of the biggest surprises I had when I finally reached top management was how much personality quirks influence corporate decision making.

In early 2000, a dog-eared document began making the rounds of

AT&T's executive offices like a corporate samizdat, the underground press of Communist Russia. Several copy generations old, it was blotchy, and parts of it were hard to read. The copy I received was underlined and had scribbled asterisks and exclamation points in the margin.

It was an article from the January-February issue of the *Harvard Business Review* by psychoanalyst Michael Maccoby entitled "Narcissistic Leaders: The Incredible Pros, the Inevitable Cons."[1] While Maccoby had done work for AT&T in the past, he had not, as far as I knew, contacted us in the preparation of his article. Nevertheless, his article read as if he had been hovering, sight unseen, just above our management meetings for the past two years.

Maccoby was not using the term *narcissistic* pejoratively. In fact, the examples he cited—Jack Welch, George Soros, Bill Gates, Andy Grove—are admirable figures. In the context of business leadership, he saw narcissists as "gifted and creative strategists who see the big picture and find meaning in the risky challenge of changing the world and leaving behind a legacy." He suggested that what he called "productive narcissists" were just what the doctor ordered when companies were facing fundamental changes in their markets or technologies.

That certainly described AT&T, and the board (or chance) had given us two narcissists in a row to get us through the transition: first John Walter, then Mike Armstrong. "Productive narcissists," Maccoby wrote, "are not only risk takers willing to get the job done but also charmers who can convert the masses with their rhetoric." That also described both Walter and Armstrong. Both were highly effective salesmen and were very popular with rank-and-file employees, whose dissatisfaction with bureaucracy and impatience with the pace of change the two leaders seemed to mirror.

Maccoby saw an Achilles heel in narcissists, however: They are not very introspective and tend to lack self-knowledge. They set audacious goals, but they don't listen to the very people who have to achieve them. They are highly competitive and see threats everywhere, and when some of their schemes fail, they are hypersensitive to criticism, blaming others and never themselves.

Armstrong appeared to understand these dangers intuitively. He wasn't very introspective, but he seemed to understand that he intimidated some people, and he had trained himself to be a patient listener. In meetings, he seldom interrupted anyone and always apologized if he inadvertently started speaking before someone had finished, urging that person to go on. The quickest way to lose his confidence was to roll over when he challenged you. I can attest from personal experience that he respected people who disagreed with him openly—even heatedly—as long as their arguments were logical and fact-based. He quickly tired of people who whined or lacked conviction. He was highly competitive, pushing people to accelerate their deadlines or raise their targets, but when things went wrong, he was not inclined to waste time finding people to blame.

Uncharacteristically for someone brimming with such confidence, Armstrong was the exception to Galbraith's Law that "faced with the choice of changing one's mind and proving that there is no need to do so, almost everyone gets busy on the proof." Given a new set of facts, Armstrong would confidently change course. However, as we will see, he wasn't always quick to admit that he had done so, no matter what the compass readings said. He was not the kind of CEO who hated to be given bad news, and he had no trouble distinguishing between the message and the messenger. He simply ignored setbacks, focusing on fixing the problem and moving on. He was not naturally suspicious of those around him; he might question their competence, but he seldom questioned their motives.

In fact, in view of later events, one could argue that he was too trusting. In his early years at AT&T, he was not particularly sensitive to criticism, striving, in his own words, to "rise above it." But in the end, the sheer quantity of the negative press, some of it highly personal, weighed him down. Whatever calluses he had acquired over the years wore off, exposing raw nerves.

At one point, I had brought him such a string of bad news that if I showed up in his office unexpectedly, I could tell from his expression that his stomach had begun to knot. That alarmed me because, by nature, Armstrong was one of the most optimistic people I had ever met. Brimming with confidence, he refused to dwell on problems or let adversity paralyze him, even if he had been backed into a corner, as he ultimately was.

It also would be wrong to assume that Armstrong and Walter were cut from the same cloth. Armstrong had far greater depth. While not an intellectual, he was highly intelligent, understood technology at both a practical and a conceptual level, and could more than hold his own in a discussion of global macroeconomic issues. He had a steel-trap mind for numbers, and he understood the subsurface hydraulics of financial statements. He was also tireless, regularly putting in twelve- to fifteen-hour days five days a week and spending good chunks of the weekend on conference calls. By comparison, John Walter was a cardboard cutout.

Dealing with Narcissists

Maccoby's article offered practical advice for dealing with a productive narcissist, ranging from consistently empathizing with his feelings to letting him take credit for your ideas and ignoring any requests of his that don't make sense, as you can be confident that he will forget them. But his most helpful advice was to find a narcissistic boss's sidekick, the one person whom he listens to and who keeps him grounded in reality. Such a person often becomes an extension of the narcissist, but is infinitely more approachable.

No one can apply for this role (and one wonders who would), but Maccoby's research suggests that many productive narcissists choose just such a person to define the operational requirements of their vision and to anchor their more soaring flights of fancy. Chosen well, a sidekick can reinforce a narcissistic leader's strengths and compensate for the leader's weaknesses.

But it can work the other way too: Some sidekicks reinforce narcissists' most dangerous tendencies, feed their fantasies, and carry out their wishes whether or not those wishes make sense. And because narcissists are so self-confident, they can also be undermined by people who lack the courage to confront them, but are clever enough to manipulate them. Armstrong's sidekicks came in all three flavors, as we will see.

John Walter's sidekick arrived in the person of Steve Bono, who had been one of the PR people at Donnelly. Marilyn Laurie and I met with Bono in early November, just two weeks after Walter's appointment. Naturally, we were curious about Walter's expectations—how many speeches did he give, how many media interviews did he do, how did he like to be briefed?

We were surprised to learn that at Donnelly, Walter gave relatively few outside speeches, maybe half a dozen a year, and did not do many interviews either, maybe one every other month. By contrast, Bob

Allen gave about twenty-four major public addresses a year, not count-ing grace notes at various charity dinners. The interview requests were virtually endless. He could spend part of every day on the phone with one reporter or another. On the other hand, Allen required little hand-holding. He knew what he wanted to say, and he knew when it was important that he take a direct hand in shaping what he said. Other-wise, he let us assemble the wisdom of the organization on the subject at hand and present it to him for review, comment, and approval in a largely mechanical process.

Bono warned us that Walter, in contrast, preferred an iterative process with a very long lead time. He wanted to see detailed planning on any event in which he was being asked to participate, including background on the other participants. He wanted to understand the "so what" of anything he was being asked to do, starting with the business goal it served. He never spoke extemporaneously. He always wanted talking points, even for small internal meetings. And he wouldn't say or sign anything before he was comfortable with it, but he couldn't always express what caused his discomfort. He preferred an in-person briefing on all this, but if a briefing had to be in writing, it couldn't go on for more than a page. He always stayed on message, repeating the same points and anecdotes until his audience could get to the punch line before he did. Finally, he was highly critical, always looking for a better way to do things.

Bono eventually moved to AT&T's payroll, taking a relatively unde-fined job in Human Resources. His official portfolio was broadly de-fined as "culture change," but he spent most of his time interpreting Walter to us and us to Walter. (He left when Walter did and eventually became senior vice president of corporate communications for the ServiceMaster Company.)

CEO Management

Companies don't make decisions, people do. It's folly to assume that all CEOs are alike or that you can learn anything truly meaningful about CEOs by reading their biographies. The two AT&T CEOs and three presidents that I knew most intimately—Bob Allen, Mike Arm-strong, Alex Mandl, John Walter, and John Zeglis—could not have been more different, although, interestingly, four of the five were Mid-westerners. (Armstrong and Walter had even graduated from the same college, Miami of Ohio.) Each had his own style. Some were morning people; others were night owls. Some were cerebral; others were more intuitive. Two were salesmen; one was a lawyer; one started in finance; one in the telephone business, supervisor of operators old enough to be his mother. None were engineers, even though they spent the peak of their careers in the most technical of industries in the period of greatest technological change.

In psychoanalytic terms, Walter and Armstrong showed many of the characteristics of productive narcissists; Allen, Zeglis, and Mandl showed the characteristics of productive obsessives in their conscientious focus on operations and on bringing order to a chaotic environment. All five men were smart, despite what has been written about some of them. None was particularly greedy, at least by today's standards, and I personally never had reason to question the integrity of any of them. The two who became CEO of AT&T were done in by bad casting decisions.

Board Duties

It's said that the most important responsibility of a board of directors is to select the right CEO. My experience suggests that that's only half the job. The people who immediately surround the CEO will make or break the company. If they compensate for the CEO's weaknesses, they will help to ensure that the company is led by a complete executive. If, in addition, they reinforce the CEO's strengths, they will greatly magnify his or her effectiveness. But if they suffer from the same weaknesses and mindlessly follow directions, they will put the CEO and the company on a path to disaster.

In recent years, boards have reasserted that selecting a CEO's successor is their prerogative and theirs alone. To that end, most boards have devoted substantial time to reviewing the performance and capabilities of their company's most senior team. But much of their input comes from the sitting CEO, and when there's a problem, the board is unlikely to look for the cause in the dynamic between the CEO and his or her subordinates. Indeed, if the dynamic were too poisonous to ignore, it would almost certainly be the subordinate who would be let go. Having made the most significant decision of their tenure—the selection of a CEO—most boards suffer from cognitive dissonance if subsequent events suggest that they were wrong, or even not as right as they might have been.

When the AT&T board reviewed Mike Armstrong's performance for the year 2000 (the year in which the company revised its earnings guidance twice, saw its stock price tumble by 17 percent, flirted with a liquidity crisis, and ultimately announced a massive restructuring that would undo billions of dollars in acquisitions), it deliberated for more than two hours and then called him into the boardroom to give him a standing ovation.

The board members were not applauding his mistakes, or even his performance. They were acknowledging his courage and the obstacles he had overcome. Not one of them would have wanted to be in his shoes. Of course, they cut his bonus. What they should have done was figure out what had gone wrong. Part of it was unknowable at that point—WorldCom's fraud had created pricing pressure that deprived the company of the earnings it needed to sustain its investments in cable and wireless. But part of it had been in the room with them; in the first two years of Armstrong's tenure, the company was long on vision but short on financial discipline in its acquisitions and divestitures. The problems of 2000 had been sown in the years before. The board had hired a great CEO, but it had waited too long to complete him with a great CFO.

Part of that responsibility also falls on a CEO's PR counselor. The best advice I received when I assumed responsibility for AT&T's public relations came from my predecessor twice removed. Ed Block had been senior vice president of public relations at AT&T when AT&T still enjoyed a monopoly and was the largest company in the world, with influence that was felt from the corridors of Capitol Hill to rural village halls. Block reminded me that my job was to be a physical extension of the CEO. Good public relations was *his* responsibility. My job was to help him fulfill it. He was my only client, and I had better get used to his whims, eccentricities, strengths, weaknesses, and foibles, because I would be living with them for as long as I had my job. And if I didn't get used to them, I wouldn't have it for long.

But as Block pointed out, my job was not simply to *keep* my job. Successful CEOs are like thoroughbred racehorses: They wear blinders to block out distractions and stay focused on the finish line. My job was to provide peripheral vision, even if it was occasionally at the price of being nipped. My biggest regret is that, while I had moments of clarity, I was seduced by the allure of the stock markets, as were most of my colleagues. This was not simply a function of my growing pile of stock options. It was the ethos of an era in which success was measured by the stock tables, anything with a "dot-com" in its name was doubling or tripling in value, and our company seemed hopelessly out of step.

5

Expect the Dumbing Down of Reality

The media set the agenda for public discourse and define the environment within which CEOs operate. But the media work on a level well beyond an outsider's reach—what they say is often less important than how they say it and what they have said before. Their impact can't be tallied in clippings. They serve no master but a public that values entertainment as well as information, and sometimes mistakes the one for the other.

The Beginning of the End

John Walter looked tired. He was scheduled to speak to a large group of employees at AT&T's corporate education center. We had arranged a series of these meetings to give him a feel for the company and, especially, to show employees that he wasn't the Bozo that the media had made him out to be.

This meeting was early in the new year, and Walter had just flown back from Chicago, where he had spent the Christmas holidays with his family. He started out by waving a sheaf of papers at the group.

"This is what PR wanted me to say," he said. "It's worthless. I don't think these PR people know anything."

Then he threw the papers on the podium and walked out in front of it, saying, "If they do to me what they did to Bob Allen, I'm in trouble."

He didn't know it yet, but he *was* in trouble. And PR had played a small, if unknowing, role in putting him there.

Reporters had been pestering us to interview Walter from the day of his appointment. Normally, the safest time to do interviews is when an executive is new to the job. No one really expects him to know anything, so you don't have to worry about dealing with substantive issues. But the coverage of Walter's appointment had been so cheeky that we had adopted a strategy of making him available for one-on-one interviews only when the interview was about a specific accomplishment, such as a new service. We had steadfastly maintained this position through the first two months of Walter's tenure, and, as we approached the traditional lull between Christmas and New Year's, we assumed that we were out of the woods for a while.

We never expected that Walter would fire the head of the company's consumer long-distance business as his own way of celebrating Christmas. But that's what he did—or almost did—on Friday, December 20, just before leaving for the holidays.

Nacchio

Joe Nacchio had been named one of the youngest officers in AT&T's history based on in-your-face marketing and a golden gut for what sells. Born and raised on Staten Island, he developed the Brooklyn accent common in the Italian community of Bensonhurst, just across the bridge. In any case, he used it effectively in rallying his troops commando-style. Only about five and a half feet tall, he seemed to grow in stature as he bounced on the balls of his feet. He combined street smarts with near-encyclopedic knowledge of the telephone business. He was brash, fast-talking, competitive, and quick to take offense. He expected people to show him respect, and it was said that the only thing harder than working for Nacchio was to have him working for you. Throughout his career, he had left a trail of crippled bosses in his wake.

Nacchio had been openly derisive about Walter's appointment. Knowing that he now would never have a shot at the job himself, he was highly receptive when his friend Jack Grubman put him in touch with billionaire Philip Anschutz, who was looking for someone to turn the high-capacity fiber optic cables he had buried along railroad rights-of-way into a business. In fact, by the time of the AT&T officers'

Christmas party in early December 1997, Nacchio was not so quietly bragging that he was leaving the company to become CEO of a competitor.

Walter heard about Nacchio's posturing as well as the potshots Nacchio had taken at him. On Friday morning, December 20, just before lunch, he called Nacchio into his office and told him that he had decided to make a change. Gail McGovern, who had worked for Nacchio in Business Services and now led it, would be moving over to lead the consumer long-distance business. Walter left open what Nacchio would be doing. "Burlingame has some ideas," he said.

In fact, Burlingame had no ideas. He had been told that Nacchio was being let go and that he should prepare an exit package. Nacchio left Walter's office and the building for a previously scheduled lunch. Burlingame, who expected to meet with Nacchio to discuss the formalities of his departure, was dumbfounded. He spent the rest of the afternoon trying to track Nacchio down, finally reaching him late in the day and convincing him to come back to the office.

When Nacchio got there, he thought it was to discuss an interim position while he solidified plans for his new job, as he and Anschutz had not yet completed their negotiations. Burlingame had to tell him that there was no other job and that we planned to issue the news release that night. I could hear the screams from Marilyn Laurie's office, a floor away. "You mean McGovern already knows about this?" he shouted. "PR is already drafting a release?" After a while, Burlingame's secretary, ashen-faced, came down and asked Laurie to join Burlingame and Nacchio. Laurie agreed to postpone any news release for twenty-four hours to allow Nacchio to complete negotiations for his new position.

We issued the release late Sunday afternoon, December 22, simultaneously with the release by Nacchio's new company, Qwest Communications. Our release said simply that McGovern was replacing Nacchio, who was leaving to become CEO of Qwest. But when Walter, who by then was back in Chicago, got on the phone with reporters, he made a point of saying that he had "fired" Nacchio. The *Wall Street Journal* used the management change as the lead for a Christmas Eve profile of Walter.[1]

Allen was embarrassed by the *Journal* story because it said that Walter had "summarily removed" Nacchio from his position. In fact, Allen had told Walter that one of his first acts should be to replace Nacchio, whom Allen considered immature and impulsive, but he hadn't asked for a public execution. On Christmas Eve, Allen called Nacchio at home and apologized for the way the announcement had been handled.

Allen was also troubled by several other assertions in the story. "To hear AT&T's new president tell it," the *Journal* said, "he is pretty much free to run the business without a lot of second-guessing from Mr. Allen." Furthermore, it quoted a marketing manager as saying, "[Walter] seems to be dismantling everything Bob Allen put in place, like the separate business units and the corporate culture." And the story began by saying, "[Walter] already is acting as AT&T's de facto CEO, the post he isn't supposed to assume until January 1998."

Allen didn't think Walter was overreaching. He knew how the media worked, and he himself had been caught off guard more than once. But he was worried that when Walter was pushed into areas in which he wasn't yet competent (which, after less than ninety days, was most areas), he was vulnerable to mistakes and to being misinterpreted. Allen asked us to "throttle back" the wind machine.

SBC Comes Calling

As it happens, the crafty CEO of SBC Communications, Ed Whitacre, also read the *Wall Street Journal* story. Donnelly printed his company's phone books, as it did for most of the other Bell companies, so he knew John Walter well. In fact, they had gone bird hunting together on Whitacre's 1,800-acre ranch eighty miles north of San Antonio. Although he had sent Walter a friendly note when his appointment at AT&T was announced, he frankly didn't understand it. Walter was a nice enough guy and certainly a good salesman, but, as Whitacre put it to his executive team, "he didn't know diddly-shit about the telephone business." Now the *Journal* made it sound as if he was in charge.

Whitacre, a lanky six feet four with a southern drawl and a crusty demeanor, was probably the shrewdest of the Bell company CEOs. Although Southwestern Bell, as the regional phone company was first known, was initially considered the runt of the Baby Bells and had none of the sexy cities, such as Los Angeles or New York, in its service area, Whitacre had followed his predecessor's model and stuck to his knitting, refusing to be tempted into flashy ventures. On the contrary, he poured money into bolstering his local monopoly, expanding his wireless business, and taking a 10 percent stake in the Mexican phone company, Telefonos de Mexico, whose customers shared a community of interest with many of his own customers. He expanded that community of interest by announcing the acquisition of Pacific Telesis in April of 1996.

But Whitacre knew that he still had not achieved critical mass, especially if he wanted to serve businesses outside his operating territory in the west and southwest. And by consistently raising revenue, earnings, and dividends every year for twelve years, he had made his own stock a currency that could be used to broaden his base even further. After thinking about it for a few days, Whitacre put in a call to his hunting buddy, John Walter.

Walter initially thought that Whitacre was following up on his congratulatory note and was mildly surprised when he began asking him about the *Wall Street Journal* article. "Are you really in charge up there?" Whitacre asked. Walter repeated what he had told the *Journal*: He valued Allen's experience and consulted with him, but the board had agreed that he would be running things. (In fact, Walter seldom saw Allen outside of regular meetings and was slightly miffed at what he interpreted as Allen's aloofness. For his part, Allen was trying to stay out of Walter's way and was becoming increasingly impatient with Walter's focus on symbolic actions, rather than nuts-and-bolts management.) "Well, in that case," Whitacre said, "what would you think of talking about a merger between AT&T and SBC?"

To his credit, Walter said, "Now that *is* something I'd want to talk to Bob about." But even before talking to Allen, Walter knew that this could be the strategic move that would solve the biggest problem facing the company. Breaking into the local phone business was proving prohibitively expensive. AT&T had already spent $1 billion on its local effort, had only 11,000 customers to show for it, and was losing money on every one of them. Combining with SBC would give it a huge leg up in figuring out how to enter local markets nationwide. Besides, Allen was already committed to leaving in January of 1998. It would probably take at least that long to get the merger approved. Whitacre would be fifty-five by then, and Walter could imagine working the same deal with him that he had reached with Allen. By 1999, he could be atop Ma Bell reincarnated.

Thus began five months of discussion between "Star" (SBC, which was headquartered in the Lone Star State of Texas) and "Garden" (AT&T, which was headquartered in the Garden State of New Jersey). It was not the first time that AT&T had entertained the idea of merging with one of its former offspring (and it would not be the last), but it was probably the most serious effort to date. Neither company had any illusions about how high the regulatory hurdles would prove to be, but they had sharply different views on how to scale them.

SBC preferred to make the announcement and then wait for the regulators to set the height the two companies would have to jump as a condition for the merger. That was the approach that SBC had taken in negotiating its merger with Pacific Telesis, and it seemed to be working. The AT&T negotiators, on the other hand, believed that the merger would never even receive serious consideration unless its very announcement included a declaration of "model citizenship" on SBC's part. In their view, SBC should drop all objections to the Telecom Act, commit to even more rigorous standards for opening its local networks to competition than the law required, and agree not to close on the merger until it had facilities-based local competition. Further, SBC shouldn't try to offer long-distance service in its local territory until the merger closed.

SBC's negotiators saw this as a clumsy effort on the part of AT&T to tie the company's hands while the FCC, the Department of Justice, and who knew who else dithered over the merger. And what, they asked, if the merger was turned down? Once their local markets were open, there would be no way to close them again. AT&T, which would have been insulated from attacks in SBC's seven-state territory, would have lost nothing. But SBC would have lost months getting into long distance and would have aided and abetted the loss of its local market share.

By contrast, the so-called social issues—such as who would run the merged companies—were a breeze. Allen planned to stay on at AT&T for the two years the merger review would probably take and then would step down in favor of Whitacre. Left open was whether Walter would have a role in the new company. It was at about this point that Walter had a change of heart—a merger that had made sense to him just weeks before suddenly looked highly dubious. And he didn't keep his misgivings to himself. He agitated the heads of the consumer and business long-distance businesses, whom he had just installed the previous December, by warning them that their jobs were at risk if the merger went through. Never one to have difficulty putting two and two together, Allen was more than disappointed in his new president, and he shared his misgivings with the board in executive session.

The Leak

Then, on Memorial Day 1997, as I was forming hamburger patties to put on the charcoal grill, my home phone rang. It was John Keller, who told me that he was putting the final touches on a story for the next day's *Journal* that would break the news about our merger discussions with SBC. According to "sources close to the negotiations," he said, we had been in discussion for some time, but now the discussions had grown so serious that we had put some business transactions on hold. This last reference clearly concerned some wireless swaps that we had postponed because of the merger talks. That suggested someone at AT&T Wireless as the source of the leaks, but figuring out how Keller got the story was not my primary concern at the moment. Nor were the hamburgers.

I told Keller that, as he knew, we didn't comment on this kind of rumor, but just to be sure we weren't going to change our policy in this instance, I would check with Zeglis. I called Zeglis, and we decided to leave things as they were. It didn't sound as if Keller had much, and these rumors were popping up all the time. Zeglis wasn't even sure he'd call Allen about it.

The next day's *Wall Street Journal* demonstrated how a good reporter can turn the slimmest facts into a front-page 2,526-word story. What Keller knew could be put into a single compound sentence: Sources close to both companies say that merger discussions between SBC and AT&T had grown very serious in the last month, causing AT&T to postpone some wireless business transactions, even though many issues had not yet been resolved and both companies realized that approval of such a merger would face many obstacles. The other 2,474 words were based on Keller's own knowledge of the companies and interviews with people who knew nothing of the merger discussions themselves but had an opinion about them.

Of course, once the *Wall Street Journal* declares something to be news, it *is* news, even if it technically isn't. The news wires picked up the story, as did the next day's newspapers. Merrill Lynch's analyst, Dan Reingold, published an investor note saying that the deal would never be approved. Nevertheless, AT&T stock surged $1.38 (4 percent). CNBC jumped in with a report that John Walter would be CEO of the merged companies, leaving Ed Whitacre as non-executive chairman.

Allen was furious. As far as he was concerned, the leak had come from John Walter or someone close to him.[2] Whoever had leaked the information wanted to crater the deal. Allen was convinced that SBC was still interested in moving forward. In fact, Whitacre had called and suggested just that. The only person who stood to lose if a deal went through was John Walter.

Now, unfortunately, Allen was caught in a two-way negotiation as he contended not only with SBC but with all the forces opposed to a merger. In addition, he couldn't argue in favor of a deal that he couldn't acknowledge. The only voices being heard were those of competitors, consumer advocates, and other pundits who opposed the deal on the principle that big is bad.

Our policy of not commenting on such rumors was based on an SEC rule that would require us to comment whenever there was a substantial change in the situation we had commented on. So, for example, if we confirmed that we were talking to SBC, we would then have to announce it if we ended the talks. If they started again, we would have to announce that. And there was even a legal opinion that if we started talking to someone else about the same thing, we would have to announce that. And so forth. Making all these announcements would box us in, so it was easier and more prudent to avoid commenting as a matter of policy. Of course, once you have such a policy, you have to stick to it or reporters can start reading meaning into what you don't say as well as what you do say. Meanwhile, the company's critics used the merger rumors as proof that AT&T was never serious about competing with the local phone companies. It wanted to be one!

Setting the Record Straight

We decided to set the record straight. We chose as the venue a speech that Allen was scheduled to give to the CEO Club of Boston on June 9. The speech was designed to make three points: (1) We were committed to offering local service and were prepared to go it alone, even though it had been slow going because of the Bell monopolies' foot-dragging, (2) no local Bell company should be allowed into long distance until it opens its markets as required by the Telecom Act, and (3) mergers between long-distance companies and the Bell companies should not be unthinkable if they really lead to greater competition in all regions (including the Bell company's home region). And by the way, Ma Bell is dead. May she rest in peace. In other words, we had no intention of trying to recreate the Bell monopoly that had been taken apart in 1984. Forcing local markets open should be a precondition of any long-distance/local company merger—ours or anyone else's.

We arranged to get our message out as broadly as we could because we knew that the media would concentrate on the sexier parts of the story. That included delivering a copy of the speech to more than 3,000 public officials, community leaders, and other influentials on the day it was given. We also submitted an op-ed, entitled "Ma Bell Is Dead," to the *Wall Street Journal*, reprising the same basic arguments used in the speech.

Allen's speech was broadly reported. The Dow Jones news service, for example, quoted Allen as saying that mergers between long-distance companies and local Bell companies ought not to be "unthinkable" if they "enhance competition." Reuters's story led with, "A potential merger of SBC Communications Inc. and AT&T Corp. would likely include a detailed plan to open SBC's local markets to competitors." Bear Stearns issued an investor note saying, "AT&T and SBC Communications have a better-than-average chance to overcome opposition to a potential combination." Lawyers at the Department of Justice's antitrust division congratulated our lobbyists for making a compelling case that "passed the red-face test." In other words, they thought our arguments were credible. Capitol Hill staffers said that Allen had said all the right things about competition, and they would take a wait-and-see attitude on any merger.

That was not the way FCC Chairman Reed Hundt saw it. Caught after a speech in New York City, he said he thought that most antitrust experts would find a merger between AT&T and any of the regional Bell companies "unthinkable." Then, to make sure everyone got the point, he scheduled a speech at the Brookings Institution for June 19 to give a point-by-point rebuttal of Allen's speech. And, according to his memoirs, he "cut a deal with the *New York Times* to trade good coverage of [his] speech for an exclusive leak."[3] The *Times*, keeping its end of the bargain, delivered a banner headline on page one of its business section on the morning before the speech, guaranteeing that TV cameras would be in the room when Hundt walked to the podium.

Two of Hundt's colleagues on the commission said that his speech was inappropriate. The *Times* itself called it "almost unheard of for a Federal official to publicly prejudge a corporate merger"[4] and pointed out that Hundt was scheduled to step down within six months and would be unlikely to vote on it anyway. The media had another field day.

All we could do was seize on a point on the first page of Hundt's speech, in which he said that such a merger "should be considered only when and *if* it is proposed." Two days after the speech, Allen's *Journal* op-ed appeared, spiced up with references to Hundt's speech inserted at the paper's request to give it more "news value."

Then, on June 27, the FCC denied SBC's application to offer long-distance service in Oklahoma—an application to which we had filed a forty-five-page objection shortly after the *Journal*'s original story appeared. The FCC's action convinced SBC that merger approval would come at too high a price, if it was even possible. Whitacre called Allen and told him that he didn't believe a merger was in the cards. The forces opposing a merger were too great, and the two companies' approaches to dealing with them were too different. Allen agreed to call off the talks, and the two CEOs told their respective boards on Friday.

Although Allen and Whitacre agreed to maintain radio silence on the end of the discussions, by late afternoon we got wind that someone was spreading the story that SBC had called off discussions because it was fed up with the way we were handling the lobbying and PR. We stuck to our policy of not commenting, but off the record we hinted that the talks were called off because SBC wouldn't agree to open its markets. Both versions were true, and in the all-important contest to be positioned as the company that called off the talks, AT&T took a slight lead—that was the way the *New York Times* headline played it, while most other papers were more neutral.[5]

On the other hand, the *New York Times* also decided that this meant that John Walter was out of a job, quoting an unnamed AT&T board member as saying that he was in trouble. I thought I knew who the board member was. He sat on another board with Alex Mandl, and I could imagine the two of them chatting about Alex's former job at AT&T and gossiping about the current cast of characters. Mandl, in turn, knew Mark Landler, the *New York Times* reporter who wrote the story.

Exit Walter

I knew the story was accurate. In fact, I was already drafting memos recommending ways in which we could handle Walter's departure.

Walter had also known for several weeks that something was up. He had called me from Europe in mid-June, asking for a stronger response to a *Business Week* report that he was odd man out whether or not we pursued a merger with SBC. When I told him that I thought it would be a mistake to dignify such rumors by trying to get Bob Allen on the record again, Walter told me that a director had warned him that Allen had lost confidence in him and had told the board that Walter did not need to be part of the leadership following a merger with SBC.

He wanted me to make it clear to *Business Week*, and anyone else who thought he was out of the loop, that he had been active in the SBC talks, even though he knew they could "put him in harm's way."

"John," I said, "I can't say you've been active in talks we aren't acknowledging we've even had." At that point, I realized that it was past midnight in Germany, where he was calling from. "It's late. You need some rest. Don't worry about *Business Week*; it's only another rumor."

"We need to get the word out," he said as he hung up. There wasn't much else I could say. I knew he was probably on his way out. But I hoped we could handle it in a way that did minimal damage to either his reputation or ours.

I had had my first hint that Walter might be in trouble in March, when Allen called me into his office to tell me that he planned to make Zeglis a member of the board and its vice chairman. It seemed that Zeglis had been offered the CEO job at an Illinois utility. Until that moment, Allen had assumed that Zeglis was not interested in the top job. Now, he realized, not only was Zeglis interested in it, but others saw him in those terms.

When Mandl left, Zeglis had stepped in to run the company's vast consumer services organization, and had discovered that there was no particular magic to operational management. Furthermore, he had been decidedly unimpressed with John Walter and knew that he could do whatever Walter could do.

Allen, who was becoming increasingly uncomfortable with Walter, didn't want to lose Zeglis. So he offered him a vice chairmanship, if the board agreed, with the tacit assurance that the company's succession plans were not set in concrete. When I warned Allen that Zeglis's appointment would be interpreted as a lack of confidence in Walter, he simply smiled and said, "I know that." He didn't need to say more.

The fly in the ointment, however, was the company's proxy. We were already printing three million copies, and they listed all the director nominees to be voted on at the May annual meeting. Reprinting them was not an option, even if we were willing to spend the money—there wasn't enough time. And adding Zeglis's name in a special supplement to the proxy would raise even more questions. The company's bylaws permitted directors to be elected by the board between meetings. So Allen told Zeglis that he would be made vice chairman and a director as soon after the annual meeting as was practical. That turned out to be mid-June.

By then, Allen could barely stand to be in the same room as John Walter, whom he was convinced was leaking like a sieve and whom he blamed for the failure of the SBC merger discussions. Furthermore, Allen had been hearing complaints about Walter from a steady stream of executives, both company veterans and newcomers. According to them, Walter seemed unable to focus on any subject for more than twenty minutes and was quick to criticize, but offered no solutions. They said he still didn't have a grasp of the business's fundamentals and didn't seem to be making any effort to learn them. He had made little progress on basic operating issues, such as fixing the billing systems, despite his early expressions of disbelief at their inadequacy.

Walter had particularly alienated the former McCaw wireless executives when he complained about having to fly all the way to Seattle for a briefing on their fixed wireless project and cut short a tour of the secret manufacturing plant they had built in a Redmond office park. In fact, he openly questioned the company's wireless investment. His efforts to make a show of "firing people" offended many executives and caused some to question his integrity.

Allen himself was beginning to believe Walter was a brilliant salesman but superficial, dealing in tired bromides. At one board meeting just before the executive session when Allen met alone with the outside members, Allen asked Walter to give an operational review. He spent twenty minutes talking about his efforts to instill a sense of ownership into the company's employees, told Ross Perot's snake story, and ended by declaring that AT&T had all the elements to be a winning, learning organization. When he left the room, Allen simply said, "See what I mean?"

Unfortunately, back in April we had scheduled Allen, Walter, and Zeglis to attend an editorial board meeting with *USA Today* on June 30. Putting the three of them in front of a group of reporters would be like dangling raw meat in front of lions, but we decided to keep the date in order to avoid fueling more speculation about succession. I flew down with Allen. Walter and Zeglis took a separate company plane, in keeping with corporate security's policy on key executives flying together. But when we got to Washington, Allen and Walter somehow ended up in the same car. Walter apparently spent the short trip to *USA Today*'s headquarters complaining about media leaks and vowing to get to the bottom of them. For the car ride back, Allen frantically waved me into his car so he wouldn't have to relive the same conversation.

Somewhere in the hour and a half we spent with *USA Today*, someone asked what Allen thought of Hundt's speech. Allen said, "I thought it was inappropriate, and I don't think I should say more." That was the sum total of what he said.

The next day's paper screamed that he had "ripped into Hundt"; "assailed the FCC"; and "blamed regulators for the collapse of the SBC deal."[6] I called the editors, and they apologized profusely. It seems that someone had written all the headlines and subheads at the stroke of midnight, just before the paper was beamed up to the satellites for transmission to their printing plants. The editors and writers who attended the editorial board meeting were all at home by then, safely tucked into their beds, and didn't see the final version until they got to work the next day.

Although I pretended to be upset, I was secretly delighted that they had chosen to beat a dead horse rather than pick up on the real story that was sitting across the table from them—John Walter would be gone before the company announced its second-quarter results on July 21.

I had drawn that line in the sand because making the announcement after we issued our financial results would unnecessarily give Walter another opportunity to position himself during the conference call that typically accompanied our release, and we would be stuck with whatever he said in interviews. Besides, once the board had reached even a tentative decision on succession, I couldn't continue to say that "nothing has changed" since we announced his appointment the previous October. The board was scheduled to meet on Wednesday, July 16.

John Walter called me at home twice over the July 4 holiday weekend, showing increasing impatience with me for not taking a more active stance in stopping speculation about his status within the company. I was becoming concerned that he might take unilateral action to reaffirm his intention of staying on at AT&T, making it more difficult to announce his leaving in a face-saving way.

On the evening of July 15, there were two sets of meetings in New York City that brought this drama to a close. The outside members of AT&T's board had gathered in one of the conference rooms at the Wachtell Lipton law firm. After meeting with Allen and hearing his concerns about Walter, they excused him and interviewed several other senior executives. In the end, they sat by themselves late into the night, wondering how they had gotten into this mess.

In a hotel restaurant across town, John Walter was dining with the chairman of Korn Ferry, one of the executive search firms that had brought him to AT&T. He explained that there would be a showdown at the next day's board meeting. He would tell the board to choose between him and Bob Allen. He expected the board to side with him, and he would need to replace a number of executives. My name was at the top of the list.

How People Relate to the Media

The practice of public relations is not defined solely by media relations. But that's what every CEO I've known has focused on, almost to the exclusion of other functions such as employee communications and community relations. One of my predecessors even defined the job as "making it possible for the CEO to read the *Wall Street Journal* in the morning without getting heartburn."

While my own definition of public relations is a little more expansive, there is no doubt that what is reported about individuals and organizations can become the environment within which they operate. And with twenty-four-hour news channels, the Internet, and instant communication, that environment can swing rapidly from sunny skies to storm clouds and every climate in between. However, the dinosaurs were not done in by a rapid drop in temperature. They slipped off their evolutionary path because they were incapable of reacting to those changing conditions.

The interlinked saga of John Walter and our merger discussions with SBC was one more demonstration of how media coverage affects an organization's operational freedom and constraints.

People have a very complicated relationship with the news media. For example, the Israeli psychologists Daniel Kahneman and Amos

Tversky demonstrated that people's attitudes and behavior depend in good measure on how information is presented to them. Until they have been put into the framework of a news story, most facts are blessedly neutral, but a story's framing is actually a more reliable predictor of a reader's subsequent beliefs than the substance of the story itself. Familiar or vivid examples can skew judgments more than abstract—but more accurate—data, and first impressions shape subsequent attitudes. Kahneman and Tversky called this the "availability error," and it explains why it can be so difficult to reverse a long string of negative news or to correct a story's slant after it has taken hold.[7]

Mathematician John Allen Paulos points out that public response to most big stories is strongly colored by past stories, even if those past stories are only superficially similar, because they are "psychologically available."[8] What he calls "anchoring effects" inhibit people from moving too far from "conventional wisdom" or from the latest "facts" that they have been presented with, even if those "facts" are wrong. The "halo effect" causes people to judge a person or a company in terms of one salient characteristic, which may be positive (e.g., graduating from a prestigious university) or negative (e.g., being associated with a string of negative news stories). We generally see what we expect to see.[9]

All this helps to explain how the media put John Walter in short pants from the day of his announcement as AT&T's new president. At Donnelly, he had been seen as a visionary and highly effective leader. Many newspapers, in fact, presented his credentials accurately. The *Wall Street Journal* story, for example, was arguably quite positive in substance. It described him as "a charismatic manager who coupled teamwork and technology with an iron-fisted focus on profit growth at Chicago-based Donnelley."[10] But the sarcasm of the headline in that paper—"Bell's Curve: A Telecom Novice Is Handed Challenge of Remaking AT&T"—along with similar jibes elsewhere created a first impression that was hard to correct.

In hindsight, we should have kept to our first strategy of allowing all this to die down by focusing Walter on the nuts and bolts of the business and making him available only when he had something concrete to announce. There were several such opportunities in the first quarter of 1997—we announced a new "PocketNet" wireless phone with Internet capabilities, for example—but Walter had already alienated the leadership of the wireless division and played no role in its introduction. By contrast, when AT&T Wireless introduced the first single-rate nationwide calling plan, Digital One Rate, Mike Armstrong hosted the news conference and made the announcement on behalf of the entire company.

Ironically, the PocketNet phone accounted for 11 percent of AT&T's news coverage in the first four months of 1997 and had a perfect favorability rating, as measured by an outside researcher, Delahaye MediaLink. Walter, on the other hand, was more closely associated with the "firing" of Joe Nacchio in the last month of 1996, the announcement of the prior year's lackluster earnings in the first month of the new year, the defection of an international partner to a rival, a 30 percent drop in first-quarter earnings, and a financial analysts' conference at which he predicted that the company would earn "$5 or $6 a share within five years."

Those announcements accounted for 54 percent of AT&T's coverage in the first four months of the year, and, according to MediaLink, their average favorability was 2.0 on a five-point scale on which 1 is entirely negative. By the time we took control of Walter's media appearances and forced the wireless people to let him announce their fixed wireless project, he had been firmly associated with "bad news." Although the announcement of a wireless end run around the Bell companies garnered highly positive press (4.99 on MediaLink's favorability scale), it was too little too late to help John Walter's image.

This also explains why we were so determined to get some measure of control over the speculation about our merger discussions with SBC. As always happens in these cases, after everyone had reported on the *Wall Street Journal*'s report, most reporters started looking for a fresh angle, calling their own sources, and writing their own speculative stories. Everyone with an agenda ended up in print, and three major themes evolved: (1) AT&T isn't so serious about competitive local markets, (2) this harebrained idea is unthinkable and should be dead on arrival, and (3) it's the last desperate act of a chairman who wants to retire in a blaze of glory.

This was not a good position to be in. People started interpreting our actions through the lens of what they thought was really going on. For example, when we ended local marketing in California because of Pacific Telesis's clumsy ordering systems, the generally accepted wisdom was that this was somehow related to our negotiations with SBC. That was not very well received in other states where we were arguing for lower wholesale rates.

Agenda setting is probably the most significant role that the media play in public discourse. Political scientist Bernard Cohen put it most succinctly when he wrote that the press "may not be successful much of the time in telling people what to think, but it is stunningly successful in telling its readers what to think *about*."[11] The media's agenda setting also has another effect: Studies show that the volume of coverage dedicated to a subject seems to have an impact completely separate from the substantive content of that coverage. In addition to giving a topic salience, heavy media coverage can heighten the attitudes associated with the topic. The sheer volume of coverage reinforces first impressions.[12]

When we spoke out on the rumors of our discussions with SBC, FCC Chairman Hundt said that we "broke the first rule of Information Age politics. Don't go first."[13] But from our perspective, we were not going first. We were trying desperately to refocus what had already become a raging debate. Our goal was not so much to win anyone over on the merits of an AT&T/SBC merger as to change the subject, shifting the argument to the admittedly complicated public policy issue of opening local markets.

We wanted to make AT&T's position on local competition crystal clear so that rumors of the merger discussions with SBC didn't further complicate our efforts to enter local markets or allow the Bell companies to slip through into long distance. And we were willing to do this at the possible expense of the merger discussions themselves, since we knew that if our arguments gained traction publicly, they would be easier to argue privately at the negotiating table. On the other hand, if they fell on deaf ears in the public arena, it didn't matter how successful we were in San Antonio.

We were relatively successful in reordering the public agenda. When the merger talks broke down, most of the media blamed their failure on SBC's unwillingness to open its local markets. Unfortunately, we did not succeed in correcting the impression that AT&T was acting out of desperation, from a position of weakness. Our public policy message was too esoteric and too complicated. The subtlety of legal arguments may work in a courtroom or in the quiet of a judge's chambers, but the court of public opinion is swayed by simpler ideas, especially if they are tied to emotionally charged symbols.

6

Work Inside Out
Toward Your Customers

A new CEO should devote the first 180 days to intense learning, first from employees, then from customers. His or her entire focus should be on building employee morale and aligning the workforce behind a single vision of what, together, they can do for the company's customers. Only when that seed has taken root, should a CEO's attention include the media or sell-side financial analysts. A new CEO who defines success in terms of the company share price will pay attention to all the wrong things.

Armstrong

Mike Armstrong used to say that Mondays were his favorite day of the week. It wasn't just for effect; it was obvious he really meant it. He would literally bounce as he walked from his Porsche to the elevator that would take him to his fourth-floor office in Basking Ridge. It wasn't that he had a hard time filling his weekend—the two or three briefcases under his arms were evidence of the mail and memos he had churned through when he wasn't on the golf course, doting on his grandchildren at home, or motorcycling with his sons-in-law through the Connecticut countryside. He simply relished the challenges the work week would bring. In fact, it was the sheer challenge of re-righting an American icon that had drawn him to AT&T in the first place.

Armstrong and his wife Anne had just completed building and furnishing their dream house in Manhattan Beach, California, a short ride from his office at Hughes Electronics. They had lived in it for seven days when the headhunters representing AT&T called him for a second time in less than a year. Things were going well at Hughes. In fact, better than "well"—Hughes, which was controlled by General Motors but had public shareowners, was GM's best-performing unit and its stock price had increased 300 percent since Armstrong had taken over.

Although he thought of himself as a CEO and had his own board of directors, Armstrong knew that he really reported to GM vice chairman, Harry Pearce. He had always wanted to be a full-fledged CEO, but he had missed the opportunity at IBM. Although he had tried to convince GM's CEO, Jack Smith, to spin off Hughes, Smith had made it clear that he wasn't interested in pursing the idea.

So now that the AT&T search was for a CEO, rather than for his understudy, it was tempting on several levels. Armstrong would not only be a full-fledged CEO, but the CEO of a company of historical significance. From what he had read in the papers, the company was in sad shape. The challenge of fixing it appealed to his competitive instincts. And, also based on what he had read, he could hardly make things worse.

For their part, AT&T's employees were duly impressed with Armstrong's early press. But what really won them over was something he did before he even formally arrived at AT&T. Impatient to get started, but unwilling to saddle his wife with single-handedly packing up their household belongings for the second time in a year, Armstrong spent the week after the announcement of his appointment in California. But as soon as a free afternoon presented itself, he decided to visit a local AT&T sales office near his home. Instead of pulling up in a limousine, he drove there in his Porsche, evaded the waiting AT&T dignitaries waiting for him in the front lobby by talking his way past the guard at the employee entrance, and wandered around the building introducing himself to startled clerks and sales people. AT&T's rumor mill spread the story across the company before he had left the building.

The Early Days

Armstrong's instincts to start inside and work his way out were consistent with our own. We adopted a formal strategy of keeping a relatively low external profile during Armstrong's first ninety days. In addition to the obvious consideration that he had little to say at that early stage, we hoped that this would allow him to regain his footing. Because he took office within two weeks of joining the company, Armstrong had virtually no "getting ready" period. He needed time to develop personal chemistry and a practical working arrangement with the biggest blind date of his life, John Zeglis, who had been his rival for the CEO job and was now ostensibly his second in command.

He needed to take his own measure of the rest of the senior executive team. All he had seen so far was a package of biographies that the head of the board's search committee had asked me to pull together. Since Armstrong was already 59, he knew that he had five or six years at the outside for whatever he was going to do. He didn't think he would have the time to simultaneously change out the top management and re-focus the company. If he had to make any changes, he would have to make them fast. (In the end, by the time he left in 2002, only three of the senior managers who were there when he arrived were still on the payroll. He had gone through two chief financial officers, five heads each of business and consumer services, and three heads each of wireless and broadband services.)

Even more importantly, to my mind, he needed to master AT&T's vast bureaucracy and restore a sense of confidence to a badly demoralized body of employees. We had been measuring employee attitudes for decades, and we had been advised by researchers who specialized in these things that, after years of downsizing, AT&T was the equivalent of a "trauma company," that is, a business that has gone through a major crisis such as a bankruptcy. Employees had very low feelings of job security, did not trust senior management, and got most of their information from what the researcher called the company's "prison-quality rumor mill."

Following John Walter's resignation, only 10 percent of employees said they had confidence in senior management, our lowest reading ever—even lower than the 45 percent who expressed confidence in management following the disastrous downsizing announcement of January 1996. Whatever his shortcomings, Walter had succeeded in connecting with rank-and-file employees by adopting and giving voice to many of their complaints about AT&T's traditional hierarchy. When he was forced out, employees were left feeling like cards in a deck that was being shuffled. One of my rules of thumb is that half of what employees learn about their own company comes from reading the business media, but that this information is ten times more credible than what they are told by the company itself. Given the year AT&T had just gone through, it was no wonder that employees were shell-shocked.

Armstrong had developed his own theories on leading change as CEO of Hughes Electronics. He had joined Hughes when the Cold War ended and defense contracts, its traditional source of revenue, were withering. Over the course of several years, he led Hughes in simultaneously downsizing, spinning off businesses, and building a new source of earnings around satellites broadcasting entertainment programming into people's homes. It was a radical departure for the proud aviation and electronics company that traced its roots back to Howard Hughes. But it was arguably only a dress rehearsal for the challenges at AT&T.

Armstrong said that the biggest lesson he had learned at Hughes was that "People make change happen; achieving successful change depends on winning people over."[1] He knew that he had to simultaneously restore AT&T employees' confidence in their own competence and convince them that they had to embrace radical change. He knew that everyone understood the problem the company faced: Its principal source of revenue and profits, long-distance service, was slowly melting and when the Bell companies were free to offer long distance, AT&T's revenue would practically evaporate. But if defining the problem was easy; the solution was not so obvious. And developing a sense of urgency about solving it was even more difficult.

AT&T's Culture

AT&T people had been living with the issue of declining market share for more than a decade. They had become cynical about the "program *du jour*" designed to address it. Although many AT&T employees had something of a defeatist attitude, they were blissfully unaware of it. The consumer long distance people, in particular, were almost smug, glorying in their role as the single greatest source of company profits. When he led the consumer business, Joe Nacchio bragged that it was one of the most profitable legal businesses in the world. "In fact," he said, "cocaine dealers were moving into the distribution of counterfeit pre-paid cards because the profits are as good and there is less danger of being rubbed out." If anything, the consumer long-distance people resented the annual demands for still better margins that were pressed upon them. In a way, they had an embedded self-interest in keeping prior strategies alive, even at the expense of new ones. So they were much more likely to embrace partial fixes, such as bundling multiple existing services on a single bill—rather than efforts to redesign the business from scratch.

It would be a mistake, however, to assume that there was a monolithic "AT&T culture" and to lay all the blame for the company's problems there. Culture makes a difference, but it has been oversold as an excuse for corporate failure. AT&T had many traits common to large companies. It was slow-moving, internally focused, and religiously hierarchical. Given its long history, AT&T also had some unique characteristics. Its monopoly days left employees with deep feelings of entitlement as well as higher ideals—such as a spirit of service and a sense of family. But within this general social envelope were strains of sharply different cultures that defined how people perceived the world and how they behaved.

AT&T Labs, for example, still had much more in common with Bell Labs, from which it had been carved in the 1996 Trivestiture, than with the rest of AT&T. Its 6,000 employees lived in a semi-academic environment, largely disconnected from the fortunes of the businesses they ostensibly served.

Similarly, the corporate staffs—law, government affairs, human resources, finance, and public relations—were huge bureaucracies in their own right moving in and out of the businesses' gravitational pull. For example, the law department, which Zeglis had once led, thought of itself as the company's true intellectual leadership. It tried to have the final word on nearly every business decision, shaped strategy by interpreting laws and regulations and the extent to which they could be stretched, and had successfully resisted attempts to put it under the control of anyone but the CEO.

The people in Network Operations, which ran the vast AT&T network, had an engineering mentality. Highly regimented, they were process-oriented and did everything by the book, especially after a disastrous period in the late 1990s when relentless downsizing had contributed to a series of highly publicized network failures.

The people in Business Services had a sales culture and were typically at war with the internal organizations responsible for developing the services they sold or for installing and maintaining them.

While he never completely understood AT&T's culture (and had an especially tin ear for its consumer business), Armstrong instinctively knew that its strongest strands ran through a Gordian knot of sometimes competing mental models and patterns of behavior. Somehow, he had to move all the people of AT&T in the same direction by pulling on the strands that tied them together without becoming ensnared in the threads of competing interests. He began with his most senior team.

Ninety-Day Retreat

After Armstrong arrived in November of 1997 he literally put the top fifteen operational and functional managers in a windowless conference room and told us that we wouldn't leave until we figured out what it would take to make AT&T a great global communications company. It took ninety days even though some of us went in there thinking that we already *were* a great global communications company.

By now, Marilyn Laurie had told Armstrong of her plans to retire and I succeeded her as executive vice president of public relations. We met around a U-shaped table from 8 A.M. to 6 P.M. nearly every day with only a brief break to grab a sandwich from a table set up in a corner of the room. There were no other time-outs unless Armstrong's secretary brought in a message that he had an important phone call.

The ostensible agenda for these meetings was a review of the current year's operating results and the next year's plan. Normally, that would take a day. Under Armstrong, it took weeks as he taught us the importance of "drilling down." If the consumer long distance business was projecting an average price decline, he wanted to know the prices by service line and calling plan, then he wanted to know revenue by customer segment and time of day, and so forth. Small armies churned out the numbers in the bowels of the building, often overnight, and committed them to transparencies known as "viewgraphs" at AT&T. Managers at the level just below those of us in the room would work their way through the transparencies on an overhead projector while being peppered with questions. Every presentation had the same conclusion—a "come-back" that required more "drilling down."

In the process, we all developed a better understanding of our business and the threats it faced. First, most of the company's profits were coming from the consumer long-distance business. The company had been steadily losing market share, but the same competition that had forced it to lower prices had stimulated demand, increasing total revenue. Since 1984, AT&T had been getting a smaller slice of a bigger pie. But now it seemed that prices had declined so much that further reductions would stimulate no more demand. The most optimistic projections called for small declines in revenue on the order of 1 or 2 percent a year. And if the Bell operating companies were allowed to offer long-distance service, which we all believed was likely before the end of the decade, consumer long-distance revenue would decline even more.

Second, to compete with the Bells, AT&T had to find a practical way to offer its own local service in addition to long-distance. Stringing wire from central offices to people's homes was hopelessly expensive and couldn't be justified by the revenue it could generate on phone calls. That's why AT&T had concentrated on re-selling the Bells' local service under the AT&T brand, as provided for in the Telecom Act. But the Bell's so-called wholesale rate was set so high, AT&T lost at least $10 a month on every customer it signed. And the company's efforts to bring its own cables into office buildings, where the potential revenue could justify it, were painfully slow.

Third, as Armstrong put it, he had not seen such a bloated cost structure since the heyday of the mainframe computer business. The company's sales, general, and administrative expenses were nearly 30 percent of revenue compared to an average of 22 percent for our competitors. And AT&T's biggest single cost was simply reimbursing the local telephone companies for originating and completing long-distance calls. In 1996, the last full year before Armstrong arrived, that amounted to $16 billion in so-called access charges—an average of more than five cents on every minute of every long-distance call. Long-distance competition was forcing the price of calls down, but the cost of access had changed little because its provision was still a monopoly and it accounted for much of the local telephone companies' profits.

Fourth, no one knew what the Internet really meant for the telephone business, but the pundits claimed that it would "change everything," making phone calls free. We knew that, at minimum, its underlying digital technologies would have a profound affect on our biggest customers and not only were we stuck in an analog world, but we were spending $4 billion in capital every year to cement our position there.

Finally, while international calls represented only 10 percent of the traffic on AT&T's network, they accounted for about 20 percent of the company's revenue and nearly 30 percent of its profits. Yet the company's international strategy was a confusing amalgam of loose alliances with foreign phone companies that spent most of their time arguing about account control rather than signing up and serving customers. Furthermore, international prices were coming down even faster than domestic prices as small entrepreneurial companies found ways to game the system that was supposed to compensate foreign companies for completing calls. For example, some companies routed calls over private lines to their own switches in a foreign country avoiding the local operator's "landing charges" entirely. There were call back services that turned a call from Africa to the United States into a call from the United States to Africa, taking advantage of the lower U.S. rates. And if it cost less to originate a call to France from Sweden than from the United States, they would route calls through that country.

Armstrong did not have the solution for all these threats but, as John Zeglis once pointed out to a reporter who was trying to understand the management dynamic of these early days, "we had lots of ideas of our own."[2] Armstrong was a sponge who soaked up all those ideas, drilled through them to bedrock and then systematically knitted a strategy around them. He was relentless, uninhibited by any preconceptions of what was taboo. In hindsight, his early decisions amounted to picking low-hanging fruit—cut costs, end the money-losing effort to resell local telephone service, stop investing in analog switching, establish a physical link to our best customers, and increase consumer long distance's margins to fund an expansion of the wireless and data businesses.

Risk Takers

Few of these decisions were without risk. For example, I argued that we should not commit to eliminating jobs without first deciding how we were going to get the work done with a smaller workforce. Armstrong decreed that the only way managers would figure out how to get along with fewer people was by giving them fewer people. Besides,

Human Resources chief Hal Burlingame had come up with an early retirement incentive that could make the process virtually painless. The actuaries had warned that the plan might prove so popular that we would have to put limits on who could take it. Nearly every other decision carried similar risks, described in gory detail by managers who had been taught to imagine the worse and then plan for it until there was no longer a need to take the risk in the first place.

Armstrong's willingness to take calculated risks was precisely the opposite of the AT&T culture. When AT&T was a monopoly no one was rewarded for taking risks. On the contrary, people were rewarded for identifying risks and avoiding them. People based their careers on analyzing and planning, not on executing, which was simply assumed to be the product of momentum. There was no particular urgency to making decisions; opportunities would wait until the analysis was completed and published in a thick binder. In general, the company adhered to the cesspool theory of decision-making, refusing to deal with an issue until it floated to the surface. When problems arose—as they occasionally did even in a monopoly—resources would be thrown at them until they went away. A monopoly has plenty of resources.

Also, a company without competitors naturally turns inward. AT&T developed complex standards to tell it what was going on in the outside world of its customers in the form of blocked calls, held orders, and the seconds it took an operator to answer a call. AT&T executives pored over these performance indices, looking for areas that fell significantly below or above average. The internal competition that this process fostered provided the best telephone service in the world, but it was slow and inflexible. And the spirit of internal competition hung on in the management psyche like a virus, long after it had outlived its usefulness, making cross-unit collaboration difficult and tedious.

A Future

Armstrong knew that he had less than five years to deliver on the singular request the board had made of him. At his very first board meeting, he had asked the directors what they expected of him. Ralph Larsen, the CEO of Johnson & Johnson, put it simply. "A future," he said. "We expect you to give AT&T a future."

In pursuit of that goal, Armstrong was willing to take risks and make decisions before all the data were in. He believed that "companies suffered more damage from consistently delayed decisions than from occasionally wrong" ones.[3] Rather than waiting for all the data, he was willing to risk mistakes, reasoning that they could be repaired, but a missed opportunity in this fast-changing industry was gone forever.

Closeting himself with his senior team for ninety days was not just a means of educating himself on the business and its leaders; it was also a calculated attempt to break through organizational walls. By putting everyone in the same room, he pulverized the old channels of thinking. And he used the "come-back" as an expression of urgency.

While Armstrong's leadership style had an *ad hoc* appearance, it put pressure on an organization where, in the words of one consultant, "the road to advancement has often been paved with negation, that is, clever reasons for not doing things, not being responsive and not being bold."[4] Armstrong himself complained that AT&T excelled at one-stop shopping—no matter what the question, no one could say yes, but anyone could say no. By literally putting significant questions to a vote, he brought to an end the days of "going along by humming along."[5]

Armstrong also knew that he couldn't depend exclusively on middle managers—who were most tightly ensnarled in those competing threads and therefore most resistant to change—to bring his strategy to the general body of employees. To some extent, he had to do it himself if only to model the communications behavior he expected from his senior team and others. Knowing that there would be multiple demands on his calendar, we set a specific budget for the time he would devote to "leadership communications" as distinct from "business operations." In all, he would spend the equivalent of four or five days a month (20 to 25 percent of his time) in communications-focused activities. At least half of that time would be devoted to internal communications, as opposed to meetings with financial analysts, reporters, or public officials or giving outside speeches.

Our theory was that in the early days, re-building external confidence in AT&T was less important than mobilizing the employees, who would have to deliver on the promises that we made externally.

Communication, Not Information

That does not mean a company's top PR counselor should try to become an internal press baron. Employee information is not the same as employee communications. Information flows off presses and out of personal computers. Real communication flows two ways. Paradoxically, the best way for the CEO to engage employees initially is not to give a rousing speech, but to listen. When the CEO has established his *bona fides* as someone who "gets it," he can begin to articulate a common purpose that builds on the company's strengths and heritage. Rushing this part of a CEO transition leaves hidden voids that will crack under pressure.

We looked for ways to get Armstrong in front of the people on the front lines from his first day on the job. He usually went to these sessions alone, without an entourage and with no prepared remarks. He began by introducing himself, summarized what he heard at his last stop and then he essentially asked "what would you do if you were me?" Of course, as time went on, he couldn't resist moving from "receive" mode to "transmit." He's a powerful speaker, brimming with confidence and he inspires it in others. He also wrote a column for the employee newspaper, issued e-mails called "As I See It" on timely issues he knew were making their way through the rumor mill, and carved blocks of time out of his calendar so he could simply "show up" in locations outside New Jersey. Armstrong understood that some managers might skip his memos or be distracted at his meetings, but they would watch every move he made.

So even during the ninety-day forced march through our business reviews, he forced himself to get out of the office and spend time with customers and employees. We leveraged this informal communications network by arranging for Armstrong to send brief, often handwritten, "thank you" notes to people at all levels of the company for landing a major account, solving a customer problem, or simply reaching an unusual service milestone. Often, the people wrote back asking for an autographed photo of Armstrong leaning against his Harley. As I accompanied him on some of his field trips, I was often impressed by how many of these notes and photos were pinned to cubicle walls, even in the most stridently anti-management, union strongholds.

Other Voices

Armstrong was not totally hostage to the ideas that came up in that windowless conference room. One of the first calls he received on the day we announced his appointment as CEO was from Iain Vallance, the urbane chairman of British Telecommunications. BT had recently been bested in its efforts to merge with MCI by a small upstart called WorldCom. Vallance knew Armstrong from his days as head of IBM World Trade, based in Paris.

"Maybe we can do something together," Vallance said. Would Armstrong be willing to meet?

Within days, Armstrong booked a flight on the Concorde and met with Vallance in the British Airways lounge at Heathrow. Nothing was to come of their on-again, off-again discussions for more than six months. That was not the case with the other field trip Armstrong took.

On his way back from one of his trips to the west coast, Armstrong dropped in on John Malone in Denver. Armstrong's path had crossed Malone's in his days at Hughes, but they were not close. For his part, Malone had tried several times to do a deal with AT&T only to be frustrated in the end.

Malone has the rugged good looks of someone who has just swung off Old Paint after a day of clearing brush on the lower forty. He has a square jaw and flinty eyes. He is a quiet man, not given to arm waving or table pounding. He commands attention simply through the sheer force of the mathematical certainty with which he expresses himself. He spins complex financial strategies with the ease of a cowboy telling stories around the campfire.

Malone actually began his career at AT&T's Bell Labs, which paid for his Ph.D. in operations research. But he was so discouraged by the company's inflexibility he resigned and moved out west where he eventually fell into the orbit of Bob Magness, a swashbuckling cable entrepreneur as unlike anyone at AT&T as Malone was likely to find on the face of the earth. By 1997, Malone was CEO of Tele-Communications, Inc., (TCI) the country's largest cable system operator. TCI had also acquired an ownership stake in various programming networks as the price for putting them on its cable systems. And together with other members of the tight-knit cable fraternity, Cox Communications and Comcast Corporation, TCI controlled the country's largest high-speed Internet provider, the AtHome Corporation, and one of the largest competitive local telephone companies, the Teleport Communications Group (TCG).

One of Malone's favorite sayings is "never become romantically involved with a business." He is not an investor. He is a trader. The difference is significant. An investor has a long-term horizon and values a company at the net present value of its future earnings stream. A trader's horizon is no longer than his next trade and he believes a company has no intrinsic value at all. It's worth only what someone else is willing to pay for it and the trick is figuring out what makes it valuable to them.

Like Vallance, Malone was sure that TCI and AT&T should "do something together," but he not only knew what it was, but knew the order in which it should happen. AT&T had looked at TCG about a year earlier, but had come to the conclusion that the asking price (about $4 billion) was too high. Since then, the values of competitive local exchange companies had soared.

Malone suggested that Armstrong send in a new team to discuss a trade of AT&T shares for TCG. If the deal could be structured as a merger, rather than an acquisition, it would be nearly tax-free. That could set the companies up to do a follow-on deal with the AtHome Corporation; this would make AT&T the leader in high-speed Internet access, leapfrogging over America Online's much slower dial-up service. And, who knows, maybe TCI itself could form a joint venture with AT&T to provide phone service over its cable lines in an end run around the Bell companies that could be a model for deals with other cable providers.

With this rough road map in his head, Armstrong returned to Basking Ridge and charged his chief financial officer, Dan Somers, with getting the first element—the acquisition of TCG—sewed up by the beginning of 1998. It would not be easy—TCG was growing so fast that it was difficult to get a firm fix on anything, its assets, customer count, receivables, and so on. Furthermore, some of the AT&T operating people had looked under TCG's hood before and were decidedly unimpressed. The operation had a fly-by-the-seat-of-your-pants quality. But Somers fancied himself a deal-maker. He would make this deal happen.

Dan Somers

Somers had joined AT&T as CFO in the summer of 1997, just five months before Armstrong's appointment. Hired to replace Rick Miller, who had left shortly after John Walter's arrival, Somers had spent six years at Bell Canada, four as CFO of its international division and the last two running a small cable television company that it owned in England. Prior to that he had worked for an investment bank, run a chain of Hardee's franchises in North Carolina, and been president of a small radio station group in Nova Scotia.

While Miller had weighed each number on a spreadsheet individually, Somers tried to hear the rhythm of the numbers. He was not big on details. Maybe it was his astigmatism—reading a column of numbers, he would push his glasses up on his forehead, bend down to his desk until his chin was practically on the surface, and squint. In any case, he tended to use round numbers in the style of the investment banker he had been early in his career.

When Somers joined the discussion about merging TCG into our own local operations, he found a roomful of engineers and lawyers arguing about "indefeasible rights of use," "rights of way," and "building penetrations." His accountants were struggling to make sense of TCG's financial statements. And the investment bankers were running comparables as if the company were considering the purchase of a beach house at the Jersey Shore.

In any acquisition, the key question to be answered is whether the property being purchased will increase the purchaser's value. It is not unusual for a purchase to lower, or dilute, a company's earnings per share in the early years. But at some point it should contribute to earnings by either increasing revenue, decreasing expenses, or both. Otherwise, why do it?

Sometimes, the purchase price itself can become a drag on earnings as "goodwill," or the difference between the acquisition's purchase price and the fair value of its assets and liabilities, is amortized over a period that, in those days, could range up to forty years.

The TCG purchase was to be accounted for as a "pooling of interests," which meant its operations would simply be combined with AT&T's, triggering no goodwill amortization. However, the AT&T stock issued for the purchase would dilute earnings per share since they would be added to the base of outstanding shares. So the big question was how adding TCG's revenue, expenses, and costs to AT&T's would affect the combined companies' earnings divided by the new number of outstanding AT&T shares.

Looking backward, that was not difficult to assess, assuming different purchase prices. But looking forward required a series of judgment calls that would help define the price that AT&T could afford to pay for TCG: Would TCG's revenue growth continue at the same rate, or would it accelerate as AT&T's larger sales force included its services in its product portfolio? Would TCG and AT&T's expenses simply be additive, or would they decline as redundant organizations were eliminated? And how would the costs of the two companies' local operations be affected by economies of scale?

As Somers listened to his team's assessment, he realized that their proposed offer was less than what he thought Malone would accept based on what his (and, for that matter, Somers' own) investment bankers said TCG was worth—upwards of $11 billion. So he pulled his key people aside and, in his smoker's voice, told them to cross all the t's and dot all the i's to make sure that they had uncovered TCG's true value. The not invented here syndrome (which seemed to have been invented at AT&T) must be getting in their way. TCG had to have more value to AT&T than what the deal team had turned up so far.

Sometime during the Christmas holidays of 1997, Somers' team found that value. So when the New Year dawned, we started writing the announcement of what had now been code-named Project Woody while the company's lawyers nailed down just what we were buying and drew up the agreement.

On the evening of January 8, 1998, on the hairy edge of making the announcement in time for the next morning's papers, we issued the news release and held a hastily organized teleconference. Armstrong's quote in the news release bowed in the directions of Wall Street, which would be looking for an indication of his financial strategy, and Washington, D.C., which would be looking for an indication of his intentions regarding local service:

> This is a great match with powerful financial and strategic synergies for both companies. Joining forces with TCG will speed AT&T's entry into the local business market, reduce our costs and enable us to provide businesses the any-distance services they want.

The deal would lower earnings per share in the current calendar year, but only slightly, and it would produce sufficient synergies to increase earnings in subsequent years. Little more than two months into the job, Armstrong had begun to reshape the company by attacking its greatest vulnerability. Wall Street showed its enthusiasm for the deal as AT&T's stock price increased from $60 a share the day before the announcement to $65 seven trading days later.

Taking It to the Street

By the end of January 1998, Armstrong was ready to host a meeting with financial analysts to outline the rest of his plan. To set the stage, we gave an exclusive interview to *BusinessWeek* that was timed to appear just before our January 26 analyst meeting. The headline of the story, which appeared on the cover and also included a one-page "chat" with Armstrong, was "New Boss, New Plan"[3] and it outlined the general themes that Armstrong would address at the analyst meeting in six categories: costs, local service, long distance, international, wireless, and the Internet. It featured a big picture of Zeglis saying "Everything we do takes about a third of the time it used to take." And the seven-page story ended with the magazine's own assessment— "[Armstrong's] off to a good start."

On January 26, AT&T announced a better than expected increase in fourth quarter earnings, plans to reduce expenses by $1.6 billion in the current year alone, and major changes to the AT&T network that would vastly increase its data-handling capacity at a sharply lower cost.

Analysts termed the meeting, held in the cavernous ballroom of the New York Hilton, more upbeat than the previous year's, yet the stock declined about $4 a share over the course of the day, largely because of a report by Jack Grubman that the company was thinking about buying a cable company. When Armstrong stepped off the escalator at the New York Hilton on his way into the ballroom, he ran into Grubman.

"Why did you put out that crazy note," he asked, semi-playfully.

"Because you're planning a crazy move," Grubman replied dead seriously.

Luckily, the flow of analysts off the escalator pushed the two men in different directions. Cable was just one of the technologies mentioned in the formal presentations during the meeting—and in the question period that followed, Armstrong went out of his way to say he was thinking of partnerships, not acquisitions. Nevertheless, the stock price did not return to pre-meeting levels until mid-March, just three months before we actually *did* announce a merger agreement with the TCI cable company.

Meanwhile, when we announced that the targeted expense reductions would be accomplished by eliminating about 18,000 jobs, news trucks raced to our Basking Ridge, New Jersey, headquarters to tape what they expected would be distraught employees. The only upset people they found were those managers who were not eligible for the voluntary early retirement offer which included a 20 percent pension sweetener. Armstrong had broadcast the plan to employees just before the analyst meeting from a borrowed television studio in CBS' headquarters building just across the street from the Hilton.

Change Management

The changes Armstrong set in motion during his first 90 days were consistent with his principles of managing risk—they built on AT&T's strengths. "To be credible and therefore doable," Armstrong has said, "change must draw from institutional and individual strength."[6] In other words, it needs a solid foundation. The more radical the change, the deeper the foundation must be. People have to believe that they are capable of doing what is asked of them and they have to see a future for themselves in the new world that they are being asked to create.

While what Armstrong asked of AT&T's people in his first eight months as CEO was challenging, it was in no way inconsistent with their sense of competency. Indeed, even the acquisition of TCG (which would later prove financially imprudent) was consistent with their sense of Mission. This would not necessarily be the case for Armstrong's next major move—the acquisition of the country's largest cable television system.

None of us noticed it at the time, but as Armstrong was pulled deeper into Malone's orbit, he became increasingly pre-occupied with the company's share price, especially as companies with a fraction of AT&T's revenue or earnings surpassed it in market capitalization.

But for now, in February of 1998, 41 percent of employees expressed strong confidence in senior management and 58 percent believed the company was moving in the right direction. Armstrong had succeeded in beginning to build a strong internal base for the changes ahead. We know now that it did not hold.

7

Don't Let Plugging Leaks Become an Obsession

Whether they spring from carelessness or from a malicious streak, leaks complicate a company's life. But some CEOs let leaks drive the timing—and sometimes the substance—of their decision making. No one purposely sets sail on a leaky vessel, but adopting a Queeg-like obsession with leaks won't plug them, and it could run the ship aground.

Projects Paris and Flower

By the middle of 1998, Armstrong's conversations with John Malone of TCI and Iain Vallance of BT had evolved into full-fledged projects with code names, blackout lists, and squads of investment bankers and lawyers who would periodically take over a floor at the Wachtell Lipton law firm.

The code names were intended to disguise the projects' true purposes if anyone happened to see one of the presentations the bankers were churning out. The blackout lists were supposed to identify the only people who were authorized to know that Project Paris was the merger discussions with TCI (Italy) and Project Flower was a proposed joint venture with British Telecom (Thistle) or, as it preferred to be known, BT. AT&T was respectively "Brazil" and "Violet."

Armstrong was worried that news of one or both of these deals would leak, but after Grubman's January note, he was particularly paranoid that rumors of the cable deal would sink the company's shares before he had a chance to explain it. Besides, both deals had already taken 180-degree turns, and no one was betting that this wouldn't happen again. The discussions with Malone had started as an exploration of ways in which the two companies might partner to meet their respective objectives. AT&T needed access to TCI's customers and hoped to ride its cables, offering phone service alongside the cable company's TV programming and high-speed Internet service. TCI needed capital to modernize its cable plant so that it could add channels and new services. In fact, at first, Malone thought the AtHome Corporation might be a model that AT&T could follow. The majority of AtHome was owned by the cable companies that carried its high-speed Internet service, and it gave 40 percent of its revenue to them in exchange for using their cables. Malone even arranged for Armstrong to secretly meet the heads of the other cable companies at their annual industry convention in Atlanta in May of 1998.

Armstrong made his pitch on a conceptual basis, and they knocked it down on practical terms.[1] If they had another dollar to invest, they would put it into something like pay-per-view movies, which they understood, not phone service. Besides, their experts said that practical phone-over-cable service was still several years away, when they would have completed the switch from analog to digital technology. Investing in analog phone service was throwing money away.[2]

Back in 1998, the one cable company, other than TCI, that had dabbled in providing analog phone service over cable—Cox Communications—didn't think it needed AT&T's help. So TCI was the only girl at the party who wanted to dance. But when the two companies tried to work out a joint venture, they got hung up on details such as how much bandwidth to dedicate to communications service, how to allocate capital costs, how to split revenue, and so on. These were precisely the issues that had cratered discussions with several cable companies under Bob Allen several years earlier.

In the end, Armstrong decided that it would be easier to simply merge the two companies. He had the flexibility to buy TCI because Bob Allen had left AT&T with a pristine balance sheet. Even after assuming $1.1 billion in Teleport debt, the company had enough cash on hand (nearly $8.5 billion) to cover nearly all its outstanding debt. The TCI deal would add $16.5 billion in debt to the company's books, but AT&T's net debt would still be only a modest 22 percent of its total capitalization.

However, when Armstrong met with Malone at AT&T's airport hangar in Morristown, New Jersey, in early June, neither of them discussed such numbers. They discussed the strategic logic of a merger, and they grew so excited about its potential that they took turns passing a yellow legal pad back and forth as they sketched out how the merged companies would work. At the end of the meeting, they agreed to charge AT&T's CFO, Dan Somers, and TCI's president, Leo Hindery, with working out the details in absolute secrecy. What had started as a conversation about joint ventures turned into one of the biggest corporate acquisitions of 1998.

The BT discussions had traveled exactly the opposite path. BT's chairman, Iain Vallance, had felt personally defeated when his proposed merger with MCI had been trumped by WorldCom. It had been the second time he had failed to gain entry to the largest communications market in the world—the United States—and he was still smarting. (Ironically, AT&T had been the first spoiler when it acquired McCaw Cellular, in which BT had a 20 percent interest that it hoped to increase when U.S. law allowed.)

Vallance proposed a full merger almost from the first meeting. Teams of lawyers and bankers from both sides of the Atlantic worked on a potential deal, but it soon became clear that combining the two companies was likely to create a huge tax liability for AT&T shareowners. So the talks turned from a full merger to a joint venture, with John Zeglis leading the AT&T team.

I was aware of both sets of discussions, but not the details. In fact, Armstrong asked me to consider which deal I would announce first if we had a choice. I think I would have gone with the BT joint venture first, but while I was tossing it around in my head one Friday afternoon, my phone rang. It was Somers, and from the noise in the background, I knew he was either in an airport waiting lounge or in one of Wachtell Lipton's conference rooms. "Listen," he said, "can you come in here Sunday? I think it's time."

While Armstrong had eliminated chauffeur-driven commuting, most of the company's top officers had themselves driven almost everywhere else, especially into New York City, so that they could read their mail, work the phone, and otherwise avoid stretching out what were already twelve-hour days for most of us. The back of a company car was the perfect place to lose myself in the Sunday *New York Times*. To my surprise, the business section featured a 2,800-word profile of the man I would be spending the next few days with: Leo J. Hindery,

Jr., the president and chief operating officer of TeleCommunications, Inc.

The profile acknowledged Hindery's management skills and gave him credit for the company's soaring stock price (which had increased 149 percent since his arrival). But it also portrayed him as a "story-teller" who, among other things, embellished his past to make it seem more difficult than it really was. It said that his brother, one of his Jesuit college professors, and even his own mother had contradicted his claims that he "left home when he was 13"; "lost touch with his family" because "they just didn't care"; and "joined the merchant marine at 16." It also said that he "worked like a maniac," getting into the office or on the phone by 5 A.M. every day. In fact, the *Times* said, Hindery attributed his work habits to his "weird childhood," since he "started paying for everything" when he was nine years old, "working in the fields." The story said that Hindery's wife likened living with him to "having an eccentric uncle in the attic." "Eccentricity," concluded the *Times*, "might well be Mr. Hindery's defining characteristic."[3] I couldn't wait to meet him.

Hindery

Hindery turned out to be a slightly paunchy man with a doughy complexion and a short but intense attention span. He had a courtly manner (he was "awed by the opportunity and respectful of the challenge"), a weakness for Krispy Kreme donuts that increased in direct proportion to the length of negotiations, and he seemed to own a single navy blue pin-striped suit, which he wore whenever he was not racing one of the stock cars he owned.

Even off the racetrack, he was constantly in motion, flying between his home base in San Francisco, where his wife and teenage daughter lived; a condo in Denver, where TCI's headquarters were; and a company apartment in New York City's Waldorf-Astoria, where he camped out when he was doing deals or schmoozing media moguls in contemplation of one. FedEx packages of paperwork chased him around the country, and during the brief period when he attended Armstrong's day-long Monday meetings, he would stay only long enough to sort through one such package. Then he had to either "take a phone call" or "get to a meeting in the city."

In our first conversation that Sunday afternoon, he wanted to discuss media strategy for the announcement. "I'd like to give the story to Leslie Cauley at the *Wall Street Journal*," he said, "but I know John Keller covers your beat, so I propose we give it to the two of them." Cauley covered the cable industry for the *Journal*, and I knew her from her earlier assignment writing about the Bell companies. She was smart, very aggressive, and highly opinionated. But I also knew something else about her: Keller didn't trust her. He had once been her boss, and he had been convinced that she was going easy on Bell Atlantic because one of its executives was leaking information to her. Keller had no problem accepting leaks—they were his stock in trade—but he had a schoolmarmy abhorrence of playing favorites, especially when it reflected on his coverage of the industry. So he had her moved off the beat.

Knowing this, I didn't think Hindery's plan of a joint leak would work, but beyond that, I was troubled about leaking a story this big to anyone. If the *Journal* wrote anything that was halfway accurate, every other reporter in town would know that we had leaked it, and it would make our ongoing relationship with them more difficult. And if the main news were out before our formal announcement, the rest of the media would have no choice but to expand their analysis rather than simply repeat already known facts.

"No way," I said. "The story is too complicated. We need to have first swing at telling it without depending on a reporter who will bring her own biases to it." Unexpectedly, this "eccentric" man, whose net worth the *Times* that very day had pegged at $70 million, which would surely soar if this deal went through, readily agreed. "I never thought of that," he said. Discussion over.

I went back to trying to understand the convoluted deal itself. AT&T was not simply acquiring TCI; it was combining it with its long-distance and wireless businesses to create a new company that would be known as AT&T Consumer Services (ACS). ACS would have revenue of about $33 billion and would not be simply a division of AT&T—it would be a separate tracking stock that would trade in its own right, reflecting its own economic performance separate from AT&T's, just as Hughes Electronics traded separately from General Motors. The theory was that ACS tracking stock would be attractive to investors who were more interested in growth than in current earnings. That happened to describe a lot of the people who owned TCI and, following the merger, would end up with AT&T stock. Plus, it described the kind of business that AT&T Consumer Services would become: One that was focused on turning TCI's cable TV lines into broadband pipes carrying digital entertainment, high-speed Internet, and any-distance communication services.

AT&T would finally have a direct connection to the 33 million homes that were passed by its own cable systems or those of companies in which it had a stake. It could reach the rest of its long-distance customers through fixed wireless, by leasing the Bells' lines, or through partnerships with other cable companies. And it would inherit TCI's controlling interest in AtHome.

AT&T Consumer Services would have earnings before interest, taxes, depreciation, and amortization (EBITDA) of about $7.5 billion, growing more than 20 percent a year even without considering synergies. These were growth businesses with real customers and real revenue. The rest of AT&T, the parent, would consist of its business segments and its network infrastructure. In fact, one of its biggest customers would be AT&T Consumer Services, which would own no long-distance networks of its own. It would have about $36 billion in revenue, growing about 9 percent a year and generating net income of $4 to $5 billion in its first year.

There were, however, a few complications. Malone didn't want to give up TCI's programming interests, so they would be merged into Liberty Media, which he controlled, and it too would become a tracking stock of AT&T. AT&T would benefit from Liberty Media's tax losses but would write a check every year to reimburse Liberty for the privilege of using them, in effect allowing Malone to turn tax losses into cash. The deal document was peppered with this sort of thing, in which Malone reveled.

The board approved the deal in the late afternoon of June 23, 1998, and we prepared to announce it before the markets opened the next day. AT&T ended up paying the going rate for cable companies in the spring of that year, somewhere between the $2,600 that Paul Allen had paid for Marcus Cable in April and the $3,500 per subscriber that Cox Communications had paid for Community Cable in May. How much the company paid (or, depending on your point of view, overpaid) would become a hot issue in the weeks to come, along with wild estimates of the cost of upgrading TCI's cable systems.

But at a little past midnight on the morning of June 24, my biggest concern was nailing down exactly how many shares of TCI John Malone owned so that we could finalize the news release. His dealings with the company were so convoluted, with so many options and warrants triggered by various contingencies, that no one seemed to know. Around 1:00 A.M., while AT&T's bankers were pulling TCI's bankers out of bed, someone handed me a printout off the *Wall Street Journal's* Web site. "AT&T Appears Close to a Deal to Acquire TCI for $30 Billion—Merger Would Provide Long-Distance Giant with an Easy Route Around the Baby Bells," its headlines read. At about 2,300 words, it was actually three times longer than the company news release we planned to issue in the morning, and it had nearly all the details, including the tracking stock structure.

When to Expect Leaks

Outside of the White House, there may not have been an institution in the world with more leaks than AT&T in the 1990s and early 2000s. Armstrong once joked that if he had a reflective thought while he was shaving, he would often read it in the *Wall Street Journal* at breakfast. While, as at the White House, these leaks spawned a furious search for the sources, I know of only one instance in which the culprit was caught. But the effect of the leaks was painful. As on a true naval vessel, they often made it nearly impossible for the company to leave the dock.

The company had a very clear policy: No one was authorized to speak to a reporter or to a financial analyst without first consulting with Media Relations or Investor Relations. And, of course, someone from PR or Investor Relations would always sit in on the interview, even with the company's most senior officers, including the CEO. That way, not only was there an extra pair of ears on our side, but there was someone other than the executive who could follow up, clarify answers, or get additional information. Plus, the Media Relations or IR person would also prepare a brief memo outlining what was asked and answered for the benefit of anyone else the reporter or analyst would be speaking to.

The company usually pointed to SEC rules regulating the disclosure of insider information to justify these strict controls, although even when the Securities and Exchange Commission tightened rules on financial disclosure in 2000, it wasn't at all clear that they applied to journalists. The real reason for the controls, of course, was that in fast-moving industries, information is power. Releasing information at the wrong time or in the wrong way can put the company at a distinct competitive or regulatory disadvantage. For example, in 1996, when word of a new wireless service leaked the day before AT&T's scheduled announcement, several competitors were able to throw water on it before it even happened.

Leaks fall into two categories: the malicious and the careless. Deliberate leaks increase in inverse proportion to company loyalty, so any company that is experiencing high stress is vulnerable, and as in one's personal life, even positive change is stressful. Outsiders, of course, are never confused about where their loyalty belongs—they will trade on a company's private information whenever it benefits them.

AT&T was essentially a case history of seemingly malicious leaks. At one point, I had my staff review every major AT&T announcement between 1995 and 1997. The biggest ones—Trivestiture, John Walter's hiring and resignation, changes in our earnings outlook—never leaked. Almost all the stories that did leak involved people who were new to the company or weren't getting along with the "headquarters" types. For example, every major announcement involving AT&T Wireless leaked prematurely. And the Internet talent hired to goose the company's nascent efforts in that area played their Rolodexes as hard as their PCs.

Many leaks are simply rumors with a press pass. When employees know that something is going on, but can't get anyone to tell them what it is, they fill in the blanks for themselves. Since they are on the inside and understand the company at least as well as their bosses do, their educated guesses are often correct. When rumors fly freely, one of those rumors is bound to land on a reporter's desk.

There is really only one sure way to fight rumors: Keep employees informed. If a rumor starts, nip it in the bud as honestly as you can. Make sure supervisors talk to chronic rumormongers individually. And do what you can to lower the stress levels in which rumors breed. Hypercompetitive cultures that have people watching their backs are more rumor-prone than supportive environments that value teamwork.

One technique that we used very effectively at AT&T was to publish employee letters questioning corporate policy or even criticizing company actions in our daily electronic newsletter and monthly print publication. And when we broadcast Allen's or Armstrong's employee town meetings, we made no effort to censor the questions, many of which came in over an open telephone line. While this made some executives uncomfortable at first, it proved to be an effective safety valve that helped reduce the tension in which rumors proliferate. And over the years, only one or two of these letters were ever reprinted outside the company.

Most leaks, though, are the result of simple carelessness or naïve exuberance. Some information reaches the wrong people simply because employees lower their guard—they read confidential papers on airplanes, discuss private deals in restaurants, send confidential faxes to hotels, and so on. More often, an executive takes one or two trusted lieutenants into her confidence. Before you know it, they have each taken one or two trusted people into their confidence. And so on until the supposedly private information ripples throughout the organization.

Everyone loves a secret. Few people can keep one, especially if it appears that everyone else is in on it. And once something has been the subject of media speculation, many people assume that there is no longer a reason not to discuss it with colleagues and family. In fact, many people get some ego gratification from acknowledging that they are "in the know." It's a status symbol.

Over the years, we developed three principles for managing confidential information:

1. *Secrecy must be planned.* Project code names and blackout lists of people authorized to have information cannot guarantee security by themselves, but they heighten awareness of the need for vigilance.

2. *Confidential information must be closely held.* Insiders should be limited to those who need to know the information in order to do their job. Even then, information should be compartmentalized so that people know only what they need to know. Outside consultants and suppliers should be limited to those whose loyalty is unquestioned and whose personal agendas are clear. Even then, they should be required to sign a nondisclosure agreement for each project.

3. *Confidentiality should not be limited to critical projects.* Employees should be periodically reminded that they should not discuss company business in public places and should always keep company material under lock and key.

Enforcing these basic rules—with periodic audits—will reinforce the seriousness of your intentions.

One Person's "Leak" Is Another's "Right to Know"

If these techniques are less than foolproof, it is because many people don't understand how a good reporter does his job. AT&T used to be in the exclusive club of companies that have full-time reporters dedicated to following their every move. The *Wall Street Journal*'s John Keller majored in AT&T. He probably had more sources inside and outside the company than any other single person in the history of the company.

Keller consciously positioned himself to capitalize on carelessness, disaffection, and ego gratification. He operated like a detective, talking to dozens of people a week, at all hours, nearly every evening and most weekends. He cultivated "friends" at all levels in AT&T and within the industry, keeping in regular touch with dozens of contacts and learning about their families, jobs, and interests. He would call them—often at home—seemingly just to chat, then test incomplete theories on them, gauging their reactions and filing the information away.

He would watch people's movements, going on the alert if it took longer than usual for someone to return a phone call or if an executive was out of town or had otherwise altered her schedule. When he got a thread of information from one person, he tested it on another, confirmed it with the next person, and then weaved it together with threads from other sources.

He shared information to get information, acting as if he knew more than he did in order to trick people into telling him things. If he thought his source (such as an analyst) wanted to be mentioned in the pages of the *Journal*, he'd offer such a mention in return for information. But he was also very careful to protect his sources. Someone who provided sensitive information for one story would sometimes be quoted only in a separate unrelated story.

Because he was so well known, having covered the company for more than a decade at three different publications, he received regular tips from the company's employees. Over time, the tips became a litany of complaints as he assumed the role of unofficial external ombudsman. If employees heard rumors of a layoff, they left him voicemail messages. When he saw a consistent pattern in the messages, he would try to develop his own sources and finally seek the company's official comment. The resulting story reinforced the employees' view that the *Journal* was the most reliable source of information about AT&T.

Many employees made Bob Allen the personification of their complaints and fears. Keller knew that he was being used and discounted many of the anonymous complaints left on his voicemail. But they could not have failed to influence his reporting.

The *Journal* was proud of Keller's scoops, and he was probably one of its highest-paid reporters at the time, but that didn't exempt him from rigorous cross-examination when someone raised questions about his sources. When AT&T Director Walter Elisha sent a letter to the *Journal* rebutting Keller's October 1997 page-one story on the board's decision to "make a change at the top," the paper's managing editor, Paul Steiger, asked his ace reporter to drop by. "Bring your notes," he said.

When Keller reached Steiger's office, he was directed to a nearby conference room, where the top editors had all gathered to pick his story apart line by line. For a solid hour, they challenged Keller to back up every assertion in the story by citing his sources and reading from his notes. When it was done, Steiger thanked him, and that was the last he heard of it. The paper ran Elisha's letter the next day just as he had written it, except for the last sentence: "Your reporter should be ashamed of himself."

Shortly after the TCI acquisition, Keller left the *Journal* to take a position with the Spencer Stuart executive search firm. His AT&T beat was assigned to a different editor and several other writers. But Leslie Cauley continued to cover the cable industry, and, since AT&T was now one of the biggest players in cable, the company fell into her crosshairs. Hindery had already figured that out, and, by giving her one of the biggest business scoops of the year, he not only ingratiated himself with her but established himself as a trusted source within the highest councils of AT&T. Furthermore, he helped significantly enhance Cauley's position with the *Journal*'s editors. Her coverage of the company over the next three years never failed to reflect Hindery's point of view, and when it was all over, he returned the favor— Hindery chose Cauley to write his memoirs, *The Biggest Game of All*. Of course, we anticipated none of this when we issued the news release announcing the AT&T–TCI merger early on the morning of June 24, 1998.

TCI

When the *Wall Street Journal* posted the merger story on its Web site shortly after midnight, editors in newsrooms across the country dragged reporters out of bed to write their own take for the next morning's editions. Their Day One stories, which appeared in many papers' late editions even before we issued the news release at 6:30 A.M., reprised most of the *Journal* story.

I knew that meant that the Day Two stories would be even more challenging as every writer tried to find a new angle. This made the analyst meeting planned for 9:00 A.M. and the news conference planned for noon even more critical. Armstrong and Malone would both speak, and then Zeglis and Hindery would join them for the question period. With one eye on the regulators in Washington, D.C., I wanted Armstrong and Malone to emphasize the consumer benefits of the merger. With the deal's price tag in mind, I wanted them both to demonstrate how the merger would create value for both companies' shareowners. And knowing that the Day Two stories would inevitably look for winners and losers, I wanted to be sure that no space showed between Hindery's and Zeglis's shoulders. Hindery's apparent leak to the *Journal* didn't fill me with confidence on that score.

The news conference went without a hitch once Malone and Armstrong worked their way through a phalanx of photographers waiting for them outside the auditorium. Reporters noted that Malone, who had come out of semiretirement when TCI ran into financial difficulties eighteen months before, was more "effusive" and "bubbly" than they had seen him in recent years. Armstrong, seeing an opportunity to demonstrate the changes he was making in AT&T's culture, bragged that he got the deal done in only "eight days." Knowing that neither Armstrong nor Malone would toss any of the questions to anyone else, I told Zeglis to grab the second question no matter what the subject, answer it, and invite Hindery to add his own thoughts. Even that seemed to work. We kept all four of them tied up through the afternoon and evening in one-on-one interviews. Members of my staff kept everyone coordinated by using a wireless telephone conference call that we kept open for twelve hours.

An unnamed money manager was rumored to have said, "I'd stay away from anything Malone is selling or AT&T is buying. This deal has both curses." Nevertheless, the next day's media coverage was generally positive, with most stories emphasizing the consumer benefits. The *Chicago Tribune* credited Armstrong with "delivering on expectations [of] turning lemons into lemonade." The *Washington Times* called the deal "a hookup for the millennium." *BusinessWeek* proclaimed, "At Last: Telecom Unbound." *Time* magazine said simply,

"Gulliver has stirred." The chairman of the FCC declared the proposed merger "eminently thinkable." The *New York Times* even ran an editorial in its July 5 edition crediting the deal with ushering in an era of "better service and lower prices for consumers."[4] But by then AT&T's stock price had declined 16 percent, prompting Malone to say that the fall-off "scares me to death."[5]

What happened? The immediate problem was that our announcement did not adequately address the widespread belief that TCI's cable plant was a shambles and that the cost of upgrading it would be monumental. On top of that, we failed to anticipate the full impact of a seismic shift in the thesis under which most people and institutions had invested in AT&T stock.

Cable Upgrades

Although our news release said that the new company would "significantly accelerate the upgrading of its cable infrastructure," it gave no estimate of the cost. Yet that was the subject of the third question asked at the news conference, which came from one of the cable trade reporters, John Higgins of *Broadcasting and Cable*:[6]

HIGGINS: From what you are talking about doing with the cable systems, TCI's plant is relatively poorly equipped compared to some of the other operators in terms of its two-way capabilities and the conditions of its plant. . . . Why is this going to work the way you all say it's going to work?

MALONE: That's a pretty unfriendly statement, John.

(LAUGHTER)

MALONE: No, I think TCI's plant upgrade plans, which got a lot of publicity when we decided to rethink it about 18 months ago, you know, are pretty well on track. TCI, by the end of the year 2000, will be fully rebuilt to two-way fiber to the node. And our current capacity, in terms of two-way and fiber capacity, is sufficient to launch more than we have enough human beings to launch, in terms of the services at the present time, and was designed to be done that way, to phase in the upgrade.

That hardly settled the question, and *BusinessWeek*, in the middle of an otherwise glowing story, filled the void with its own estimate of the cost of upgrading TCI's cables. "The costs of upgrading TCI's entire infrastructure so that it can provide telephony and high-speed Internet access are enormous," *BusinessWeek* wrote, "about $15 billion for TCI and its affiliates, by Armstrong's reckoning. And some analysts think those numbers are low. They forecast that the costs could hit $20 billion or more."[7] Armstrong couldn't remember saying anything remotely like that, nor could any of us who were with him in all his interviews.

The briefing packages the company had prepared for the financial analysts included no estimates, although the company had tentatively planned to include $1.8 billion for the upgrade in its capital plans for the first three years following the acquisition, in addition to the $1.5 billion that TCI had yet to spend as part of its own upgrade plan. But because "some analysts" quoted an even higher number, we knew that our problem required more than a simple letter to the editor. So we charged AT&T Labs with developing the definitive story on how the upgrade would be accomplished and what it would cost.

By June 30, the presentation was ready to go, and we organized a conference call with industry analysts. In five charts, it described how a traditional one-way cable TV system worked, how it could be upgraded to increase capacity and create two-way capabilities, how traditional telephone service could be provided over the upgraded cable using off-the-shelf equipment, how a "packet data solution" could be integrated into that upgraded plant when it was available, and finally what all this would cost by category. The industry analysts remained wary, especially about the estimated time frame that AT&T Labs offered for the availability of packet data technology. Some of them had also heard horror stories about the earliest cable telephony experiments. The analysts who were familiar with the cable industry were skeptical that a cable plant could ever meet AT&T's service standards. The analysts who were familiar with the telephone industry questioned whether AT&T could ever meld its cumbersome billing systems with TCI's. The stock slid another 37.5 cents, and Somers told us to repeat the briefing for the media.

The media, who had been aware of the first briefing, assumed that we were panicking. In fact, the next day's *Wall Street Journal* headline read, "AT&T Tries Again to Clarify TCI Deal."[8] Given the same information, reporters added up the figures on the last page and came up with a total of over \$4 billion to provide phone service. It was less than \$15 to \$20 billion, but it was far more than the \$1.8 billion in AT&T's capital budget for the first three years of the merger. As we tried to explain in a letter to the editor, most of the costs listed in AT&T Labs' presentation were already in TCI's existing construction budget so that it could add channels and offer high-speed data. The cost of adding phone service to that was \$300 to \$500 per household, depending on whether or not a household was a video customer.

The charts had actually spelled all that out, but because the presenters from AT&T Labs had approached the question as engineers, rather than as marketers or even reporters, they had never made it clear. And those of us in PR who should have known better didn't do an adequate job of following up. After the second briefing, AT&T's stock slid another \$1.88 to the lowest price since Armstrong took over.

We made at least three mistakes here. First, to solve a short-term problem (lack of information on the cost of upgrading TCI's cable systems to provide phone service), we chose a channel with a long-term focus. Industry analysts are a source of information that the media use, but they do not publish on a daily basis. Most of their analysis comes in thick technical reports commissioned by clients or in monthly newsletters that are primarily designed to promote their capabilities by being provocative.

Second, we created the impression that we were reeling from one strategy to another by scheduling two briefings in such close proximity. If it was necessary to hold separate briefings for analysts and reporters because the former would tend toward highly technical questions that would be of little interest (and incomprehensible) to the latter, the two briefings should have been announced simultaneously.

Finally, the briefer should probably have been someone from operations. While the AT&T Labs executives have great credibility with the media and analysts, they live in a nuanced world and seldom make flatly declarative statements. And like many engineers, if you ask them what time it is, they are programmed to tell you how to build a clock—or, in this case, a cable system.

Luckily, we had also been pursuing a parallel strategy. Howard Anderson, founder of the most credible industry research firm, the Yankee Group, was an enthusiastic supporter of the TCI acquisition. The day of the merger announcement, he sent me an e-mail with "Fortune Favors the Bold" in the subject line. I told him that if the Yankee Group were to publish an analysis of the merged companies' prospects, including the likely cost of upgrades, we would pay for its distribution.

The Yankee Group published its white paper on July 15. The title was "AT&T and TCI: Fortune Favors the Bold." While admitting that the deal was "not perfect," the report said that it was AT&T's "last best option" and moved the company's "grade for long-term strategy" from "a C to an A." It quoted the cost of upgrading the cable plant as "$1.8 billion" over three years.[9] On the very same day, the telephone and cable analysts at Morgan Stanley, which had not been involved in the merger discussions, issued a joint report strongly supporting the merger. Within days, analysts at other investment banks followed.

Yet even when investors had perfect information, the company's stock price did not recover. It hovered around $57 or $58 a share through most of July, well below its peak of $65.38 on the day before the merger announcement.

The Tracker

John Malone, who would become AT&T's biggest individual shareholder when the merger closed, was unhappy about the stock slide, but he thought he knew the real cause: "Right now," Malone told *Broadcasting and Cable* magazine in early July, "if you're an AT&T shareholder, you're sitting there saying, 'Holy cow, I'm giving up 21 percent dilution on stock to get a company (TCI) with no earnings and to pick up a huge amount of goodwill amortization.' So the impact on AT&T's earnings, the way you would think this thing works, is serious."[10] But the problem, in Malone's view, was temporary.

The theory behind the tracking stock structure of the TCI deal was to insulate AT&T's traditional shareowners, who considered it essentially a utility stock, from the volatility of the cable business, which was still in its early investment phase and not generating earnings. Unfortunately, even the most sophisticated investors had difficulty getting their minds around the concept of a tracking stock. It was certainly beyond the ken of the widows and orphans who were thought to hold AT&T's stock. And frankly, even the institutions that had large positions in AT&T did not know what to make of it. We had not announced how much of the tracking stock AT&T would hold in its own account, except to say that the public would hold a "significant portion." (At this stage, General Motors owned more than a third of the economic interest in Hughes Electronics.)

Hindery tried to step into this vacuum by telling the *Los Angeles Times* that he expected AT&T to retain "little or no economic interest"[11] in the tracker, only to be promptly contradicted by a company spokesperson, further contributing to investor confusion. In retrospect, many of these twists and turns might have been avoided if the announcement of the merger had not been rushed out before all the details had been worked out. Nothing that was known was withheld, but not everything was known. That's one of the downsides of working in an environment of leaks and rumors.

In the absence of more detailed information on the capital structure of the tracking stock, investors moved in and out of AT&T stock based on their changing assumptions of how the merged companies would conform to their investment style. There was a seismic shift in the investment thesis surrounding AT&T as it morphed from a boring but steady utility to a company with much of the volatility of a high-growth start-up. But, for the most part, that shift went unnoticed because institutional investors report their holdings only quarterly.

AT&T watchers were left to their own devices to explain its moribund stock price. And the reasons they came up with—AT&T overpaid, the cable upgrade will be very expensive, the technology is uncertain, and so on—soon became common wisdom, along with a persistent suspicion that AT&T had moved too fast, throwing caution to the winds. "It was very clear to me that the deal was put together in eight days," said Brian Adamik of the Yankee Group. "There are a lot of rocks that haven't been turned over."[12]

The next issue to crawl out from under those rocks would have a negligible effect on the company's share price but a profound impact on its efforts to transform its consumer business.

8

Casting Is Everything

The biggest mistake a CEO can make is a bad casting decision—
either dumping somebody simply because she was part of the old
team or waiting too long to replace an executive who doesn't
share the same vision or values. Given enough time, an incompe-
tent executive can be coached and retrained. Given enough time,
an executive who is working at cross purposes with the CEO will
poison the entire organization. CEOs should treat hirings and
firings as teaching moments to reinforce their goals and strategies.

Hindery and Zeglis

Although John Zeglis was president of the company, on the weekend
before the TCI merger was announced, he didn't know much more
about the negotiations than I did. He had, in fact, been preoccupied
with the BT discussions, which seemed to be going well but were
entering sticky valuation negotiations. To make it a true 50/50 venture, as BT insisted it must be, AT&T actually had to exclude some of
its international assets. BT, on the other hand, was pushing to put a
very high value on some of its European distribution networks that,
while potentially valuable, didn't yet have many customers.

Zeglis and Peter Bonfield, BT's president, had great personal
chemistry, but their lieutenants were still a little suspicious of each
other. Just weeks earlier, after all, they had been bitter enemies. AT&T
had a subsidiary in the United Kingdom that was competing with BT
on its home turf, and BT's managers were still smarting from being

left at the altar by MCI. As a result, Zeglis found himself much more deeply involved in the details of the negotiations than normal. It suited his analytic mind, but it was grueling work.

So Zeglis was a little surprised to learn that Somers had managed to wring a deal from the Malone-Hindery combo in less than two weeks. He had more than an academic interest in the terms of the TCI deal. Armstrong had proposed that Zeglis assume the post of chairman and CEO of AT&T Consumer Services, which would include TCI. "You'll run your own show," he said, "just like I did at Hughes." Having witnessed the relish with which Armstrong dove into business-unit operational reviews, Zeglis must have taken that with a grain of salt, but he also knew that once he had his own shareowners, he could use his fiduciary responsibility to them to build some distance between himself and Armstrong.

No one could argue with the logic of the deal—using cable to reestablish a direct connection with its customers was something that the company had been exploring for several years. Its engineers were convinced that it could be done technically. The biggest question was at what cost and how quickly. If Somers' team had crossed that bridge, the only thing standing in the company's way was the company itself.

Zeglis had seen firsthand how intramural battles over transfer charges, account control, and cost allocations could become an endless-loop detour from actually delivering service to customers. Launching a wireless plan that charged a flat fee for local and long-distance calls without roaming charges had been a real nosebleed, even though he had direct control over all the units involved. Zeglis couldn't help wondering how Hindery, whom he barely knew, would feel about reporting to him.

The first hint came in an interview Malone gave to a cable trade magazine following the merger announcement. Asked how Hindery would feel about working for the "Bellheads" at AT&T, Malone said, "Leo's got a big ego . . . [but he] responds to a challenge . . . [and] AT&T ain't a Bellhead company when this deal closes. . . . Armstrong ain't a Bellhead. Dan Somers ain't a Bellhead. [Teleport Chairman] Bob Annunziata sure as hell ain't a Bellhead. Leo Hindery sure as hell ain't a Bellhead. I just named all the top executives."[1] All but Hindery's putative boss—John Zeglis.

Hindery himself played a passive-aggressive game with Zeglis through much of the summer. Whenever Zeglis called a meeting, Hindery had to be somewhere else; whenever he asked for details on cable upgrade plans, he received incomplete information; when he sent organization charts to Hindery for comment, they went unanswered. In the summer of 1998, when Hindery was trying to get out of reporting to Zeglis, he told Leslie Cauley of the *Wall Street Journal* about his problems with "the Bellheads" at AT&T, especially Zeglis, who was really "just a lawyer."

Hindery had given Cauley so many scoops and inside anecdotes over the years that it was not surprising that she was inclined to believe him. Deciding that she had another scoop, she asked to interview Armstrong and Zeglis. I went one better, insisting that all three executives would talk to her, but only together. We all gathered in Armstrong's office around his speakerphone as Cauley tossed questions at Armstrong, Zeglis, and Hindery in turn. Her story left open the question of their ability to work together, but she was forced to quote Hindery downplaying the cultural differences between TCI and AT&T. "Messrs. Zeglis and Hindery said they didn't think cultural differences would be a barrier to working well together," Cauley wrote. "Mr. Hindery played down the notion that cable companies still act like buccaneers, adding that TCI's operations are similar to those of the phone company. The two executives noted they . . . will have a collaborative approach to running things."[2]

Eventually, Armstrong had to settle the issue. He took Zeglis and Hindery to lunch at a nearby restaurant, where they presented their points of view. Hindery said that he had great respect for Zeglis, but that Zeglis didn't add any value to the cable business and Hindery had no intention of reporting to him. Zeglis said that he didn't care who ran the cable business, but someone had to have the responsibility for integrating customer offers. History had shown how difficult that was even when line executives reported to the same boss. It would be impossible if there were no reporting relationship at all. Armstrong said he would have to think about it.

On September 28, Armstrong blinked. Calling his top advisers together in the boardroom, he went over his thinking. The investment bankers had been telling him that an IPO for a $33 billion company would be difficult to sell. Furthermore, investors were concerned that we were proposing to put a sick business (long distance) into the tracker. Saying that there's a difference between being bold and being dumb, he decided to keep long distance out of the tracker and fix it. We could still go to market with bundles. Hindery would report directly to Armstrong.

Casting Is Everything

At stake here was not which executive should be in charge or who should report to whom. The central question was much larger: What was the nature of the company's consumer long-distance business?

Armstrong had been clear about one thing: Consumer long-distance service was a commodity. Whether years of price competition had made it so or whether it had been destined to become so when the Bells subsumed the business into an "any-distance" offer was arguable. But what was beyond argument was that the business was in decline. Armstrong's strategy to "decommoditize" long distance depended first on building or buying physical connections to its customers. The very first page of the deal package for the TCI merger that the bankers had prepared said that the merger was part of an initiative "to shift Brazil (AT&T) to a facilities-based, broadband, all-distance consumer strategy that procures direct access to the residential market through ownership of multiple broadband platforms."

That objective recognized that AT&T's consumer long-distance *business* (as distinct from the service it provided) was essentially a vast marketing machine—more than 225 million direct-marketing pieces and 140 million telemarketing calls per year. Few understood that it owned no networks. Its services ran over its parent's national and transoceanic networks and the local networks of various regional telephone companies here and abroad. Its principal assets were some 50 million customer relationships and the systems to care for them.

The TCI acquisition was part of a plan to give the consumer business a mosaic of distribution networks over which it could offer any-distance communication services. TCI's systems covered only about a third of the country but would serve as a "proof of concept" to persuade other cable providers to form joint ventures with AT&T. Where the company didn't own or lease cables, it would use wireless. In between, it would keep trying to lease the Bells' lines at reasonable rates.

It's hard to understand why Armstrong abandoned this plan. It could be that he didn't think Zeglis, who had limited operational experience at that point, was up to the job. In fact, in explaining his change of heart to Zeglis, he pointed out that Zeglis would still have ample opportunity to prove his operational mettle by directing AT&T's international, consumer, and wireless businesses. Plus, he said, Zeglis would still have responsibility for the company's so-called consumer franchise, integrating offers wherever it made sense.

It could also be that Armstrong didn't believe he could afford to have Hindery bolt. The flack he had taken over the TCI acquisition had convinced him that his reputation hung on the merger's success, which in turn depended on meeting aggressive goals for upgrading TCI's cables. Ironically, although Armstrong didn't want Hindery to leave until he had completed the cable upgrade, he was becoming so irritated at Hindery's increasing independence that he told the board that Hindery would be gone within a year. Whatever the reason, a seemingly expedient staffing decision had far-reaching strategic implications. Instead of a single consumer services business that could optimize its distribution networks, AT&T had *three* consumer businesses, all competing for the same customers.

Little Boxes

It's a management axiom that an organizational design cannot guarantee success, and it's a mistake to seek a silver bullet in the arrangement of little boxes on an organization chart. On the other hand, the right organization design can correct unproductive behavior. Bob Allen's move to business units in 1989 uncovered the true sources of the company's profits and helped each of its businesses better understand its costs, especially compared to those of its competitors.

Of course, every organizational design introduces its own behavioral problems. Once Allen had organized AT&T into business units and paid their leaders based on their individual units' performance, it became much more difficult to get the business units to work together. Armstrong did little, if anything, to change this. On the contrary, treating the cable, consumer long-distance, and wireless businesses as separate units almost ensured that they would consider each other toxic viruses.

Everyone up and down the line took their cue from the people at the top. Hindery did not have to write a memo about his political victory. But everyone at TCI soon knew that it would be business as usual following the merger. An employee broadcast the day after the merger announcement was the last time TCI employees saw Zeglis and Hindery together.

The consumer long-distance business's only hope now was to convince regulators to let it lease parts of the Bell companies' networks at reasonable rates. To his credit, Armstrong threw himself into that battle with all the urgency of a third-party candidate with unlimited public financing. For example, when it appeared that the Bells would win federal legislation freeing them from a requirement that they lease their networks to others, he met with fully half the members of the U.S. Senate in a single day.

But it would be early 2002 before AT&T convinced the regulators in one large state (New York) to reduce the Bells' wholesale rates enough for it to make a small profit. Meanwhile, the consumer long-distance business slashed prices and tried packaging itself with everything from cable TV service to oil changes to slow down its erosion. However, the first cable TV discount package it offered was not in partnership with AT&T's own cable company, but with New York's Cablevision. Zeglis was right: An executive can meet goals only if he controls the necessary resources. Armstrong had made Zeglis responsible for something called "the consumer franchise" without really defining what that meant and had put one of its fastest-growing businesses, cable, out of his reach.

I suspected that Zeglis would leave the company in late 2000, when the balance of a retention grant that the board had given him—now worth about $1.5 million—would vest. Zeglis was becoming increasingly indiscreet in criticizing Armstrong in front of subordinates, but was all smiles when sitting at his side in meetings. My dilemma was what to do with him in the meantime. If I raised his profile, it would create a bigger hole when he left. If I lowered his profile, it would contribute to the sense that he had somehow been demoted, but it would lower the perception of loss.

It was a highly personal question for me. Zeglis had had more to do with my promotion to executive vice president in November of 1997 than Armstrong, who had known me for less than a month at that point. I liked Zeglis and considered him a friend. But my job was to protect the company. So whereas in the 1997 annual report, Zeglis appeared standing beside Armstrong at the end of the letter to shareowners, in the 1998 report, I tucked him into an inside page, comparing cell phones with the head of the wireless business.

When Armstrong decided to issue tracking stock for the wireless business in late 1999, the president of that division tried to shove Zeglis aside as Hindery had done. By then, however, Armstrong had learned a lesson from the Hindery saga. Zeglis stayed; the wireless head left. For his part, Zeglis followed the example set by Armstrong himself when he had been CEO of GM's tracking stock, Hughes Electronics: He never stopped trying to separate the wireless business even more decisively from its parent, AT&T.

Meanwhile, TCI introduced cable telephone service when the merger closed, and by the end of 1998, it had nearly 100,000 customers. But the consumer long-distance business received none of the benefit. The cable business took its new phone customers off whatever AT&T calling plan they were on. It bought its long-distance carriage from AT&T's business unit. Rather than using wireless or cable to get to its customers, AT&T Consumer Services watched those units take its customers away. AT&T's most profitable business became a wet nurse for units that were hemorrhaging losses. Consumer long-distance revenue dropped by more than half in just five years—from $23 billion in 1998 to $9.5 billion in 2003.

Meanwhile, Armstrong had placed his trust in Hindery, who shared neither his vision nor his values. And he had made an enemy of Zeglis, who was now determined to leave the company and would eventually find a way to take a big part of it with him.

Fresh Exuberance

Over the summer and fall of 1998, AT&T's investor base stabilized. The company's stock was now in the hands of investors who were comfortable with the notion of a tracking stock. The cost of upgrading TCI's cable systems became clearer. And then AT&T announced a series of deals that capitalized on its acknowledged strengths and filled perceived voids. First came the joint venture with BT, which gave the company an in-country presence in economic centers outside the United States and a deep-pocketed partner to share the cost of building a new data network to connect them. Then AT&T acquired Vanguard Cellular Systems, Inc., adding 625,000 wireless customers and greatly expanding its footprint in the eastern United States. Finally, in early December 1998, the company acquired the IBM Global Network, which extended to more than 850 cities in 59 countries. And as part of that deal, the company signed IBM to a separate five-year, $5 billion outsourcing agreement.

No one really understands what moves the stock market, but AT&T's experience in 1998 suggests that stock prices often move in three stages. First, the skeptics bail out. Eventually, the stock reaches a point of equilibrium. And then something ignites buying interest. The deals

AT&T completed in the summer and fall of 1998 acted as a positive accelerant for its stock price. By the Christmas holidays of 1998, it hovered in the mid- to high $70s.

Sitting at his ski house in Telluride, Colorado, Armstrong had an epiphany: He didn't need the tracker. The market seemed to have been able to value AT&T without it. He called John Malone and found him surprisingly comfortable with the idea. Then, on the first day of business in 1999, Armstrong called all the senior managers together once more and explained his reasoning.

The tracker had been attractive to him because it would force investors to value AT&T as the sum of its parts, rather than as a single earnings per share machine. It also represented a currency that the company could use in acquisitions: "Want to sell your cable company? Take part of our tracker in return." But in November and December 1998, as AT&T's stock price moved from the mid-$50s to the high $70s, it became clear that the market was already recognizing the company's segment values. And at those prices, AT&T itself became a currency that could be used in further acquisitions if cable partnerships didn't materialize. Furthermore, everyone knew that tracking stocks added one more layer of complexity to managing a company. He had seen that firsthand at Hughes. So if we didn't need the currency of a tracker and we didn't want the seams that come with it, why do it? We would cancel plans to create a tracking stock, reconsidering it when and if necessary.

The people who had worked on the SEC filings for the tracker through the holidays could only take solace in the knowledge that there would be plenty of other filing to prepare.

At the end of the week, AT&T scheduled an analyst meeting to announce the change in plans for a tracking stock and to begin putting flesh on the rough outlines of a "new" AT&T that was increasing cash flow from its traditional businesses at double-digit rates while reducing its dependence on long-distance service by growing top-line revenue from its new lines of business, including wireless, cable, and outsourcing, by 20 to 25 percent annually. John Malone was there to endorse the company's plans, including the decision to defer the creation of a tracking stock. Armstrong capped things by announcing a $4 billion stock repurchase and a three-for-two stock split, the first in thirty-five years. The stock soared by $2.81 a share, closing at an all-time high of $85.06.

But the *Los Angeles Times*'s Sallie Hoffmeister, who many of us suspected had been the recipient of several Hindery leaks over the years, could find a dark cloud even in that cheery news. "Company sources," she wrote, "said the plan was scrapped last week because of unresolved internal disputes."[3]

Cable Craziness

On September 30, 1999, I received a handwritten fax from the New York office of the Baker & Botts law firm. "This is crazy!" it began in Leo Hindery's scrawl. "There is *no* way that I committed to this, which came to me unsolicited over the transom, without first talking with AT&T general counsel Jim (Cicconi) and then with Mike, both of which I did *before* I got back to Riordan." Hindery was reacting to a note from Armstrong chiding him for trying to charge the AT&T Foundation, which I headed, for a $1,000,000 grant to "LA 2000," a pet project of Los Angeles mayor Dick Riordan to celebrate the millennium with a sports and entertainment festival. Apparently, somebody had decided that a donation would be helpful in securing the mayor's support for the MediaOne license transfer that was being considered by the city council. But there was no way the foundation could be used for something like that, and I had complained to Armstrong.

Hindery's note tried to shift the blame. "The use of the Foundation was *not* my idea, I assure you, nor was the decision to proceed mine." I wondered what Hindery was doing at Baker & Botts. As far as I knew, that firm wasn't representing AT&T in any current matter. I knew that John Malone used Baker & Botts, and I wondered if Hindery was getting its advice on how to get out of his employment contract with AT&T without losing options worth millions.

The day before the TCI merger was announced, TCI had given Hindery a new contract with a grant of one million restricted shares, worth $38.7 million. On the very day of the announcement, AT&T entered into its own employment contract with Hindery. It reduced the term of his employment to a flat five years, promised him two years' compensation if he were fired, and allowed him to retain his restricted stock grant, which, by the fall of 1999, was worth about $65 million, nearly double its original value. But to reap the full benefit of these shares, Hindery would have to either stay at AT&T until June 2003 or have himself terminated without cause. Since, as a practical matter, "cause" was essentially limited to conviction of a felony, the path that Hindery would take was not difficult to figure out. In fact, Armstrong and Hindery had been increasingly at odds in the past few months, and most of us had concluded that Hindery was actually *trying* to get fired. Like Zeglis, Hindery had begun openly criticizing Armstrong, complaining about his long meetings and his tendency to micromanage.

Then, in June 1999, without consulting Armstrong, he agreed to distribute NBC digital television services, a pact that had wide-ranging implications for the company. The Federal Communications Commission's "must carry" rules require cable companies to carry broadcasters' local analog signals for free, but there are no regulations covering their new digital signals. Armstrong thought that he—and even the board of directors—should have had a voice in settling the issue with the nation's leading television network. I don't know if Armstrong spoke to Hindery about it, but I was told to warn my PR team in Denver that we needed advance notice of such major announcements.

Then, in late September, Armstrong was surprised to find Hindery quoted in the pages of the *Wall Street Journal* as endorsing merger talks between Motorola and General Instrument.[4] TCI—now AT&T—was General Instrument's largest customer. But more troubling, TCI had acquired warrants for General Instrument shares when it essentially standardized on GI's set-top boxes. Those warrants had gone to Liberty Media, which was now General Instrument's biggest shareowner. The *Journal* story said that AT&T was soon expected to announce the purchase of as many as two million additional cable TV set-top boxes from General Instrument and one million cable modems from Motorola, in a deal valued at about $1 billion.

Armstrong smelled a rat. Although Hindery would later say that he had memos proving that he had briefed Armstrong on the purchase, AT&T's CEO clearly didn't know anything about it. Under the company's schedule of authorizations, any purchase of that size had to be reviewed by its board of directors. This time Armstrong sent off a fiery memo demanding to know what was going on. But over the weekend, as he was still waiting to hear from Hindery, Armstrong received reports that Hindery had been criticizing him to the company's largest institutional investor. Armstrong decided he'd had enough. He called me at home on Sunday night and told me to prepare a news release. Hindery would be leaving the company.

Exit Hindery

When Hindery came in for Armstrong's regular Monday meeting on October 4, he didn't seem to have a care in the world. They were closeted together at lunch, and when Hindery emerged, he seemed as ebullient as ever. I gave him a draft of the news release I had prepared, with space for his quote. He gave me a brief paragraph expressing his confidence in "Mike's strategy" and stating what a pleasure it had been to work with him, what an honor it had been to be president of AT&T's broadband division and TCI, how much he would miss the cable industry, and how much he cherished the people who worked for him. Then Hindery flew back to Denver to be with his people when the announcement was made.

For once, the story did not leak. We issued the news release at 7:30 A.M. on October 6. CNBC's David Faber said that while Hindery's departure might seem abrupt, "sources" told him that he had been "openly talking about leaving for months."[5] Hindery himself told Dow Jones that it was "the most natural consequence of a big merger" once he had accomplished what he had been asked to do. AT&T's stock went up about 4 percent on the news, after months of trading sideways. The next day's major newspapers, however, stressed the personality conflicts between Hindery and Armstrong, the culture clash between the cable and telephone companies, and an especially curious event of the prior week when Hindery spoke at Trinity College.

After his formal remarks at the college, Hindery was asked about rumors that AT&T and AOL were discussing a deal to give the online service giant enhanced access to its cable lines, perhaps by selling it the Excite Web portal. In response, he used a line he had used once in the past, in a joint appearance with Armstrong. "Absolutely not," he told Reuters. But then he went on to say, "There have been no discussions underway whatsoever." It was practically an offhand comment, but it was picked up by Reuters, and the resulting story sent Excite@-Home's share price down when the market opened the next day.

The alarm bells in AT&T's Washington office were even louder, however. FCC Chairman Bill Kennard had asked AT&T to try to work out a commercial agreement with Internet service providers (ISPs) to demonstrate that regulatory intervention was unnecessary. The company was working with one of the largest independent ISPs, Mind-Spring, to hammer out just such an agreement, which would go into effect once AtHome's exclusivity expired in mid-2002. And, in fact, it was also talking to AOL about the same deal. Hindery's comment that "there have been no discussions underway whatsoever" was too all-encompassing. Hindery didn't see what all the fuss was about. He knew that AOL would never agree to wait for access to AT&T's cable systems. Besides, he was answering a question about discussions to sell the Excite Web portal to AOL, which was not yet formally on the table. Yes, the lawyers said, but if it ever *does* becomes an option that we want to pursue, we'll have to announce it because you've ruled it out. To Hindery, this was just another example of staffs ruling the roost at the phone company, which had been one of the themes of his talk to the kids at Trinity College.

Later in the day, the company issued an artfully worded statement that essentially said, "Never mind." Under the headline "Internet Strategy Statement" issued "in light of continuing rumors," it read:

> We have periodically explored, and we continue to explore, many alternatives with respect to our Internet strategy and our ownership interest in Excite@Home. The alternatives include internal options as well as discussions with third parties. The exploration of alternatives remains at the very preliminary stage, and at this time, AT&T has not made any decision to pursue any particular alternative or transaction. There is no assurance that any transaction will occur, and we do not intend to comment further unless and until we decide definitively to proceed with one or more alternatives, if any.

AT&T's AtHome cable partners knew about the discussions with MindSpring and, in fact, had been briefed at every turn, if only because opening cable plant to multiple ISPs was a technical challenge. AtHome's chief engineer had even provided technical advice during the negotiations. They also knew that AT&T would have liked to separate the Excite Web portal from the underlying high-speed data network service. Doing so, however, would have required their agreement, and at least one of the cable companies wasn't prepared to go along. But many in the media convinced themselves that Hindery's statement at Trinity College, the next day's curious retraction, and his departure—all within one week of each other—were somehow connected. Hindery himself encouraged the notion. In his own book, *The Biggest Game of All*, he claimed that he left because AT&T had gone back on its word to the second largest cable company, Time Warner, not to talk to AOL. Given subsequent events, there is more than a little irony to this version of events. When the MindSpring agreement was finally announced in early December, AOL called it "a step in the right direction"—probably because at that point it was only weeks away from announcing its own merger with Time Warner.

Use Executive Exits as Teaching Moments

There's a natural tendency to focus on the media's reaction to the vicissitudes of corporate life. No one likes to be criticized, especially in front of one's family, friends, and colleagues. But when one of a business's leaders leaves, the rawest point of vulnerability is not in the outside world. It is within the company itself, among the employees left behind, many of whom had some level of allegiance to the faithful departed. Hindery had replaced virtually the entire TCI senior management team when he joined the company; nearly all the executives there owed their jobs to him, and he had rewarded them all with fat retention bonuses and option grants when the AT&T merger was announced. Similarly, the rank and file loved to read about their boss dashing from one deal to another.

Armstrong tackled that issue head on in a note to the people of AT&T Broadband that tried to take some of the curse off the corporate euphemism "pursue other interests." It followed Hindery's own e-mail to the troops by minutes. "As you know, our news release said that Leo Hindery 'is leaving to pursue other interests,'" Armstrong wrote.

> That is literally true, although for all the hours and energy he has put into our business, it's hard to believe that Leo *has* any other interests. But he does. And a family that he has seen too little of over the last few years. So it's not hard to understand why he's getting off the merry-go-round. But in a real sense Leo leaves behind an important part of himself—his vision and the team he built to realize it. AT&T remains committed to that vision and to you. . . . We have made a big bet on cable and on each of you. A lot of people are watching to see if we can make that bet pay off. I know that you have skills and the determination to show that we can. You can count on my full support.

And to signal at least some level of stability, Armstrong also announced that Amos Hostetter would become more actively involved in the company's cable business while we searched for a permanent leader. Many of AT&T's cable employees had worked for Hostetter at the company he founded, Continental Cable. Meanwhile, Dan Somers, the company's CFO, who had run a small cable company in the United Kingdom, would be temporarily in charge.

Somers wasted no time asserting himself in the cable business. He rented a furnished house near its Denver headquarters and by the end of November had already spent more time there than Hindery had all year. Within weeks, he had brought in his own chief financial officer, replaced other senior executives, and began complaining to Armstrong that Hostetter's presence was "confusing" people inside and outside the company. But no one was confused about Somers's intention of keeping the cable job.

On the one hand, Somers's aggressive posture helped reassure the employees of AT&T Broadband. He held a series of employee town meetings around the country, and by simply showing up at the Denver headquarters, rather than managing by FedEx, he communicated a sense of leadership continuity. But he was no improvement when it came to working with the other AT&T units. For example, he resisted efforts to lease his unit's cables to AT&T's business services division, while laying his own plans to offer communication services to small businesses. Armstrong, who had bet his reputation on the success of the cable business, was so obsessed with the pace of system upgrades and telephony penetration that he chalked up any complaints to traditional AT&T intramural skirmishes over turf.

Focusing on the internal fallout over Hindery's leaving was exactly the right thing to do. However, we failed to do it right. How Hindery's leaving would affect the people within his own unit was a no-brainer and received a lot of attention. What was less obvious—and just as critical—was how it would affect the broader universe of AT&T employees. Here was an opportunity to signal that Hindery's failing had not been his thumbing his nose at the schedule of authorizations or forcing an embarrassing retraction about third-party discussions, but his inability to collaborate with the other AT&T businesses in any meaningful way.

Armstrong was fond of saying that "AT&T has the broadest capabilities of any communications company in the world but what sets us apart is the way [we] put them together." To date, however, it was the cable business that stood apart. Cable could have been a distribution channel and network services provider to the company's consumer and business divisions. Instead, under Hindery, it became a stand-alone business, creating its own portfolio of service bundles.

Even if he didn't want to change the business model completely, Armstrong could have signaled that he expected the cable business to partner with the other AT&T units to a greater extent. In fact, the first draft of the news release and his letter to the employees of AT&T Broadband included such an expectation. "Our job now," I had him saying, "is to focus more on building teamwork across the entire AT&T enterprise." While this was subtle, Somers and the other AT&T business leaders would have caught its significance. Armstrong scratched it out.

When executives leave a company, especially if they have been eased out, the company's lawyers will caution against saying or doing anything that might trigger a lawsuit. CEOs themselves often have mixed feelings about high-level firings, realizing that in many cases they share some of the blame for an executive's failure. Armstrong reduced the executive ranks at AT&T by 30 percent, but in almost all cases the officers affected were allowed to pick the circumstances under which they left, often after landing a job somewhere else. While this softened the blow for many of the affected executives, it created the impression of "brain drain" as some of the most familiar names within the company's ranks left for other jobs. At one point, Armstrong was even blamed for departures, such as Joe Nacchio's, that had occurred before he had arrived on the scene.

Eventually, we let it be known that many of the departures were planned, but by then the pattern had been set. Of all the top-level executives who left, Armstrong seemed to be disappointed by only one: an executive who came to AT&T when we acquired his company and left when a competitor offered him a $15 million signing bonus, a Jaguar, and monthly first-class air tickets to its home base on the West Coast for his aging mother.

Executive departures (planned or not) can be a powerful teaching tool for an organization. Instead of papering over the underlying reasons for such a departure, you should seize the opportunity to signal the changes it enables. People may ignore CEOs' memos, but they scrutinize their actions. When Armstrong gave executives the third degree in meetings, but let Hindery skip out of meetings with barely a nod at his spot on the agenda, he lost credibility with his senior team. When Hindery left, Armstrong lost his last chance to recapture the vision he had sold to AT&T's people just a year before.

9

Pay Attention to the Power of the Few

Never underestimate the power of small groups with big interests, especially when they demand that you measure up to your own rhetoric. They cannot be bought off or outspent because they do not run on money. They get their power from the righteousness of their cause and the people who are drawn to it. Never get dragged into a fight with true believers unless the stakes are so high that the only realistic alternative is to win. But be prepared to go the distance for that small number of issues that are central to your company's values or business strategy.

The Hot Network

After Hindery's departure, Armstrong made a point of traveling to Denver at least every other week for full-day performance reviews. At one of those meetings early in 2000, Somers ran through a series of actions he was planning to take to increase cable revenue. They ranged from price increases to a more aggressive program to track down and prosecute people who splice into a neighbor's TV cable and piggyback for free.

At the end of the meeting, Somers excused most of his team and told Armstrong that there was one more step he proposed to take: an expansion of the "adult entertainment" on AT&T's cable systems. The adult channels on the company's cable systems were relatively tame, featuring lots of nudity and occasionally simulated sex, but nothing truly hard-core. But DirecTV and the Dish network, which were the cable industry's only real competitors, had started offering something called the "Hot Network" that was much more explicit. The profit margins on the Hot Network were 85 to 90 percent, and, since there didn't seem to be much price sensitivity in this market niche, it carried a price of about $8 a night, twice that of the soft-core channels. AT&T was one of only two cable operators that did not offer the Hot Network (the other was Adelphia), and Somers was convinced that some subscribers were giving up their cable service for DirecTV just to receive it. He had a sample of the programming in the VCR if Armstrong wanted to see it. Saying that that was unnecessary, Armstrong gave the go-ahead to add the Hot Network to the adult pay-per-view program tier.

I didn't learn any of this until I stepped off an airplane in Phoenix, Arizona, three months later, in May of 2000. Adele Ambrose, the company's media relations vice president, called my cell phone and told me that Leslie Cauley of the *Wall Street Journal* was working on a story saying that our cable systems were planning to carry hard-core movies to boost revenue. "Is it true?" I asked. Well, apparently it was, and, as keeper of the AT&T brand, I couldn't understand why I hadn't been told about it.

As soon as I got to my room, I called Armstrong, who was at home and still a little groggy from anesthesia for a full colonoscopy he had undergone earlier in the day as part of his annual physical. "Mike, did you know that Somers plans to run something called the Hot Network?" "What of it?" he said. "We carried it at DirecTV. It's junk, but there's an audience for it, and it has great margins." I then gave him a quick summary of AT&T's prior experience with the sex industry.

In the 1990s, the company introduced something called "900 service," which provided billing services for telephone-based businesses. The idea was that a company that gave information over the phone— live or recorded—could bill the people who called it through AT&T on their long-distance bill. The per-minute charge could be whatever the business thought the market would bear, as long as it explained the charge up front and didn't start charging until the customer agreed. The service proved so popular that there was a waiting list for it while we added facilities to our network. But it soon became clear that the majority of the message services were providing not weather reports or sports scores, but sexually explicit content, including live conversations.

When the Religious Right discovered the service, it began a letter-writing campaign, and we were eventually forced to withdraw the service from organizations that reflected negatively on our brand, which included not only pornographers but also neo-Nazis and other hate groups A small group of managers in one of our customer care centers inherited the thankless task of monitoring ads at the back of adult publications to ensure that no porn services were clandestinely using the service under a pseudonym.

I promised Armstrong that the *Journal* article alone would stimulate a similar backlash. It would be far better to cancel the service now, before it was launched, than to be forced to cave later. Armstrong agreed and instructed me to tell Somers to cancel the launch. When I reached Somers by phone at his office in Denver, his reaction was not unexpected—he accused me of trying to hang him out to dry. "Not at all," I replied. "You can make the announcement. It doesn't have to come from headquarters. Just say the story is premature. You had considered it, but you've decided not to launch the channel because it's inconsistent with our values." Somers wasn't mollified and accused me of panicking for no reason. But his punch line was clear: If Armstrong wanted him to pass on the income that would flow from the Hot Network, he'd have to tell Somers himself. I decided to wait until the next morning to call Armstrong.

The next day's *Wall Street Journal* was worse than I feared. In addition to describing the Hot Network as "hard-core" and "explicit," the story quoted Time Warner cable's programming chief as saying that it "doesn't comport with the values our company wishes to exhibit." Comcast, according to the article, also passed on carrying the Hot Network. In fact, Comcast and Time Warner did carry similar explicit programming on some of their systems, but the story went on to describe AT&T's decision as "a marked contrast from policies of the former Tele-Communications, Inc., . . . which eschewed programming that featured explicit sex or extreme violence." The *Journal* went on to characterize our programming decision as a desperation move.[1]

I hated the article, but I thought it might help convince Armstrong to stand behind his decision of the night before. When I called in to the office, however, I discovered that Somers was no longer in Denver, but in New Jersey. He had already been in to see Armstrong.

When I had my call transferred to Armstrong's office, he said, "You know how when you feel like crap, everything looks like crap? That's how it was last night when you called. This morning I feel better, and I don't think we should let one lousy article panic us. Somers has plans in place to give customers unprecedented control over adult programming. You should get together with him to discuss it, and then we should talk again." Somers had demonstrated the advantages of having access to a corporate jet. I usually flew commercial.

Be True to Your Values

In the first two weeks following the *Journal* story, AT&T received 2,243 complaints about its decision to carry the Hot Network. Over 100 shareholders said they would sell their stock. Over 300 customers threatened to cancel their service. And 200 employees sent e-mails expressing disbelief that the company would "distribute pornography." The American Family Association asked the Department of Justice to investigate the company for possibly violating federal pornography statutes. A coalition of twenty-seven socially responsible investment funds that claimed to own $100 million in AT&T shares began drafting a shareowner resolution voicing opposition to distribution of the Hot Network.

One could (and in fact some did) argue that this was a relatively small number of complaints for a company with upwards of 50 million customers, and that $100 million was just a fraction of the company's overall market value. Indeed, our own tracking research indicated that only 3 percent of the public associated AT&T with the stories about the distribution of pornography on cable TV. That figure would drop to less than 1 percent over the coming months despite sporadic news stories as various groups jumped into the fray. But no one should have drawn solace from any of those numbers.

A brand is a complex blend of associations and impressions that are formed unconsciously as consumers interact with a product or representations of that product in advertising and in the media. While few single events are potent enough to alter a brand's image fundamentally, a succession of actions that are inconsistent with a brand's values can undermine it just as quietly and just as surely as slowly dissolving limestone can suddenly create a sinkhole. The dilemma that Armstrong now faced was accurately described by the *Financial Times*: "Does he decide . . . not to carry the channel and risk being seen as succumbing to censorship? Or does he stick to his guns and risk tarnishing one of America's best known brands in a long-running battle with outraged believers?"[2] But even that analysis missed the real point: However lucrative it might be and however common the practice, distributing pornography simply was not consistent with the values that the AT&T brand represented.

Many people in the United States grew up with the AT&T brand. The experiences and feelings they associate with it tend to be centered on their family at important moments in their lives. Only a generation or two ago, a long-distance call was a Big Deal that usually indicated that something significant was happening at one end of the line. Dads announced the birth of new babies; soldiers called home from the front; little Johnny introduced Grandma to his new puppy over the phone. It was warm; it was fuzzy; it was AT&T.

Much of the company's imagery was inherited simply because it had the good fortune to have been around for 100 years. But a good deal of it was also the result of deliberate calculation—carefully selecting, defining, and modulating rational and emotional associations until AT&T was a member of the family. For example, the company sponsored the 1984 Torch Run, which brought the Olympic Flame through every state on its way to the Summer Games in Los Angeles. More recently, contestants on *Who Wants to Be a Millionaire* got help answering questions "thanks to our friends at AT&T."

AT&T's apparent embrace of pornography—especially compared to the claimed reluctance of other cable companies to carry it (which proved to be largely untrue)—sent the mother of all mixed signals to consumers. It was like parading Ma Bell down Main Street clad only in a thong and pasties.

The AT&T board recognized this and asked for a full briefing on the Hot Network issue. Somers's case essentially boiled down to three points: There is a large demand for this programming, we've taken unusual steps to keep it out of the hands of minors, and it makes us upwards of $50 million a year in profit. He chose not to show them an industry chart that described in clinical detail the difference between "soft" and "hard core" adult entertainment in terms of permitted sexual activity, anatomy, and camera angles. In the end—with assurances that the AT&T brand would never be used in proximity to the adult channels, either in program guides or on the screen—the board left it to Armstrong to manage the fallout.

There was little direct impact. By 2001, less than 1 percent of the public associated AT&T with pornography. But the *Financial Times* predicted a "long-running battle with outraged believers,"[3] and that was indeed what it turned out to be. In a letter dated June 20, 2000, an organization called the Religious Alliance Against Pornography demanded a meeting with Armstrong to express its concerns.

The letter was forwarded to AT&T Broadband and apparently was ignored because when the group wrote again in February 2001, it advised us it was planning to hold a news conference just before our annual meeting, which by another stroke of bad luck was scheduled to be held in the same city as its national headquarters, Cincinnati.

The organizers of the group did not seem to be the typical rabble-rousers who were attracted to this kind of issue as a way to raise funds. The co-chair of the group's executive committee was the Catholic Cardinal Archbishop of Baltimore, and its membership was drawn from such diverse groups as the Southern Baptist Convention, the National Council of Churches, the Salvation Army, the American Society of Muslims, the Greek Orthodox Church, and the Jewish Theological Seminary.

Concerned that a news conference to announce that we wouldn't even meet with this group would be worse than one to announce that we had met and couldn't agree, I convinced Armstrong that we should apologize for not responding to the group's first letter and agree to a meeting. On that basis, it called off its news conference. Armstrong and I met with the group twice, once in 2001 and again in 2002. The closest the alliance came to militant behavior was when its executive director was interviewed on Dr. James Dobson's *Focus on the Family* radio show, generating a flurry of letters. Otherwise, the members of the alliance proved to be thoughtful, sincere people whose message came down to this: Others may distribute pornography, but we expect more of AT&T.

They had a better grasp of AT&T's values than some of the company's leaders.

Single-Issue Groups

Back in 1989, management guru Peter Drucker identified a social phenomenon that he thought would change the political landscape. In his book *The New Realities*, he cautioned managers about "the tyranny of the small minority"[4]—single-issue groups that gain political influence simply because they are very vocal and know how to capture media attention in a way that magnifies their presence. Such groups don't exist to win over public opinion or to create a consensus; they exist to defeat a candidate, block an action, or simply sustain their own existence. They exercise negative political power for causes on the left as well as on the right. And they have learned to harness the power of the Internet to increase their potency.

The Religious Alliance Against Pornography had all the makings of a single-issue political group, but there was one essential difference: Its stated goal was the same as its real goal. The members of the alliance wanted AT&T to stop distributing pornography. Period. They were not willing to negotiate the terms, they couldn't be bought off, and they were convinced that if they appealed to the better part of our character, they could persuade us that they were right. For example, the group refused to allow a distinction between the hard-core programming of the Hot Network—which literally was an endless loop of people engaging in various sex acts with little pretense of a story line—and the tamer fare of the Playboy Channel.

The group brought about a dozen people to our second meeting who told vivid stories of their past "addiction" to pornography. Armstrong and I were genuinely moved as these people detailed how their compulsion had ruined their marriages and their lives, but their anguished stories didn't have the desired effect. While I still opposed running the Hot Network because it was basically at odds with our brand values, Armstrong and I felt no more responsible for feeding sexual addiction than the people who make Ho-Ho's might feel at a meeting of Overeaters Anonymous. On the contrary, it reinforced our determination to develop even more effective parental controls. But the alliance seemed to consider the dialogue constructive, and, while it occasionally threatened to take some form of action, it never did.

We will never know if the group held back because we engaged it in dialogue, but I feel sure that this contributed. On the day we announced the sale of our cable systems to Comcast, I called the alliance's executive director to tell him that we were "getting out of the pornography business."

Rainbow/PUSH

Some groups, however, see a big company as simply a long lever they can use to lift their cause. Jesse Jackson's Rainbow/PUSH Coalition didn't really know what it wanted when Jackson first contacted us following the announcement of our plans to acquire TCI. It just knew that the required regulatory approval created an opening for it.

The letter that Jackson sent had a total of ten questions, ranging from the company's ethnic diversity to its banking relationships. Rather than ignore the letter or send a canned reply, I recommended that we use Sandy Weill, co-CEO of Citigroup at the time and a member of AT&T's board of directors, as an intermediary with Jackson. Weill was one of the founding sponsors of Jackson's Wall Street Project, and I thought that if he could get Jackson to sit down with Armstrong, without an entourage on either side and without the mediation of their handlers, we might be able to build a constructive relationship. Weill agreed, and a breakfast was scheduled at the Regency Hotel in New York City.

Armstrong and Weill went without assistants; Jackson was accompanied by Karin Stanford, the executive director of his Citizenship Education Program, the nonprofit foundation through which he financed many of his activities. Stanford wrote her Ph.D. thesis on Jackson and then went to work for him in Washington. Breakfast ended with an agreement that Stanford would contact me to explore the questions posed in Jackson's initial letter. I arranged for Stanford and some of her colleagues to spend a full day in Basking Ridge, interviewing the subject matter experts in each area where they had questions. I made it clear that these were not to be negotiating sessions, but sessions to educate Jackson's people. At the same time, the sessions would give us some insight into the group's goals.

By the end of the day, we not only knew what Jackson and his group wanted but knew how to give it to them at practically no cost. While he was still easily seduced by an opportunity to walk a picket line and work crowds into a frenzy, Jackson's principal goal had become economic development within the African American community, particularly its growing middle class. Two of his major tools in that effort were the Wall Street Project, an annual seminar and trade fair conducted in lower Manhattan, and an associated Trade Bureau, a loosely organized group of minority entrepreneurs and businesspeople who looked to Jackson to give them entrée to the large corporations that sponsored the Wall Street Project.

AT&T's treasurer hit on an idea that was precisely at the intersection of Jackson's interests and our own. The company had been hoping for some time to expand its investment banking relationships with minority firms. In fact, the Treasury Department had already begun identifying minority firms that might play a role in an upcoming bond offering.

The company's treasurer thought he could expedite his plans so that Armstrong could announce them at the upcoming meeting of the Wall Street Project. In fact, if the bond offering went well, the company could even schedule a smaller debt offering that would be completely managed by minority firms. Both ideas proved to be in the sweet spot of Jackson's current interests.

Armstrong made the announcement, Jackson declared him the "Branch Rickey of corporate America," and we never had a problem with Rainbow/PUSH from that point forward, despite numerous efforts by various plaintiffs' lawyers and union officials to suck him into their disputes with us.

Our dealings with single-issue groups were informed by hard-won lessons accumulated over several decades. For example, in 1990 one of the most prominent single-issue groups of all dragged AT&T into the most divisive national debate since the Vietnam War: abortion.

Planned Parenthood

AT&T had made an annual contribution to Planned Parenthood for twenty years. The donation was directed at preventing teen pregnancy, but by 1990, the organization had become a leading advocate of abortion rights. Not wanting to be part of the national debate on abortion, AT&T tried to quietly end its contributions to Planned Parenthood, while stepping up its support for other programs on teen pregnancy.

Initially, Planned Parenthood's response was muted. But then someone at the Christian Action Council leaked the information to the *Washington Times*, which was doing a round-up story on "Right to Life Victories." AT&T was only one of several companies mentioned, but it was too much for Planned Parenthood, which was outraged not only that we had informed its opponents of our decision, but especially that those opponents were claiming it as a victory.

Planned Parenthood issued a four-page news release accusing AT&T of "corporate cowardice" and asking its supporters to donate AT&T stock to the organization so that it would have more influence over us. In addition, it announced that it had cancelled a $350,000 equipment contract with the company. Within days, it ran full-page national newspaper ads vilifying AT&T for caving in to the Religious Right and asking people who believed in "The Right to Choose" to

"Hang Up on AT&T." The ads had two coupons: one to send as a protest to AT&T, the other to send money to Planned Parenthood.

Within just a few weeks we received over 53,000 letters, split about equally on both sides of the issue. We also took almost 90,000 phone calls. And we got 40,000 coupons from those Planned Parenthood ads. The ads also sparked new media interest in the controversy. Stories that had once run in the back of the paper moved to the front page, often with Planned Parenthood's ad as an illustration. Editorial writers and columnists jumped on the bandwagon. A *Boston Globe* columnist wrote that "AT&T" now stood for "Abortion, Timidity and Teeming millions more unplanned babies." Eventually, the furor wound down, although to this day AT&T occasionally receives a letter protesting that long-ago decision. The lessons live on.

Corporate Responsibility

Many companies thought that the big lesson here was to "shun controversy, avoid risks, and keep your head down." Those are *not* the lessons we drew from our experience. We continued to believe that corporate social responsibility is, as Drucker suggests, a matter of self-interest, but we did not see it as limited to the areas of philanthropy and community relations. It is at the center of *all* a company's activities, and it has a broader meaning than doing good to do well. Companies need to rigorously define their self-interest in terms of the values that are essential to their competitive success. They should support, and listen to, causes and groups that are aligned with those values. And they should be ready to go the distance on that small number of issues where they are threatened.

For example, AT&T has been attacked by the Religious Right for its inclusive employment policies. AT&T was the first major American corporation to include sexual orientation in its formal diversity policy, back in 1975. The company's diversity training includes a module on creating a productive and supportive working environment for gay, lesbian, bisexual, and transgender employees. Many of its employees celebrate Gay Pride Month, just as they do Hispanic Heritage Month or other cultural and ethnic commemorations.

All this has driven the Religious Right to distraction, causing it to accuse the company of everything from "indoctrinating" its employees in "aberrant lifestyles" to "encouraging immorality." The company receives hundreds of letters every year protesting its inclusive employment practices. The Reverend Donald Wildmon of Tupelo, Mississippi, who heads the American Family Association, even backed a long-distance reseller called LifeLine, which he promoted as a "Christian alternative" to AT&T.

Despite the full force of the Religious Right's indignation, the company has not caved on its diversity policy. That's not because these efforts have no economic impact. In fact, AT&T has lost hundreds of thousands of customers to LifeLine and other resellers that kick back a portion of their revenue to church groups. And the company doesn't simply ignore these groups. AT&T executives have met with Reverend Wildmon and others a number of times to explain the company's position and have listened respectfully as they described theirs.

But the issue here is so fundamental to AT&T's corporate values and to its own self-interest that there is no room for compromise. To compete in an industry whose principal engine is human creativity, AT&T simply must attract and keep the best talent available, without regard to race, gender, disability, religion, sexual orientation, or any other irrelevant circumstance.

If you base decisions on a deep understanding of your company's self-interest and values, you will pick your battles carefully and avoid getting drawn into fights that you don't intend to win. By walking down the middle of the road during the Planned Parenthood controversy—neither appearing to cave in to the Religious Right nor siding with the proponents of abortion—we left AT&T vulnerable on both sides.

The *Focus* Incident

Furthermore, the exercise of corporate social responsibility should not be based on making regular deposits in a mythical "trust bank"—for example, by sentencing its CEO to chair charity dinners—against the inevitable day when it will need to make a withdrawal. AT&T learned the futility of this quid pro quo approach in a firestorm of criticism it suffered in 1993 over a small cartoon in an employee publication called *Focus*.

When an article intended for AT&T's all-employee magazine, *Focus*, was killed just before press time, the editors substituted an innocuous quiz on AT&T's international operations, and an outside design studio inserted cartoons into a hastily prepared layout. The AT&T

production manager back in New Jersey (who happened to be a young black woman) received a blurry fax of the art and signed off on the piece. What she didn't know was that a small drawing intended to depict telephone calling around the world showed stereotypical figures, including a man in a beret in Europe—and a monkey on the phone in Africa.

As soon as the first copies arrived in our offices, the editor knew we had a problem. Ashen-faced, she brought the cartoon to her boss's attention.

The full run of 250,000 copies was already on its way to people's homes, so we did what the textbooks say you're supposed to do: Admit the mistake before someone else makes a big deal of it, accept responsibility, and apologize—which we did in our daily electronic newsletter within twenty-four hours, before the issue reached most people's mailboxes (guaranteeing, of course, that employees would tear the magazine apart looking for the offensive cartoon). Once people had seen the cartoon, the first apology was deemed insufficient. So the CEO issued another one, but many AT&T employees—African American or not—were by now embarrassed or, in many cases, enraged. The cartoon became a lightning rod for every diversity grievance that employees harbored. These grievances were shared with outsiders ranging from the NAACP to the Rev. Al Sharpton, who picketed our New York headquarters.

In a final stroke of bad luck, all of this broke on the front page of the *Washington Post* just as the Congressional Black Caucus's annual Legislative Weekend was getting underway at the Washington Convention Center. More than 2,000 African American leaders, ranging from members of the Nation of Islam to the NAACP, were in town to discuss race relations. Speaker after speaker used the cartoon as an example of corporate America's sorry diversity record. AT&T's CEO was called to testify before the Congressional Black Caucus, whose chairman dismissed all of his explanations and apologies with an expletive.

Ironically, AT&T was (and still is) one of the most generous corporate donors to African American organizations, including the NAACP, the United Negro College Fund, and the Urban League. At one point, 25 percent of all African Americans with Ph.D.s in electrical engineering had received financial support and mentoring from AT&T. The company was a pioneer in minority purchasing and spends more than $1 billion a year with firms owned by people of color or women. Furthermore, even during the extensive downsizing of recent years, AT&T took pains to ensure that the company's diversity profile wasn't adversely affected. In fact, it actually improved.

But, despite all these good efforts, there were still few black executives in top positions. Consequently, our pool of goodwill with African Americans was broad but not deep, and it evaporated in the heat of the controversy. Leaders at the organizations we supported did little more than express surprise and sorrow at what had happened. Among our own employees of color, the incident ignited flames of discontent because so few of them were moving into the higher ranks of management. The furor did not die down until the company enacted a new diversity program with specific goals for promoting people of color, and only after we stopped publishing the employee magazine entirely and transferred the editors to other jobs.

An interesting corollary to this incident showed that the controversy was about more than a thoughtless cartoon, that it was the result of our failure to address the legitimate needs of one of our most critical groups of stakeholders. At about the same time that the cartoon ran in our employee magazine, a similar drawing by the same artist appeared in the alumni magazine of Rutgers University,[5] illustrating a story about graduates working around the world. The 104 Rutgers alumni in Nigeria were represented by the same, now-pennant-waving monkey. There was no public outcry. Indeed, as far as I know, no one even complained.

The PR counselor's role is to help bring the company's policies and practices into harmony with its stakeholders' needs and expectations. Sometimes that means winning public agreement or, at a minimum, acceptance. At other times, it means getting the company to change its plans. But it always means having acute antennae and anticipating where interests might collide. One of my predecessors described it as "seeing around corners." That's an apt description, because for the senior PR counselor, the world is all corners, all roads are narrow, and all bridges have tolls.

10

Don't Confuse Politics and Public Relations

Politics is all about parades, creating the impression that hordes are on the march in support of the most transaction-oriented of goals—winning a vote. No company can afford to ignore a parade outside its window, but it shouldn't follow the example of some politicians who confuse running for office with holding office. Public relations is about building and nurturing long-term relationships. Public trust is more important than any short-term political gain.

Capitol Hill

The witness table, covered in humble green felt, looked insignificant under the high ceiling and before the two-tiered mahogany dais of the Senate Hearing Room. Other men might have been intimidated, but Mike Armstrong bounded into the room and smiled broadly as he took his seat before the Antitrust, Business Rights, and Competition Subcommittee of the Senate Judiciary Committee on July 7, 1998. The subcommittee had scheduled a hearing on "technological convergence" weeks before AT&T announced its merger with TCI, and the company's lobbyists had jumped at the chance to testify before a friendly committee that was relatively unprepared to ask probing questions.

Armstrong's testimony that day was directed not only at forestalling objections to the TCI merger, but also at an even more significant issue: holding the Bell companies' feet to the fire to open their local markets. As expected, within twenty-four hours of the merger announcement, every Bell company had issued a statement calling for its immediate release from the requirements of the Telecom Act. They were not alone in seeking to leverage the merger announcement for their own purposes. Consumer groups wanted cable rates rolled back, frozen, or re-regulated. The National Association of Broadcasters wanted the FCC to require the merged company to carry local TV stations' high-definition digital signals. AT&T's unions saw the merger as a side door into the notoriously antiunion cable industry. America Online saw it as a way to gain access to the merged company's cable lines.

Many of these issues would be argued not only at the Department of Justice and the FCC, but in the town halls of 950 different municipalities, ranging from Boston, Atlanta, and Los Angles to Multnomah County, Oregon, and Skokie, Illinois. Cable franchise agreements generally cannot be transferred without local approval. The way AT&T's lawyers read the law, a locality could challenge a transfer only if the new franchisee were of dubious character or financial means. AT&T had not reached that point yet. TCI's lawyers, who were more used to dealing with local politicians, knew that at least some of those politicians would see the merger as a golden opportunity to renegotiate the franchises. The same thought occurred to George Vrandenberg, AOL's wily chief counsel.

AOL was the world's leading online services company. However, its service operated at relatively low data speeds and thus could not easily accommodate the streaming audio and video applications that were becoming common on the Internet. Cable TV systems, of course, could provide that bandwidth, and several cable companies had created their own high-speed Internet service, AtHome, and given it exclusive rights to use their cables for online content. AOL feared that without access to those cable lines, its membership numbers not only would stall but could actually be surpassed by AtHome's numbers.

Vrandenberg saw an opportunity to hoist AT&T by its own petard. Why shouldn't AOL have the same "equal access" to AT&T's cable lines that AT&T was seeking on the Bells' local telephone lines? And to make the argument seem less self-serving, he helped create a coalition of like-minded companies to carry the question around not only within the Beltway, but into town halls across the country, or at least those where AT&T and TCI would be applying for franchise transfers.

Called the "Open-Net Coalition," the membership included America Online, MCI WorldCom, and a number of smaller Internet service providers such as MindSpring Enterprises and Prodigy. The group hired a former chief staffer to Vice President Al Gore and a former Republican National Committee chairman as its co-directors so that it would have access to lawmakers on both sides of the aisle.

Jim Cicconi

Anticipating this moment, in general if not in specifics, Armstrong had spent much of 1998 looking for a superstar chief counsel. After considering several high-profile political figures, including at least one who turned out not to have a law degree, he settled on someone who was not a household name but had politics in his DNA. Jim Cicconi had worked for a Texas attorney named James Baker while he was at law school at the University of Texas. When Baker moved to the White House as President Ronald Reagan's chief of staff, Cicconi trailed along as a special assistant. He joined the Akin Gump law firm in 1985, returning to the White House for two years as deputy chief of staff to President George H. W. Bush in 1989. His specialty at Akin Gump was regulatory law, but what he really did was lobby and plot political strategy for companies like Mobil, Pfizer, and AT&T. Lean and youthful-looking, with a shock of light brown hair falling over his forehead, he still pitched for an after-hours baseball team in suburban Virginia. He also was tireless in pitching his clients' causes on Capitol Hill and at the various regulatory agencies that had fingers in their businesses or around their throats. He could have sharp elbows when he was crowded, but he generally preferred to trade favors.

Cicconi was not an obvious choice for general counsel of AT&T. He had little experience in corporate law; however, the company had plenty of attorneys on staff or on retainer who could handle such matters as contracts and litigation. But while AT&T's name was usually enough to open any door in Washington, Cicconi knew what to do when he got to the other side of the threshold better than most. He knew how to channel ergs of energy around the corridors of power until he had amassed enough to turn the great turbines of the regulatory and legislative machinery in the appropriate direction. He knew how to curry favor without appearing obsequious and how to signal annoyance with just a soupçon of menace. And he understood the importance of covering his tracks, while magnifying his presence, by organizing coalitions of like-minded organizations.

So he matched AOL's Open-Net Coalition by helping to launch and fund the Hands Off the Net Coalition, dedicated to the proposition that government regulation, such as requiring cable companies to lease their lines to Internet service providers, would kill the Internet. The coalition ran ads in communities with large numbers of broadband Internet users (and, not coincidentally, those that would be considering TCI franchise transfers). The ads showed happy families in front of their computers; while mom and dad helped junior with his homework, an ominous off-screen voice warned that monopolists such as the local phone companies were "asking the government to slow competition down." The coalition also filed *amicus* briefs supporting AT&T whenever the issue went to court and stimulated a string of editorials and op-eds.

These grassroots efforts worked. Between 1998 and 2002, nineteen states considered regulating broadband Internet access, but not one proposal moved out of committee. AT&T was hauled into court four times by those who were pushing for access to its cable lines and won all four cases. In 1999, the FCC approved the TCI merger without imposing broadband access requirements, and it has since refused to treat cable companies as common carriers, which would force them to open their cables to all comers. Of some 950 communities that had to approve the transfer of TCI's cable franchise to AT&T, only two or three tried to impose unacceptable conditions.[1]

However, the broadband access fight was really just a sideshow. While AT&T preferred to preserve the status quo in cable, the company knew that it could reach a reasonable accommodation with the likes of AOL if push came to shove. The bigger threat would come from the Bell companies. AT&T knew that their initial comments on the TCI merger were simply throat clearing. The Bells did not realistically expect anyone to equate the simple announcement of the AT&T/TCI merger with actual competition in their local markets. Besides, the Bells had already worn the FCC down and were beginning to win permission to offer long-distance service state by state. That war was over; AT&T was simply fighting a rear-guard delaying action. However, since TCI's owned and affiliated systems reached only about a third of the country at most, AT&T would need access to the Bell networks in the rest of the country. Protecting that access, under the terms set by the Telecom Act, was the company's key political goal and one of the major themes in Armstrong's testimony before the Senate subcommittee.

The Bells Attack

But the Bells saw their opening. AOL's campaign to "open the net" underlined how much Internet users coveted high-speed Internet access. Because cable companies were still deploying the systems to offer it, many areas had no high-speed service, creating the impression that demand outstripped supply. The Bells had a competing technology that could equip ordinary telephone wires to carry high-speed data, but it required huge investments and they were required by the Telecom Act to give other providers access to it. Taking a page from AT&T's playbook, beginning in 1998, they descended on Capitol Hill to push for changes in the Telecom Act that would free them from having to share their networks on the grounds that it inhibited them from deploying broadband technology.

Two long-time Bell supporters, Representatives Billy Tauzin of Louisiana and John Dingell of Michigan, accommodated them by introducing the Internet Freedom and Broadband Deployment Act, which would have amended the Telecom Act of 1996. The Tauzin-Dingell Bill went through several iterations in two different Congresses, but the Bells were determined to push it through. They funded a coalition dubbed Connect USA that commissioned white papers and recruited allies. Their trade association, the United States Telephone Association, ran ads showing how expanding broadband Internet access could boost the entire economy and create jobs. The Bells even organized employee rallies on the steps of the Capitol before calling on legislators with dozens of voters from back home in tow.

Outnumbered, but not yet outspent, AT&T helped fund and organize "Voices for Choices," a grassroots coalition of competitive telephone companies, consumer groups, and civic associations bound principally by an abiding distrust of the Bell companies. Voices for Choices not only battled the Bells' efforts to deregulate but applied political and public pressure wherever it saw an opening. For example, when SBC moved to acquire the midwestern Bell company Ameritech, Voices for Choices published a binder of news clippings explaining "How SBC Devoured PacBell." With separate tabs for articles describing "job losses," "higher rates," "poorer service," "sleazy marketing," "labor problems," "lawsuits," and "a whole new Texas culture," the binder outlined the "implications for the Midwest if SBC takes over Ameritech." Of course, the merger went through, but the coalition considered every day that SBC was fighting to get its merger approved a day that it couldn't spend trying to get into long distance.

Voices for Choices was only one of the channels that AT&T used in opposing efforts to rewrite the Telecom Act. Armstrong was a very effective spokesman for the cause in his own right. His celebrity made it easy to line up speaking engagements for him at forums as prestigious as the Detroit Economic Club, the LA Town Hall, the CEO Club of Boston, and the Chicago Executive Club.

We also took Armstrong on annual pilgrimages to meet with the editorial boards of the nation's most prominent publications, ranging from the *Wall Street Journal* and the *New York Times* to *USA Today* and the *Washington Post*, as well as *BusinessWeek, Fortune, Forbes, Money*, and the *Economist*. He was a guest on PBS's *Charlie Rose Show* (twice) and on *Lou Dobbs Moneyline* (at least four times).

And on each anniversary of the Telecom Act's passage, Armstrong was guest speaker at the Washington Press Club's Newsmaker Luncheon. (This so dismayed the Bell companies that the fourth time out they dispatched the head of their trade association to deliver a counterpoint speech immediately following Armstrong's.) We mailed copies of Armstrong's speeches to our allies and to anyone who could conceivably influence public policy. One even formed the basis for an op-ed in the *Wall Street Journal*.[2]

Armstrong was remarkably effective for two reasons. First, he is a compelling public speaker. But more importantly, he knows how to boil a message down to its essentials. While others tried to explain the arcane mechanics of the access charges that local telephone companies impose on long-distance carriers for originating and terminating calls, Armstrong simply declared them a tax and called for their reduction. The Bells' Tauzin-Dingell bill was cleverly written as a "free the Internet" act, and, in fact, few public officials really understood its implications. But they did know what monopolies were, and Armstrong dubbed the bill an effort to "re-monopolize long distance."

Efforts to rewrite the Telecom Act ultimately failed, although the Bell companies came alarmingly close when the House of Representatives passed the Tauzin-Dingell bill in 2002. It ultimately died in the Senate when Fritz Hollings, as good a friend of AT&T's as he was an ardent opponent of the Bells, declared it "blasphemous." More importantly, Voices for Choices had taken root in the states, attracting the support of local groups that were increasingly dissatisfied with the local Bell companies for letting service standards slip as they merged with each other. The state public service commissions, which had the authority to determine wholesale discounts for leasing the Bells' lines and networks, began to set rates that made offering competitive local service more realistic. When, in early 2002, the influential New York State public service commission increased the discount from an average of 10 percent to more than 30 percent, other states followed suit, and AT&T expanded its local service offerings significantly.[3]

AT&T's PR skills served its political goals. Unfortunately, in retrospect, it may have been at a high cost. Political goals tend to be narrow and transaction-oriented—discrediting an opponent or winning a vote. Public relations is supposed to be about building and nurturing long-term relationships with those who have a stake in an organization. The most insidious effect of the blurring of the distinction between politics and public relations, however, is that it can lead you to believe that any fact can be "managed." Therein lay the roots of the single biggest public relations mistake of my career.

CALLS

In 2000, our regulatory people were working on a grand scheme that would simultaneously lower the access fees that long-distance companies pay to local phone companies and allow the local companies to increase their monthly charges by an equal amount. This was a Very Big Deal. Although access charges had slowly come down over the years, they were still long-distance companies' largest single cost, amounting to 4.6 cents per minute on every long-distance call in 1999. In some cases, access charges accounted for most of the local companies' profits and subsidized the cost of providing local service.

Ever since the breakup of the Bell System, AT&T had labored mightily to lower these charges, which most economists agreed were grossly inflated, but it really had only two choices: build its own links to its customers, which was impractical in most cases, or engage in annual, contentious three-way negotiation between the Bells, the long-distance companies, and the FCC, which seldom resulted in more than incremental change. In 2000, the Bells signaled that they were prepared to agree to a more radical approach if they could be kept whole for some reasonable period. The basic idea was to shift most of the per-minute charges that were buried in long-distance rates to a monthly fee that already appeared on local phone bills.

Again, the heavy lifting was done by a coalition, the Coalition for Affordable Local and Long Distance Service (CALLS), which included most of the major local and long-distance companies. Cynics might call it a shell game, but the FCC found it attractive because the long-distance companies agreed to lower their prices as their access costs came down, so that most consumers would see lower monthly phone bills. At the last minute, however, the FCC got concerned that the deal might look like too big a win for the long-distance companies, so it insisted that AT&T roll back a $3 minimum charge that it had imposed earlier in the year. The company agreed, but pointed out that it would also have to make a series of pricing adjustments to stay whole. The FCC said it didn't care what the company did with prices as long as the $3 minimum charge was eliminated.

AT&T's "marketeers" wanted to issue a press release announcing the elimination of the minimum charge. Its regulatory attorneys wanted to stroke the FCC's collective ego, applauding their "historic action" in dramatically lowering access charges. Neither wanted to call attention to the filings we made on the same day raising the per-minute charges for calls on what was known as our "basic calling plan," which was the rate paid by about 28 million people who didn't sign up for one of our discount plans. AT&T had issued a news release every time it raised or lowered prices ever since it had been the only telephone company in town. Its competitors, on the other hand, trumpeted their price cuts, but communicated increases in very small type on their bills, if at all. This naturally irked our marketing people, who disliked the negative press that price increases stimulated. Both MCI and Sprint had raised their basic rates in recent weeks without issuing a news release—and with nary a peep from the FCC or anyone else. Why should AT&T be held to a higher standard? When all the puts and takes were computed, the average customer's bill would in fact go down.

So when I challenged the head of Consumer Services on his plan to avoid mentioning the price increases in any of our news releases, I knew what direction the argument would take. "Look," he said, "we're going to send a letter to everyone on our basic calling plan to tell them about the price increases and to offer them alternatives. Why should we issue a news release on top of that when none of our competitors do?" Against my better judgment, I settled for an oblique reference to the price increases in the news release. It would congratulate the FCC and announce the elimination of the minimum charge as part of a "restructuring" of basic rates.

News coverage the day after the announcement was highly favorable, especially for the FCC's chairman, who was cast in the role of the crusader who forced the big long-distance companies to pass their cost savings along to consumers. Most stories highlighted the elimination of AT&T's minimum fee. Consumers Union—seldom effusive in its praise of the industry—called the deal "definitely a step forward offering consumers a potential for lower prices regardless of how much calling they do."[4] But within a week, the *New York Times* ran a front-page story accusing the company—and the FCC, which admitted that it knew about the price increases—of misleading the public. "AT&T Move Means Millions Will Face Higher Phone Bill," the headline read.

Consumers Union, which by now had read the fine print, was furious, saying, "What was done by AT&T and the FCC was misleading and deceptive."[5] By mid-afternoon, we had taken more than 100 media calls and done interviews on the *CBS Evening News*, CNN, and National Public Radio, among others.

While the FCC staff reluctantly conceded that they knew about AT&T's plans to increase some prices, its chairman, Bill Kennard, put out his own six-sentence news release: "AT&T promised to pass on savings to all customers. Their new rate plan does not do that. It is in our order and I am going to enforce it. AT&T promised to tell their customers which plan would be most cost effective for them. This was not done. I will also hold AT&T to this commitment."

After all that, it was not difficult to convince Armstrong to postpone the rate increases. The next day's coverage was all about AT&T's "backing down." The FCC even got a few headlines crediting it with "hanging up on AT&T's planned rate hikes." Within two weeks, the company introduced a radically redesigned basic calling plan that eliminated minimum fees, raised most rates (though not as much as in the original plan), and gave customers their choice of three low-cost calling days. AT&T's new rates were the same as or lower than its competitors' at all times of day and even reduced the cost of anytime calling by 15 percent, with no monthly fee or minimum charge.

AT&T also sent letters to all twenty-eight million families who were on its basic calling plan or who made few long distance calls, informing them of their options. And it ran full-page ads on the price changes in more than seventy-five major newspapers around the country. Between the access reductions, the elimination of the minimum charge, the new calling plans, the cost of a twenty-eight-million-piece mailing, and the advertising, the company lost millions. But AT&T lost something even more precious: its customers' trust. And that answered the question "Why should we be held to a higher standard?" once and for all.

In PR, You Can Never Say, "I Told You So"

I wish I could say that I had foreseen the cliff at the end of the path we had taken. But even if I had—even if I had taken my warnings to Armstrong and been overruled, with the same disastrous results—I could not have said, "I told you so." My job was not only to anticipate problems, but to convince others of the seriousness of those problems and to help find solutions to them. Doing one-third of the job didn't give me any bragging rights.

Public relations is full of people who believe that their job is to be the "corporate conscience." Unfortunately, these people tend to be all mouth and no hands. They tend to forget that they represent a business. To them, price increases are a disaster. Layoffs are a catastrophe. Controversy is an occasion of sin. Like Chicken Little, they are universally ignored or, on their best days, humored. At some point, every company has to face up to economic realities.

An effective PR counselor will understand the business he or she represents as well as any of the other senior managers and will work with them to meet the needs of the company's multiple stakeholders. To be effective, PR counselors need to approach their job as business problem solving. They need to adopt a businessperson's perspective, not a journalist's. Good press is not an end in itself, and bad press is not something to be avoided at all costs—certainly not at the cost of lying. Effective PR counselors know how to balance a business's interests with those of its stakeholders to help its leaders find win-win solutions.

Truth Telling

In my years at AT&T, my biggest struggle was with the truth. Not trying to hide it or disguise it, but simply to *find* it.

In a large company, information is scattered across organizations, people hoard it and dole it out as it suits their interests, often with their own unique interpretation. It is especially difficult to distinguish what is true from what is speculative or simply wishful thinking in the heat of a crisis or when executives are protecting their own narrow interests. PR people have to be sufficiently plugged into their company's day to day operations so they can help unearth the truth in emotionally charged circumstances. Line executives have to trust them enough to let them ask the right questions.

That does not mean PR counselors should say *everything* they know in every situation. Sometimes that could also be misleading. For example, in planning layoffs, every organization is asked to prepare multiple options. Releasing all that raw information would not tell anyone anything truly useful and could lead people to the wrong conclusions. Other times, it could be needlessly damaging. When AT&T's data networks suffered a day-long outage in 1998, we quickly traced the problem to a technician who installed some faulty software. The *New York Post* wanted his name. But what purpose would releasing it have served? Management was responsible for providing the software, training the company's technicians, and ensuring the procedures they followed were fail-safe. Fingering the technician would have been irresponsible.

Ethicist Kirk Hanson notes there is a continuum of truth-telling, from lies, to incorrect interpretations, implausible interpretations, plausible interpretations, partial truths, and truth itself.[6] The PR counselor's job is to dig out the facts of a situation, assess their meaning and communicate them responsibly to relevant stakeholders. A data dump is not responsible communications, nor is abdicating their interpretation to others. An effective counselor tries to understand the facts from her stakeholders' points of view so she can give them all the information they need to act intelligently and prudently.

That was the nub of AT&T's pricing dilemma. The solution was not to try to hide it, but to put it in context.

AT&T's basic calling rates had not changed in four years. While most people thought of the company as the "high-priced spread," its basic rates were actually lower than those of its largest competitors, and would remain so after the planned price increases, even without considering the elimination of the $3 minimum charge.

As a practical matter, AT&T couldn't use its customers' monthly bills to notify them of upcoming price changes. In 2000, the Bell companies handled billing for 89 percent of AT&T's long-distance customers. The Bells limited the length of any message, even for price increases, and wanted the information months in advance. AT&T had always planned to send a letter about the price increases to affected customers, but it postponed the mailing until the FCC approved the CALLS plan so that the plan could be included.

Under those circumstances, I should have insisted that we issue a news release and even run ads on the pricing changes. It would have complicated our relationship with the FCC, which was looking for an unambiguous win. It would have taken some of the wind out of cheers for the elimination of the minimum charge. It would have been complicated and difficult to explain. But we had done it before.

In fact, when we first imposed the now-infamous minimum charge on all our basic-rate customers, we had organized a full-court press to explain the rationale behind it. Before the announcement, we met individually with 53 consumer advocates and more than 325 representatives of groups such as the AARP, the Urban League, and the National Council of La Raza. We laid out the full rationale for the move, including financial data showing that the company served 79 percent of people who made less than $10 a month in long distance calls and that it cost between $2.76 and $5.28 just to keep their accounts open. Also, we created an enhanced Life Line program that would exempt low-income customers from the charge. We issued a straightforward news release two months before the charge went into effect: "AT&T Extends $3 Usage Minimum to Basic Rate Customers, Offers Low-Usage Callers Service Options."

The Bell companies used the announcement as one more reason to push for freedom from the strictures of the Telecom Act, but everyone else—from the chairman of the FCC to the shrillest consumer advocates—was relatively restrained. While clearly not happy with the turn of events, Consumers Union issued a statement pointing out that AT&T was joining its competitors in imposing the charge and even applauded the company for exempting low-income consumers. The media coverage was straightforward and factual. It was a one-day national story, with a very brief and localized reprise months later when the charge actually started showing up on customers' bills.

But the way we handled this latest price increase generated several weeks of high-profile criticism, both for raising prices and for trying to mislead people about it. By the time the story died down, nearly half of American consumers were aware of the circumstances of

AT&T's price increases, and they were three times as likely to say that their opinion of the company had worsened. They were far less likely to buy any AT&T-branded service, whether cellular, local, long distance, online, or even cable.[7]

There are two components to trust: sincerity and competence. The 2000 CALLS fiasco called both components into question. *Newsweek* magazine's Allan Sloan was moved to ask, "Can't anyone here play this game?" The *Denver Post* editorialized that AT&T had dialed another "wrong number." And the *Los Angeles Times*'s Cal Thomas wrote that AT&T went "from Ma Bell to call girl."[8]

Several months later, I ran into Bob Allen at the local deli. I hadn't seen him in about a year. A lot had happened, not all of it pretty, but he was still shaking his head over the way we had handled the pricing changes in the basic-rate schedule. I was embarrassed, and I couldn't even say, "I told them so."

11

Say Good-Bye to the Rah-Rah Brother- and Sisterhood

With the slightest encouragement, the media and sell-side finan-cial analysts will happily become co-conspirators in blowing ex-pectations out of all proportion to your ability to deliver—the media, because this sells newspapers; the analysts, because it sells stock. But if you bring the media or analysts out on a limb with you, be prepared to break their fall if the limb breaks.

Out of Reach

With the BT joint venture and the acquisition of TCI, Armstrong had extended AT&T's reach in two directions. The BT joint venture would enable AT&T to follow its multinational customers around the world and, eventually, could give it a beachhead in non-U.S. markets that were slowly opening to competition. The TCI acquisition would give AT&T a direct link to many of its residential customers for the first time in fifteen years. And this connection would not be over poky, narrowband copper wires but over the high-speed, broadband me-dium of fiber-optic and coaxial cables. But with all that, Armstrong knew that AT&T's reach still fell short of its grasp.

AT&T's joint venture with BT, soon to be known by the same name as BT's previous partnership with MCI, Concert, began life with impressive assets under the seas and in the gateway cities of many countries. But its distribution beyond those beachheads was less impressive—a patchwork of minority holdings and loose alliances. And while it had about 300,000 miles of undersea cable, little of that cable was connected to high-speed data switches. AT&T had sought to address this gap by purchasing the IBM Global Network, but BT backed out of participating in the acquisition at the last minute. Some of the European network operators in which BT had invested actually competed with Concert in their local markets.

Furthermore, both AT&T and BT had offshore operations that were outside the scope of their joint venture. AT&T Solutions was a fast-growing systems integration and outsourcing division with 5,000 employees outside the United States. BT had an equivalent organization with people around the world. Both units were led by executives with the outsized egos and brash charm of successful Veg-o-matic salesmen. The BT joint venture was less a marriage than a dysfunctional *ménage à trois* in which all three parties (AT&T, BT, and Concert) gossip and complain about the others when they are out of earshot and have other affairs on the side.

Cable Telephony Partnerships

On the domestic side, TCI's wholly owned cable systems reached only about 10 percent of AT&T's residential customers. And because of the way the cable industry had grown, TCI's systems were scattered across the country, rarely serving an entire city. Dallas, for example, was served at that time by five different cable systems, only one of which was owned by TCI. Leo Hindery was completing a massive "clustering" program, trading, selling, and buying properties until about 80 percent of TCI's systems would be within twenty metropolitan areas. To this, Armstrong added another objective even before Hindery was officially on the payroll: forge telephony partnerships with other cable companies.

Hindery and Malone had held out the prospect that once AT&T was a member of the club, reaching deals with other cable companies would be easier than it had been when Armstrong called on the industry leaders in Atlanta just months before. Besides, if anyone had demonstrated deal-making prowess, it was Hindery. By December 1998, he had lined up agreements with five of the "affiliates" in which TCI held a minority interest. But the real precedent-setting deal, one with the next largest cable company, Time Warner, continued to elude him.

The biggest stumbling block to an agreement proved to be the kind of technical issue that most frustrated Hindery—how much bandwidth Time Warner would agree to turn over to the joint venture for telephone service. He had been in the cable business long enough to know the importance of bandwidth—it is the equivalent of floor space in a high rise. What he couldn't understand was why AT&T's negotiators wanted more than 128,000 kilobits, which was enough for at least four telephone lines into every house, and with new technology potentially even more. For their part, AT&T's bargainers did not want to be relegated to the old world of plain old telephone service (POTS). What if someone came up with practical video telephony, but it required more bandwidth? The deal was for twenty years. Who knew what could develop in that time? Hindery just rolled his eyes and reached for a Krispy Kreme donut.

The news conference planned for December 14 in a moment of optimism was postponed for a week in the hope that the negotiators could get over the impasse. Then it was postponed to an early January analyst meeting. When the squabbling continued into the new year, we went ahead with the affiliate announcements and Armstrong personally caucused with Gerry Levin, then Time Warner's chairman and CEO. The two chairmen expressed mutual annoyance with their negotiators' inability to see the forest for the trees, agreed to shove them toward the finish line, and shook hands on a conceptual deal that included the structure of a joint venture, a plan for sharing capital costs, and an initial deployment schedule.

Based on Levin and Armstrong's conviction it could all be set out in a definitive agreement within ninety days, we scheduled a full-fledged news conference for February 1 at our headquarters building on Sixth Avenue in lower Manhattan. By now, we had held so many news conferences in the small auditorium just off the building lobby that we had had it permanently wired for the network TV cameras.

Armstrong and Levin presided over the news conference. When I briefed them in Armstrong's office just before going downstairs, I gave them the now-familiar reminder that they would be surrounded by paparazzi as soon as they stepped off the elevator. "Surrounded by paparazzi?" Levin asked incredulously. "We *are* the paparazzi."

Don't Take Reporters Out on a Limb with You

Both the BT and Time Warner announcements were as much about priming the pump as about slaking AT&T's thirst for growth. The joint ventures with BT and Time Warner would demonstrate that AT&T had comprehensive international and domestic strategies. The announcements were designed to create momentum for the company, not only on Wall Street, but also among customers and potential partners. Once Time Warner signed on, other members of the cable club would fall into line. BT brought with it deep experience and business relationships on the continent of Europe and in Asia. Unfortunately, the BT joint venture began life with outsized expectations, and the one with Time Warner never left the delivery room.

Announcing the BT joint venture in July 1998 would be challenging, if only because of the time zones involved. Both companies wanted to make the announcement on their home turf, neither wanted to follow the other, and both wanted to minimize the trading hours between issuing the news release and explaining it to the media and financial analysts. So we devised a schedule that had Zeglis and Bonfield in London, and Armstrong and Vallance in New York. The news release would go out precisely at 2 A.M. in the United States, which was 7 A.M. in London. BT would then hold its analyst meeting at 11 A.M., and Bonfield and Zeglis would host a news conference at 1 P.M., both local time. Armstrong would join the London news conference by phone at 8 A.M. his time. Then he and Vallance would host an 11 A.M. news conference at AT&T's headquarters in New York.

The logistics alone gave the announcement a larger-than-life quality. Both news conferences were beamed across the Atlantic, BT arranged for the news release to be translated into dozens of languages as the announcement moved around the world, and the personalities were compelling—besides the four principals, both companies were icons in their respective countries. Many newspapers carried a photo of Bonfield and Zeglis shaking hands with the Union Jack and the Stars and Stripes behind them, as if they had just signed a peace treaty rather than a business agreement of uncertain size.

In fact, when I had gone over to London weeks before to try to finalize the news release, I had had great difficulty finding anyone who could characterize the joint venture in terms of revenue, or "turnover," as my British colleagues referred to it. Finally, in desperation, I trapped BT's principal negotiator in the elevator. "How big will this venture be?" I asked. "Oh, I don't know," he said, watching for his floor so that he could escape. "I'd say about $10 billion." That was the number I stuck in the release as a placeholder, and through dozens of subsequent reviews, it never changed. Unfortunately, by the time the venture actually closed, for various reasons having to do with a general decline in international prices, a softening of the market, and a decision to transfer fewer of its parents' customers to it, Concert's annual revenue was more like $7 billion—not a pittance, but 30 percent less than advertised. Concert began life with the unfortunate perception that it was a loser.

Underpromising does not guarantee that you will overperform, but overpromising sets the stage for certain failure. And the worst possible combination is promising more than you can deliver and making the media your co-conspirator. The *Wall Street Journal* had been speculating about AT&T's cable telephony partnerships since September 1998. Its principal cable industry reporter, Leslie Cauley, seemed to have a pipeline into the company's thinking. When we announced the joint venture with Time Warner, it seemed like one of those events that could change the course of an industry. Combined with TCI's affiliates, the two companies could reach about a third of the country's homes, including those in such large cities as New York, Los Angeles, Boston, and Houston.

The *Journal* sent three reporters to the news conference, and when they returned to the newsroom, they had a spirited discussion with their editor, who was somewhat less sanguine about the announcement. "It's only an agreement to agree," she said. "They haven't signed anything binding yet." Cauley, who had already spoken to Hindery, was convinced that the deal was done and argued that the two companies would not have put their CEOs on stage together if there was any chance that they wouldn't be able to reach agreement. When the deal later fell through, not only did we have egg on our face, but the *Journal* reporters, among others who had hyped the story to their own editors, felt burned. So when things began to go amiss for the company, we had a more difficult time controlling the damage than we would have had if we had been more modest in laying out our plans.

In itself, even the ninety-day deadline proved foolhardy. As soon as we said we "expected to reach agreement in ninety days," all the reporters and editors covering AT&T put a note in their calendars three months out. Second to writing about personalities, following up on anniversaries, deadlines, and self-imposed goals is the easiest way for the media to write about you. Set as few goals as possible, avoid imposing deadlines on yourself, and remember all your anniversaries.

MediaOne

On March 22, 1999, when I heard that Comcast had reached an agreement to buy the third-largest cable operator, MediaOne, for $60 billion in stock, I went straight to Armstrong's office to make sure he knew. He was already scribbling his thoughts on the lined pad he carried with him from meeting to meeting. "The most important thing," he said, "is that it confirms our strategy. And it recognizes the value of the TCI acquisition." (AT&T had paid about $3,000 per TCI subscriber, whereas analysts were valuing Comcast's bid at $4,000 to $5,000 per MediaOne subscriber.)

I knew that Armstrong, Hindery, and Somers had planned on taking a run at MediaOne after the dust settled on the TCI deal, which had closed just two weeks earlier. In fact, the project had been given a code name, Project Denver, months before, and they had already approached Boston investor Amos Hostetter about joining AT&T in its bid. Hostetter, who had cofounded Continental Cablevision and sold it to US West, which renamed it MediaOne, had had a falling out with the company's CEO, Chuck Lillis. Hostetter was still mulling over AT&T's offer when Comcast announced its deal. So I suspected that this was not Armstrong's last word on the matter. But for now, we were to be statesmanlike and magnanimous. When Brian Roberts, the CEO of Comcast, made a courtesy telephone call to Armstrong's office later in the afternoon, the AT&T chairman joked, "Brian, you didn't have to go to such lengths to prove I got a good deal on TCI." Roberts acted relieved that Armstrong didn't seem to mind being displaced as the nation's largest cable operator. But each man knew that the other was play-acting.

By the time of AT&T's next regularly scheduled board meeting on April 16, Armstrong's mind was made up. The discussions with Time Warner regarding the previously announced joint venture were going nowhere. If Comcast succeeded in merging with MediaOne, it would make AT&T a regional cable company. There were no other significant cable assets available. AT&T would probably have to reconsider merging with a Bell company to cover its flanks and complete a national footprint.

On the other hand, cable values had increased significantly since the TCI merger. Even after trumping Comcast's bid, the blended cost of the TCI and MediaOne properties would fall within the range of those values. MediaOne would add five million subscribers, but more importantly, it would significantly expand the company's cable foot-print in attractive areas. MediaOne's cable plant was in significantly better condition than TCI's. And it would strengthen the company's bargaining position with Time Warner through MediaOne's 25 per-cent ownership of Time Warner Entertainment, which included most of the company's cable systems, the Warner Brothers movie studio, and the Home Box Office pay service, among other assets.

Of course, there were some risks. MediaOne was a conglomerate with holdings in cable and wireless companies outside the United States. Any deal would require regulatory approval, which would re-open familiar issues such as "open cable." Plus, this time out, the com-pany would rub up uncomfortably against the FCC's cross-ownership rules. TCI and MediaOne by themselves would fall below the then-current 30 percent limit on households passed. But under a bizarre "attribution rule," if the company owned more than 5 percent of a cable system, 100 percent of the households it passed would be attrib-uted to it. With attribution for homes passed by Time Warner's cable systems, a combined TCI and MediaOne would theoretically pass 45 percent of U.S. homes, well over the cap. While the FCC's rule was being challenged in court and in any case was expected to be relaxed, no one knew what it would mean for an AT&T acquisition of Media-One.

Finally, there was financial risk. The company's earnings per share would suffer dilution of about 30 cents per share because the company would have to issue about 660 million new shares. Also, to trump Comcast, AT&T's offer would have to include cash, most of which would have to be borrowed, adding to the $4.5 billion in debt that would come with MediaOne. While many of MediaOne's nonstrategic assets could be sold, their value was uncertain, and taxes would reduce the net proceeds somewhat. The bankers expected AT&T's stock price to take a hit, but to recover even more quickly than it did after the TCI acquisition was announced.

The good news, if there was any, was that Chuck Lillis was reported to believe that a deal with AT&T was in MediaOne's best long-term interests. While Hostetter had decided not to participate directly in an AT&T bid, he said he would be supportive, as he was offended by the limited voting rights that Comcast intended to give MediaOne share-owners. The rating agencies had been briefed on the possibility of a bid for MediaOne, and so far they had not expressed any concerns.

Armstrong had discussed his thinking on MediaOne with individual directors over the course of the last few weeks, but this was the first time they were hearing the full rationale. And management was still not prepared to discuss a specific bid. Comcast's all-stock offer had declined in value, as its stock had sunk about 13 percent following the announcement. But the AT&T board was under some time pressure. When MediaOne accepted Comcast's bid, it had cleverly given itself forty-five days to consider competing offers. That period would end on May 5, so AT&T had to act by the end of the following week at the latest. Comcast could then make a new bid or walk away. Media-One could accept one of the bids or launch an auction.

And, unlike Comcast's initial bid, this would all be done in public, with other players taking sides, possibly helping to finance Comcast's bid in exchange for a piece of the spoils. Microsoft, for example, had already invested $1 billion in Comcast and was sitting on $50 billion in cash. It might join the Comcast bid in order to gain favorable access to cable lines for its MSN service, which was in a pitched battle with AOL. Time Warner was obviously interested in the outcome of a bidding war for MediaOne, which owned a 25 percent interest in its own cable systems. It was even conceivable that Disney, Viacom, or one of the other large content producers might come to Comcast's aid in return for programming agreements. In fact, anyone who was interested in MediaOne's wireless and non-U.S. cable assets might join in. Armstrong later enjoyed telling people that it was a scenario drawn straight from *Barbarians at the Gate*. The directors who had joined AT&T in quieter days could be forgiven for feeling that "AT&T has gone from Ma Bell to Pell Mell."

The board reconvened by telephone on April 22, 1999. Armstrong and the other senior officers were gathered in one of the large conference rooms at the law offices of Wachtell Lipton, where we had all been ensconced for the last week.

Goldman Sachs ran through the strategic rationale for making a bid for MediaOne, estimated the value of its piece parts, and presented a range of bids in terms of market benchmarks and the likely impact on AT&T's financial profile. The lawyers ran through the details of the Comcast merger agreement with MediaOne, outlined the major elements of AT&T's bid letter, and described the various legal and regulatory risks.

Then Somers delivered the punch line—management wanted authorization to offer $30.85 in cash and 0.95 of a share of AT&T stock for each share of MediaOne. At that day's closing price, AT&T's offer would be worth $83.375 per MediaOne share, a 17 percent premium over Comcast's offer and a 44 percent premium over MediaOne's price just prior to Comcast's original bid. The cash portion of the bid alone might have trumped Comcast's bid. After all, Comcast's share price had declined by $10 a share since it made its bid. But to sweeten AT&T's offer, Goldman Sachs recommended that the company agree to what is called a "collar," which would increase the cash portion of the company's offer to compensate for as much as a 10 percent drop in its stock price.

There were also other inducements. AT&T's shares had full voting rights, whereas Comcast's didn't; Amos Hostetter, one of MediaOne's largest shareowners, supported AT&T's bid and would join the company's board after the merger; AT&T would also add one of Media-One's existing directors to its board; and AT&T had much of its financing in place (Chase Manhattan and Goldman Sachs had committed to lend the company $10 billion and saw no problem raising more for the cash portion of the offer), so the company could move quickly. Following the bankers' presentations, the directors approved management's proposal.

Then we waited for the markets to close so that a Goldman Sachs banker could compute the up-to-the-minute value of AT&T's offer. When we had plugged that into the news release and Armstrong's letter to Lillis, Armstrong called Lillis and we put the letter on the fax machine. Within an hour, we issued the news release along with the letter.

When he learned of AT&T's offer, Comcast's treasurer and principal spokesman to the financial community reportedly sucked in his breath and said, "It's staggering." Ken McGee at the Gartner Group said, "The FCC and the Congress are not reshaping the industry anymore, it's Armstrong and AT&T." But referring to the possible bidding war he had unleashed, the *Wall Street Journal* cautioned that "Armstrong is steering AT&T into uncharted waters." The *Washington Post* asked whether AT&T were becoming "too big once again."[1] And the Bell companies all issued statements saying that the merger announcement was still more proof that they should be allowed into long distance.

The day after the announcement, Armstrong, Somers, and Hindery spent the day meeting with investors and analysts, who acknowledged the strategic rationale for the deal but were concerned about the price and particularly worried that it could go higher if Comcast countered. AT&T stock ended the day down 3 3/8 to 53 3/8, just a little more than $2 above the trigger for an additional cash payment. MediaOne was up 7 7/8 to 77 3/8, while Comcast was up 3/16 to close at 67 13/16. The Dow was down 37.5 points. It looked as if the early bets were on AT&T winning a bidding war.

But this was just the beginning of a twelve-day ride that was like being caught in the spin cycle of a washing machine.

Comcast let it be known that it had received phone calls from Microsoft, AOL, and software billionaire turned cable magnate Paul Allen. Armstrong spoke to Gates and Case. AT&T's investment bankers spoke to Allen's. Hindery called around to the major programmers. Their consensus view was that no one was really serious about joining the Comcast bid. Allen had his hands full with Charter Communications, his fledgling cable company. AOL had concluded that Comcast was even more intransigent about keeping Internet service providers off its cables than AT&T was. And, while Microsoft had an 11 percent interest in Comcast, what it really wanted was a deal to get its software into as many set-top boxes as possible.

By April 29, 1999, AT&T had secured a $30 billion loan commitment from eighteen banks to fund the cash component of its bid. On Saturday, May 1, MediaOne notified Comcast that it had accepted AT&T's bid, giving Comcast five days to top it. With that, we all moved back into Wachtell Lipton. Armstrong and Hindery had been talking to Ralph and Brian Roberts by phone ever since AT&T had made its bid. Hindery had reasoned that Comcast would drop out of the bidding if it could save face by acquiring some of the MediaOne properties. It would consider part of a loaf better than nothing—or than the whole loaf at a steeply increased price. He was right, and on the evening of May 4, AT&T and Comcast reached an agreement to "swap cable systems." In reality, Comcast was buying systems with about two million subscribers for around $5.7 billion, $1.5 billion of which would ultimately come from AT&T in the form of the MediaOne/Comcast breakup fee. It was all contingent on AT&T's completing the MediaOne purchase, and it included an agreement that Comcast would partner with AT&T in offering cable telephony if AT&T signed such a deal with two other nonaffiliated cable companies.

Technically, Comcast could still tear up the cable swap deal and try to top AT&T's offer, but that was unlikely unless some white knight rode in with truckloads of cash. The most likely rescuer, Microsoft, was negotiating its own deal in an adjacent conference room. Hindery was so eager to close that deal that the AT&T "minders" that Armstrong had put around him spent as much time negotiating with him as with Microsoft.

By the evening of May 5, the night before Comcast's deadline for topping AT&T's offer, Hindery and Somers were able to brief Armstrong, who was flying back from a speaking engagement in Los Angeles, on the deal they had worked out. AT&T would commit to putting Microsoft's software in two and a half to five million set-top boxes. In return, Microsoft would buy $5 billion in AT&T preferred shares and warrants and commit to buying MediaOne's interests in a U.K.-based cable company should AT&T's acquisition of MediaOne be successful. We issued the news release the next morning. By that afternoon, May 6, 1999, we also were able to announce that AT&T and MediaOne had reached a definitive merger agreement.

For the moment, it looked, in the words of one industry consultant, as if "there wasn't a soul who lost in this deal. Comcast won, Microsoft won, MediaOne won and AT&T won." "Armstrong," said Reuters, "turned a bargaining table into a round table."[2] But in retrospect, AT&T had made two bad bets at that table: first, that it could cash out its new investment in Time Warner Entertainment, and second, that its long-distance businesses would continue generating enough cash to support all the debt it was accumulating.

Wall Street wasn't so sure. AT&T's stock price had outperformed the overall market from the time of Armstrong's arrival until mid-1999, when it submitted its bid for MediaOne. But from that point on, the stock underperformed its major competitors'. Armstrong thought he knew why—what he came to call the "voice overhang" was obscuring very real growth in the rest of the company. AT&T's consumer long-distance business, once the goose laying basket after basket of golden eggs, was now an albatross around the company's neck.

AT&T Business's data revenue was growing in the mid- to high teens, AT&T Broadband was growing at 12 percent, and AT&T Wireless was growing at 40 percent. But it looked as if AT&T Consumer's revenue of about $20 billion would decline about 6 percent, essentially masking growth elsewhere in the company. So in February of 2000, Armstrong and Noski hired outside consultants to assess the unit's prospects and recommend strategic alternatives.

Project Pegasus

The consultants' mandate was to consider all options with no preconceptions; nothing was sacred. They explored a number of alternative strategies, but in the end one factor dominated their thinking: The consumer long-distance industry was in the middle of a severe structural decline from which it was unlikely to recover. There was really only one strategic alternative: to separate the consumer long-distance business from the rest of AT&T somehow so that it could be valued for what it was—a depleting oil well. By the consultants' analysis, no long-distance company had found a way to alter the industry's fundamentals, although they had chosen different strategies. While AT&T had carefully managed its customer losses to maximize its profitability, MCI and Sprint had sacrificed margins to gain market share. AT&T's consumer margins were about six times MCI's.

But even the consumer unit's then-projected revenue decline of 3 to 5 percent masked deeper problems. Direct-dial long distance had actually been declining 16 to 18 percent in each of the previous two or three years. That revenue decline had been offset by increases in the cost of operator-assisted and calling card calls, as well as by a slew of special fees such as the $3 minimum charge. But now consumers were resisting the extra charges. Wireless phones were replacing not only calling card calls but even long distance calls placed from home. And the FCC had forced the company to abandon its minimum charge.

Furthermore, the consultants extrapolated the impact of the Bell companies' entry into the long-distance business from AT&T's experience in areas where the local phone company was already allowed to offer a bundle of local and long-distance calling. Using the company's most optimistic views of the timing of Bell entry, they projected that the unit would lose about 30 percent of its market share in five years.

When the project was reviewed with the AT&T board at Chicago's Ritz Carlton Hotel the evening before the company's 2000 annual meeting, some of the directors seemed surprised that Armstrong was willing to walk away from a business that had such a golden franchise. Almost every survey picked AT&T as the leading consumer communications brand. Nearly half of consumers said that they would prefer receiving local service from AT&T than from their existing provider. (A significant percentage thought that AT&T already provided their local service.) The business had over 50 million customers, many of whom still hung up on competitors' telemarketing calls.

The directors asked the Pegasus Team to consider other business combinations that could leverage the AT&T brand. Armstrong promised to put the best minds on it and hired investment bankers to help value the business should the board decide to spin it off, sell it, or merge it with another company. Armstrong had difficulty thinking of the consumer business as anything but a millstone around his neck. Before the end of the month, he traveled to Boston for a meeting with Frank Governali, the powerful Goldman Sachs telecom analyst. The note that Governali issued after the meeting signaled just how determined Armstrong was to rid himself of a business that colored everything else he was trying to accomplish: "[Armstrong] recognizes the problems, is not wedded to historical decisions (or businesses), is impatient, and . . . is willing to take dramatic steps, no matter how unconventional they may seem. This applies to the consumer long distance business in particular."

When plans to separate the consumer long-distance business from AT&T leaked in the summer and fall of 2000, the reaction ranged from disbelief to horror. The *Industry Standard*, a magazine spawned in the orgiastic frenzy of the Internet craze and free of emotional attachments to anything more than a year old, surprisingly wrote, "It's hard to imagine AT&T . . . getting out of the phone business." Perhaps less unexpectedly, the company's hometown paper, the *Newark Star Ledger*, asked, "If you pull the consumer long-distance business out of AT&T Corp., is it really still AT&T?" On the other coast, the *Los Angeles Times* reported that "Wall Street showed little enthusiasm for reports . . . of spinning [off] consumer long distance." One influential industry analyst, Scott Cleland, asked, "Why would AT&T be willing to ditch its 60-million residential long-distance customers when nearly every other company sees a large customer base as the key to selling big bundles of other services such as cable and high-speed Internet access?" Even the head of the FCC bureau responsible for regulating phone companies weighed in: "I think we would definitely want to be very vigilant about the consumer ramifications."[3] Despite more than fifteen years of competition, even knowledgeable regulators and bureaucrats thought of AT&T as the carrier of last resort.

Your Customers Own Your Brand

AT&T managers were understandably proud of the company's brand. In 2000, the Interbrand consultancy ranked it the tenth most valuable brand in the world and the number one brand in communication services. To be sure, that was at least in part thanks to the more than $8 billion that the company was estimated to have spent on advertising over the previous decade. But while raw marketing power can build familiarity with and even knowledge of a company, it cannot create the customer attitude that is at the root of purchase decisions and other supportive behavior. It can't manufacture trust.

Customers trusted AT&T to an extent that surprised even those of us within the company. More than two-thirds of consumers agreed that "AT&T is a company I can trust" in surveys taken as late as the first half of 2001. As we probed those attitudes, we discovered that feelings of trust are predominantly based on a consumer's personal experience with a company's products and services, including the customer support with which it surrounds them. Other factors—advertising, word of mouth, the company's very longevity—are far less important.

While AT&T's customer base was simultaneously aging and shrinking, most people in the United States had used the company's services at one time or another. Even if they had given their long-distance business to another company, the service they had received from AT&T was the standard to which they compared their new provider. People had an unusually personal relationship with the company. One of the pollsters we hired to study investor attitudes toward AT&T was struck by the fact that even people who owned relatively large amounts of AT&T stock first wanted to know how various restructuring scenarios would affect their service, not their investment.

Work on Project Pegasus continued through the spring and summer, but by the fall other problems had pushed it onto a back burner. By the time the company announced its historic restructuring in October of 2000, it had decided to simply establish a tracking stock for the consumer business, and even that notion was later abandoned. It would be July of 2004 before AT&T would throw in the towel and stop marketing standalone long distance service to consumers. The "voice overhang," as it turned out, did not cast the only, or even the biggest, shadow across AT&T.

12

Stay Off the Treadmill of Expectations

Conspiracy theories, like mushrooms, won't grow in full sunlight. If you communicate with openness and candor, the media will give you the benefit of the doubt. On the other hand, the media have an insatiable appetite for the novel and the unexpected. Feed it, and you will soon find them chewing on your arm. Lowering expectations will not guarantee success, but overpromising is the surest path to failure.

AOL Time Warner

Early on the morning of Monday, January 10, 2000, America Online and Time Warner announced the largest merger in corporate history to that date. Time Warner owned the second largest cable television system in the United States, ran the largest portfolio of magazines, produced creative products ranging from Bugs Bunny to CNN, and held the most copyrights in the world. AOL was by far the world's leading online service company, with more than 22 million customers using its e-mail, chat, and instant messaging services.

Within minutes of hearing news of the merger, several of Armstrong's senior executives gathered in his office to discuss what it might mean to us. "Is this about content, or is it about distribution?" was the question we were batting around. In other words, did AOL do the deal in order to exploit Time Warner's vast content creation capabilities or to get access to its cable systems? And why did Time Warner agree to be acquired? Was it because the company really believed that the Internet would make its paper-and-ink products obsolete, or was it to add one more distribution system to its arsenal? It would obviously be in AT&T's interest for the deal to be seen as confirmation of cable as the premier content-distribution system. But it also raised other issues: Would this make it easier or harder for us to cash out of the Time Warner Entertainment partnership that we had inherited with the MediaOne acquisition? Would AOL change its tune on opening cable to unaffiliated Internet service providers now that it had the prospect of actually owning cable systems?

I reminded Armstrong that we would be in the second round of calls that reporters would make after they read Time Warner's news release. They would first call analysts and industry gurus for their take on what the merger meant. Then they would call us to see what we thought and how we reacted to their still-developing analysis. While I began scribbling a statement, Armstrong excused himself and disappeared into his private bathroom. Moments later, Armstrong's secretary came into the office. "Where'd he go?" she asked. "Case and Levin are on the phone." Steve Case was the CEO of America Online; Gerry Levin, the CEO of Time Warner. I knocked on the bathroom door and told Armstrong who was on the phone. He came out drying his hands and pushed the button on his speakerphone.

Levin was the first to speak. "I'm just calling to say hello," he deadpanned. "That's an expensive way to become partners," Armstrong said. Case jumped in and said that AOL was really a big communications company that would "move up the chain to content" with this merger, making it easier for the company to have a "strategic communications partner." Armstrong agreed. "Mike, AOL has *tried* to work together with AT&T," Case said. "AOL Time Warner *has* to work with you. We're a lot more complementary than we were yesterday." Levin provided an example: "Our merger announcement supports the argument that competition for the Bell companies will come through cable, Mike. This merger facilitates IP telephony." That answered one question: Levin was not really interested in offering telephony over cable until the technology was available to do it digitally.

"We ought to focus on marketing partnerships," Levin added. "We don't want to change the ownership structure of our cable systems, but we do need to figure out how to disaggregate Roadrunner and AtHome." That answered another. The Time Warner Entertainment stake that AT&T acquired with MediaOne included most of Time Warner's cable properties as well as the Roadrunner online service. Levin knew that the Department of Justice would probably require AT&T to divest its stake in Roadrunner. Armstrong parried a little. "Well, we want to be a full partner in your cable distribution systems," he said. "We thought we might exchange some of the content properties [in Time Warner Entertainment] to increase our share of the cable ownership."

"I'm not lusting for 100 percent of Warner Brothers and HBO," Levin said. "Unless you have to unload content for some regulatory reason, I'd like to ignore it for now." That answered the biggest question. Levin was satisfied with the status quo on AT&T's partial ownership of Time Warner Entertainment. Cashing out or getting more control would be no easier than it had been.

The call ended as all these calls do—with perfunctory declarations that all parties saw only great opportunities to work even more closely together, looked forward to ever deeper strategic relationships, and wished each other well.

It didn't take long for Armstrong to realize that his leverage over Time Warner had changed. AT&T had billions of dollars trapped in Time Warner Entertainment. The company was receiving absolutely nothing in return, and turning its share of the partnership into cash to pay down debt was an essential element of the MediaOne acquisition. At a minimum, AT&T had hoped to restructure AT&T's passive stake in Time Warner Entertainment by trading its programming assets for a greater say in the management of its cable systems. But while Time Warner considered the structure of Time Warner Entertainment untidy, it had no motivation to change it.

AOL's passion for ubiquity, however, was something that AT&T might exploit. AOL wanted to be everywhere, especially on high-bandwidth systems that could support streaming audio and video. The AtHome Corporation had exclusive rights to provide online service over cable systems passing 65 percent of American homes. AOL had already spent millions in hard cash and political capital to gain access to those systems. Now that it was merging with Time Warner, Armstrong could see the offer just around the bend: "I'll carry you, if you carry me." Armstrong, who knew that a network's value increased with its usage, believed that it was in AtHome's best interests to carry any content that would attract users. While AtHome's exclusivity agreements with the cable companies had been important in its start-up period, once the service was established, it could make a lot of money providing broadband access to companies like AOL.

But Armstrong was in a bind. While AT&T had theoretical control of AtHome, the other cable partners had an effective veto over any major decisions. They couldn't even agree on a strategy to fix AtHome's service problems. And they showed little inclination to open their cable systems to other Internet service providers. So Somers, who was now firmly in charge of AT&T Broadband, was given the assignment of convincing AtHome's cable partners to sing from the same sheet of music. By the end of March 2000, he had convinced Comcast and Cox to give up their veto rights in exchange for a "put" on their shares.

In essence, AT&T agreed to buy Cox and Comcast's interests in AtHome for at least $48 a share, up to an aggregate value of $3.2 billion, at any time between January 1, 2001, and June 4, 2002. Since AtHome's stock was then trading at about $33 a share and anything connected with the Internet commanded outrageous stock multiples, it didn't seem like a bad bet.

Cox and Comcast also won the right to end their exclusivity agreements early and to terminate them entirely by June 2001. But since warrants to acquire new shares were tied to increasing their distribution of the AtHome high-speed Internet service, that didn't seem like a bad bet, either.

Trouble AtHome

Precisely what happened to AtHome in the following months has been the subject of numerous court suits, but some events are uncontestable. AtHome's losses went from about $140 million at the end of 1998 to more than $7.2 *billion* at the end of 2000, including a charge of about $6 billion to write off the Excite portal, which it had bought before AT&T acquired its stake. By January 2001, as the Internet bubble deflated, AtHome's stock price had declined to $7 a share; Cox and Comcast then exercised their put, forcing AT&T to pay more than $3 billion to buy their shares. (At around the same time, Somers had structured a similarly unfortunate deal with AT&T's partners in AT&T Canada. One might have understood if Armstrong or the board of directors had instructed the maintenance staff to remove the "p," "u," and "t" keys from his computer keyboard.)

In June 2001, facing a liquidity crisis, AtHome borrowed $100 million from a group of "vulture" hedge funds that specialized in loans to companies in distress. On August 20, AtHome's outside auditor, Ernst & Young, expressed "substantial doubt" that the company would be able "to continue as a going concern." Ernst & Young was fired the next day. On August 22, AtHome's shares closed at 56 cents, 99 percent off the 1999 high.

By the end of September, facing debts of $1.2 billion and burning through about $10 million a week with only $150 million in cash on hand, including about $80 million contributed by AT&T, AtHome filed for bankruptcy and agreed to sell its assets to AT&T for $307 million. Within thirty days, AtHome's creditors objected; they demanded that AtHome close down its service immediately, claiming that the cable companies were underpaying for it. They argued that AT&T was trying to acquire AtHome's network on the cheap and estimated that it would cost the company about $1 billion to replicate the service, even though AT&T's chief technology officer had publicly estimated that it could be done in a few months for less than $100 million.

The creditors explained their reasoning in their petition to the bankruptcy court: "Only the prospect of turning off the switch will unlock [AtHome's] true value, and here is why. If AtHome terminates service to a cable company, the cable company's subscribers will all need new e-mail addresses. Additionally, the phenomenal growth and market capitalization multiples being enjoyed by the cable companies stem from the cable companies' ability to add 400,000 subscribers a quarter to AtHome's service. Simply put, the value to cable companies of their AtHome contracts is enormous, while AtHome has negative cash flow!"[1] Thus began a high-stakes game of chicken between AT&T and AtHome's creditors.

The bankruptcy court judge was scheduled to issue his ruling on Friday, November 30, 2001, and AtHome's engineers in California spent much of that day in a cat-and-mouse game with AT&T engineers: AtHome's engineers were trying to reprogram the security codes in the AT&T nodes of the AtHome network to make it more difficult to restore service if it went down. Neither Cox nor Comcast reported similar problems, so AT&T knew that it would be the likely target if the creditors won permission to begin shutting the service down.

AT&T's lawyers on both coasts, its bankers negotiating with the creditors, the engineers at its labs in California and Denver, and Armstrong's senior team in New Jersey were on a conference call through most of the day and night. When the bankruptcy court judge finally ruled that AtHome could void its cable contracts because they were unprofitable, most commentators believed that he had significantly improved its bargaining position. The cable companies would have no alternative but to accept new terms in order to continue service. To do otherwise would be to commit mutual suicide.

AtHome immediately began refusing to accept technical support calls from AT&T customers. It also started to pull down network diagnostic tools, and at midnight West Coast time, it shut off the portion of its network serving 850,000 AT&T customers, disabling their e-mail and leaving them with error messages on their computer screens. But AtHome's creditors had miscalculated. To the surprise of many inside the industry, AT&T quickly knitted its own data centers, network operations centers, and cable lines into a network that could substitute for AtHome's systems, restoring service to all 850,000 customers in less than one week.

Conspiracies Can't Grow in Full Sunlight

The mainstream national media took relatively little notice of the possibility that the AtHome service might be shut down, perhaps assuming that it was all corporate posturing, with no more at stake than in professional wrestling. The online media, on the other hand, were abuzz with the latest rumors and conspiracy theories. We made a conscious decision not to engage in sword rattling, even though, behind the scenes, we made no secret of our progress in building an alternative network.

Few people really understood what the AtHome network was. Much of it piggybacked on the same cables that carried HBO or ESPN programs to subscribers' homes. Even the modems through which customers' personal computers plugged into the high-speed network belonged to the cable companies, which leased them to subscribers. AtHome simply certified that the modems would work with the network.

AtHome's equipment was further up the line, in the "head ends" where local cables connected to high-capacity fiber-optic lines. That was where AtHome usually placed data switches to manage the network's capacity. Those switches connected to twenty-five regional data centers where AtHome stored popular content, such as Yahoo! and

CNN Web pages, so that it would be readily accessible to customers. This was also where it kept the computers for managing e-mail and routing tables for Internet domain names. On their way to the Internet, data would travel between the head ends and the data centers over a high-speed local network owned by the cable companies. For carrying data over long distances, AtHome used a private AT&T network "backbone" that minimized the traffic jams that often snarl ordinary Internet traffic.

In theory, the network could be expanded to handle any number of subscribers as long as the cable companies upgraded their lines to handle two-way data transmissions and AtHome added computers in its data centers. In practice, however, the number of subscribers grew so fast that the regional data centers couldn't handle the traffic load. By the winter of 1999, AtHome's e-mail was out of service an average of fifty-five hours a week. The cable companies hired AT&T to audit the service and make recommendations for fixing it.

Within days, AT&T's engineers concluded that AtHome's engineers were winging it. The service's capacity plan was never matched with the cable companies' estimates of demand. Furthermore, the data traffic on high-speed Internet lines has different characteristics from traffic on a dial-up service. While AtHome had only 5 percent as many users as AOL, it carried 35 percent as much traffic. As a result, the computers, called servers, on which the service ran typically operated at 85 percent of their theoretical capacity, leaving little margin for error. AtHome's cable company board members, led by Ted Rogers, the Canadian media billionaire, were furious with the company's managers and insisted that they accept supervision from AT&T's technical people. Within weeks, AT&T engineers had redesigned the network, developed a more realistic construction plan, and taught AtHome's engineers how to meet "telephone-quality" performance standards.

In September, just weeks after AtHome's auditors expressed doubt that the company could continue as a going concern, AT&T offered to buy the network as part of a "prepackaged" bankruptcy filing that would have provided a more orderly transition for all the cable companies' customers—allowing them to keep their e-mail addresses, for example. However, AT&T also hedged its bets, quietly building a network that could perform the same functions as the AtHome network and developing plans to move its customers to that network.

A week before the judge was scheduled to render his decision,

AT&T sent an e-mail to its AtHome customers warning them about the anticipated shutdown and advising them to check their e-mail every day so that messages would be saved on their local computer. The e-mail also noted that AT&T was trying to buy the AtHome network, but warned, "If the proposal to purchase the [AtHome] network is not approved, your service may be temporarily interrupted and it will be necessary to move your service to a new AT&T network." The company also established a Web site where it promised to post information as the situation developed.

AtHome Pulls the Plug

When AtHome pulled the plug, Armstrong ordered the contingency plans put into action. The morning after the decision, every customer received a recorded phone call telling them what had happened and offering a two-day credit for every day the service was out.

We knew that even if 850,000 customers without high-speed Internet service was not enough to catch the national media's attention, it would be Topic A in chat rooms and on many Web sites. Rather than endlessly trying to correct false information and empty speculation, we decided to lay out our plan to move all our former AtHome customers to our new network within two weeks and to give a daily tally of our progress.

There was a certain degree of risk in this approach. AT&T was not yet a full-fledged member of the Internet crowd that gathered at such online hangouts as "slashdot.com." Worse, the company was the object of derision and suspicion. We also knew that the migration would hit many potholes. Moving a computer from one data network to another was not simply a matter of throwing a switch. IP addresses needed to be reset, Web browsers needed to be reconfigured, and operating systems needed to be updated. And every customer's computer was unique, involving different platforms with a different mix of applications. Nevertheless, we were convinced that the only way to win over customers (and the Web media) in the long run was to be completely honest and open with them.

We did pretty well in that regard, although we were not perfect, and whenever I found out about a reporter whose call was not returned within thirty minutes, I would get in touch with him or her myself. I also assigned someone to monitor the Web chat rooms, prepared to answer questions or correct misinformation, but principally to develop a feeling for the temperature of the user community.

We issued our first update the morning of Saturday, December 1, to report that 86,000 high-speed data customers had been moved to AT&T's new network overnight. By Monday morning, more than 330,000 customers had been moved. By Tuesday, it was more than 500,000; by Wednesday morning, 750,000; and essentially all 850,000 were on the new network by Friday morning, less than a week after the bankruptcy court's ruling.

Sometime that week, AT&T withdrew its $307 million bid for AtHome's network assets. Cox and Comcast came up with $355 million to keep their customers connected for ninety days until they could build their own networks.

Of course, some people complained about the length of the holding time for customer care. There was online grumbling that the company limited download speeds to 1.5 megabits to conserve bandwidth. A few computers didn't function properly with the new AT&T service. And conspiracy theories about "who really killed AtHome" popped up here and there; in fact, like Elvis sightings, they persist to this day. But the media coverage was generally positive. Many customers were impressed with the speed with which they were back on line, even if it took a few days, and most customers said that the new service was more reliable.

If I had to do it over again, I would be more aggressive in communicating our earlier efforts to help AtHome improve its network performance. Ironically, few people, even in the technical media, understood how fragile the AtHome network had been. And no one outside the cable companies using the AtHome service understood that in the early weeks of 2001, a dedicated team of AT&T engineers had pulled it back from a slow meltdown. Of course, at the time, our primary goal was to avoid embarrassing the leadership of AtHome, who might have known how to peddle advertising, but did not have a clue as to how to build and run a network. But that reticence allowed the seeds of conspiracy theories to take root.

The final curtain fell so swiftly on AtHome that many people thought some unseen hand must have been pulling ropes to bring it down. AtHome's creditors seeded the media with grand conspiracy theories to bolster the suits they were filing against the company. They succeeded in getting both *Forbes* and *Business Week* to repeat their allegations, which accused AT&T of everything from driving AtHome into bankruptcy to stealing the design of its network. In hindsight, these stories would have had less credibility if we had been as open about our efforts to resuscitate the AtHome network as we later were about our efforts to recreate it.

Similarly, AT&T's fortunes took such a sudden turn for the worse in mid-2000 that some people wondered whether the company had been sitting on bad news hoping that some earnings alchemist would wander into its midst. Both suspicions were baseless. While neither event was the product of a conspiracy, they both demonstrated how efficiently natural forces fill a news vacuum if you allow one to develop.

May 2, 2000, Revision of Earnings Guidance

On May 2, 2000, AT&T projected that its operating earnings would be 5 percent lower than the estimates that had been announced just five months before. The company's stock declined 15 percent in a single day as investors reacted to what they believed were inflated expectations.

Those expectations had been set in a full-day extravaganza for analysts and media in a glittery ballroom at New York's Waldorf-Astoria the previous December. The presentations were choreographed to demonstrate that the company was taking aggressive action to participate in the industry's growth. With his typical penchant for "making news," Armstrong announced plans for the creation of a tracking stock for the company's wireless business, new leadership for its business services division, a major expansion of its fiber-optic network, and another near-doubling of its revenue growth rate. Operational earnings were projected to be between $2.10 and $2.15 per share.

The only hitch in his plan was a delay in naming a new chief financial officer to replace Dan Somers, whose appointment as president of the company's cable business was made permanent.

Actually, when I arrived at the Waldorf the evening before, I was carrying two versions of the main news release. In one, we would announce the appointment of Charles Noski as AT&T's chief financial officer. Noski, who had worked with Armstrong at Hughes Electronics as controller and then CFO, became that company's president and chief operating officer after Armstrong left for AT&T. Armstrong had gone after him as soon as the two-year freeze on recruiting his former

Hughes colleagues had expired. Noski had not yet talked to his children about the prospect of moving east, and, understandably, that was not something he planned to rush—even for an AT&T news release. At 11 P.M., Armstrong told me that it still hadn't happened, so I tore up that version of the release.

Noski's appointment was announced just days later, and he started work almost immediately, commuting weekly from his home in California so that his daughters could finish the school year there. He didn't realize it then, but this was a schedule that he would keep for three years as the company went through a period of financial uncertainty, romanced a series of merger partners, and ultimately split into smaller parts. There are some people (inside and outside AT&T) who believe that the company would have had a very different future had he become CFO just one year earlier. As it was, he spent his first few months trying to figure out what he had gotten himself into.

The year 2000 had begun with conflicting signals. The wireless business, which would soon be floating an initial public offering for shares tracking its performance, was doing even better than anticipated. The long-distance businesses, on the other hand, were struggling to meet financial benchmarks based on MCI WorldCom's results, which would later prove to have been grossly exaggerated. By the time Noski arrived on the scene, the long-distance unit heads were trying to renegotiate their financial targets for the year. That in itself was not unusual. Every business unit began the year with a gap between its annual targets and its latest revenue and earnings outlook. Over the course of the year, those gaps generally closed. Some businesses did better than they had been asked to do, and almost all did better than they had thought they would in the early days of the year. Every month's operational review was like an ornithological conference as business unit leaders took turns describing "bluebirds" (unforeseen windfalls) and "blackbirds" (unforeseen problems).

But by the end of April, when the units filed their latest outlooks, Noski had had enough. In the first quarter, the company's long-distance units had seldom hit the outlook they had filed just one month earlier. Something didn't smell right. Armstrong agreed and told the long-distance people to reexamine their pricing assumptions for the second half of the year until they had a business plan that they could deliver with "80 percent confidence."

Since earnings were scheduled to be announced on May 2, Armstrong wanted to see the new outlooks by Friday, April 28. I remember the date because it happened to be my birthday, and I spent it in a meeting that continued nonstop into the evening and through that weekend in the boardroom at AT&T's Basking Ridge complex.

On Friday evening, we listened to a procession of accountants using carefully prepared slides to review the latest business outlook. By Saturday evening, the presentations had become columns of figures scrawled on large easel pads, and everyone seemed to be taking a turn at crossing off numbers and inserting new ones. Hardly anyone could keep up with the changing views, and not everyone agreed. For example, Cicconi expected the access agreement he was forging with the FCC to reduce revenue, but he was surprised to hear that the consumer people now expected it to reduce earnings by as much as seven cents per share. After a day and a half of discussion that seemed to periodically circle back on itself, Armstrong was becoming increasingly impatient.

By 9 P.M., even the usually unflappable Noski was fed up. He told Armstrong that he would have his team reconcile all the different views overnight. The *Wall Street Journal* had described Noski as "bookish," but he had an intellect to match Zeglis's, an obsession with precision, and the steely determination to achieve it. But it was late Sunday evening before we were able to convince ourselves that we would miss our previous earnings estimate by as much as nine cents a share, or about $4^1/_2$ percent.

One-time events, such as the delay in closing the MediaOne deal and the newly consolidated AtHome losses, would essentially cancel each other out. But consumer long-distance revenue showed every sign of declining at an even more precipitous rate than had been anticipated at the end of the previous year, and, while business data volumes appeared to be holding, WorldCom was introducing new rock-bottom prices. Both developments portended problems in the second half of the year. There was no discussion about postponing a change in guidance, even though the consequences were not hard to predict.

When AT&T had lowered its guidance in 1996, the company's stock price had fallen 9.8 percent on the first day of trading following the announcement. When the company lowered it again in 1997, the stock had fallen 10 percent in two days. In both years, the company attributed its earnings shortfall to competitive pricing pressures and to increased investments in high-growth parts of the business. News stories, however, focused primarily on the drop in the stock price. I predicted that this time the reaction would be even more pronounced and the duration of the news coverage would probably be longer. If anything, I underestimated the reaction. None of our competitors followed suit, although we knew they must have been feeling the same pressures. Neither MCI WorldCom nor Sprint revised its full-year earnings estimates until the end of the third quarter. Who could blame them? Our stock was battered, falling 30 percent in thirty days—a loss of $54 billion in market value.

What happened? AT&T's most profitable business—long-distance voice—had always operated in a deflationary environment. But wireless plans that treated long-distance calls as "just another minute"—and even made them "free" in the evening and on weekends—were changing people's calling habits and exacerbating price competition among the long-distance carriers. But three years of budget cuts had weakened the consumer unit's vaunted "acquisition machine." Many of the customers lost to other long distance companies simply were not being replaced.

Whereas at the end of 1999, the consumer long-distance unit had expected its revenue to decline by 3 to 5 percent in 2000, just five months later it forecast a revenue decline of 5 to 7 percent; in fact, it declined nearly 10 percent. In 2001, consumer long-distance revenue was projected to decline "in the mid-teens." It actually declined 20 percent.

Worse than the slope of the revenue decline was the total inability of anyone to predict it. The consumer long-distance business was so large ($22 billion in revenue and nearly $9 billion in net income in 1999) that it cast a huge shadow over the company's other businesses, which were either far less profitable or losing money. Wireless revenue, for example, grew 44 percent in 1999, but wireless was still only about a third the size of consumer long distance and was as yet unprofitable. The stock market had figured out that in absolute dollars, AT&T's profitable businesses were declining faster than its growth businesses were growing. Further, it appeared that MCI WorldCom, even without a wireless subsidiary, had found the sweet spot in the business market—data.

In hindsight, it is now clear that MCI WorldCom was not immune to the pressures buffeting AT&T; it used accounting gimmicks and outright fraud to insulate itself from them. This not only misled investors who compared the two companies, it also created artificial price competition. If MCI WorldCom had priced its services at a level that matched the earnings it reported from 1999 to 2002, industry prices would have been about $40 billion higher. Since AT&T accounted for about 38 percent of industry revenue, it would have had about $5 billion more revenue per year. Instead of declining revenue, it would have shown growth. And history would have been very different.

Treadmill of Expectations

The lesson learned here, of course, is strictly academic: Don't compete with cheats. The more practical—and perhaps obvious—lesson is to be extremely cautious in setting expectations. AT&T, like many other companies in this era of booming stock markets, was on a treadmill of ever-increasing expectations that crested in its December 1999 analyst meeting at the Waldorf-Astoria. Again like many other companies in this era of "irrational exuberance," AT&T fed the unrealistic expectations of a market with a tapeworm in its gut. We mistook the market's nurses—the media and financial analysts who tracked the product of its digestive system—for the patient itself. And that is how we lost control of market expectations: We attempted to feed an insatiable beast.

It's a familiar story. Even now that the fever of hot new offerings and ever-rising stock prices has cooled, too many companies treat the media and financial analysts as stakeholders rather than as channels to the people whose welfare is really tied to the company's fortunes—its own employees, customers, and investors. The media, by definition, need to be fed something new on an ever-shortening news cycle. And, as Louis Lowenstein, Simon H. Rifkind Professor Emeritus of Finance and Law at Columbia University, once wrote, sell-side (brokerage) analysts "may not always see the forest for the trees, but their collective thirst for information—the information that will drive new trades and commissions—is unquenchable."[2]

The real tragedy is that some companies build their business plans, their recruiting, and even their structure around their perception of how analysts will react. And some boards mistake analysts' perceptions and biases for the reality of their own company's strategic position.

13

It's Okay to Change Your Mind

If you need to announce a fundamental change in strategy, remember that neither the media nor your company's stakeholders were on the journey that led to your decision. It will take time to bring them up to speed. Don't complicate matters by asking them to pretend that nothing has changed. Popular wisdom may be wrong, but picking a fight over it will only cost you your credibility. Sometimes it's better to be smart than right.

Loose Ends

If AT&T were a sweater, anyone who knew where to look would have seen the first threads beginning to unravel in the summer of 2000. Why it unraveled has been debated by journalists, pundits, and business school classes ever since. The man who knit the sweater, however, argued that it hadn't unraveled at all—he had merely redistributed the yarn, turning a comfortable cardigan into several snappier vests. Some of us even allowed ourselves to believe it. And therein lay another lesson: To paraphrase Albert Einstein, the only difference between genius and self-delusion is that genius has its limits.

AT&T's chief financial officer in 2000, Chuck Noski, was given to neither self-delusion nor wishful thinking. Fresh from the character-building experience of revising the company's earnings forecast for 2000, by midsummer Noski was sorting through the first estimates for 2001. They were not pretty. Sales of the company's most profitable service—long-distance voice—were declining at an even faster rate than anyone had predicted. As more long-distance calls moved to wireless networks or became e-mail messages, Sprint had introduced a new five-cents-a-minute calling plan in a desperate effort to goose usage. AT&T and MCI were forced to match it, but the new low rates did nothing to stimulate more calling. And the company's economic models indicated that things would only get worse when the Bells began offering long-distance service, even if they didn't introduce lower prices. On average, when AT&T lost ten customers to Sprint or MCI, it won eight back within six months. Customers who left for a Bell company usually stayed there.

AT&T's voice revenue, which had funded its entry into everything from credit cards to computers to wireless and now cable television, had reached an inflection point. It would never grow again. And the company's growth businesses—cable, wireless, and data—would not replace the profits generated by voice services for decades. Meanwhile, those businesses were devouring capital at an alarming rate. Depreciation alone would reduce 2001 earnings by 30 cents a share, and the combined capital requirements of the wireless, cable, and data businesses totaled $15 to $19 billion, depending on whose wish list Noski believed.

But what troubled Noski the most was the $65 billion in debt that the company had accumulated in buying its cable properties. Annual interest payments alone were about $4 billion a year, and about half the debt—some $32 billion—would come due in less than a year. It was as if the company's previous CEO, Dan Somers, had bought MediaOne with a bank credit card. The company's declining cash flow made it impossible for it to reduce its debt significantly and threatened its credit rating. Noski seriously doubted that the company could continue paying its dividend, at least not at its current level of $3.1 billion a year. Even worse, if the company's debt rating were lowered, it could be forced to negotiate new loans with its major banks, which would undoubtedly attach onerous financial and operational terms to them, further limiting the company's options. Everything boiled down to two numbers: In 2001, the company would probably generate about $22 billion in cash from operations and spend about $23 billion on capital additions, interest, and dividends. And things just got worse from there. According to one estimate, by 2005 AT&T would be spending about $13 billion a year more than it was taking in.

The company's deteriorating stock price, which had declined some

40 percent since the beginning of the year, made matters even more tenuous. With assets of $200 billion and a market cap of only $118 billion, AT&T could be a takeover target. The media and professional investors, who had hailed Armstrong just months before, began to turn on him. *BusinessWeek*, which had praised him at the beginning of 1999 for "surprise—keeping his promises to investors," in mid-2000 warned that "the jig is up for AT&T" and crowed, "AT&T can't buy its way out of this mess."[1] When rumors spread that Armstrong was on his way out, to be replaced by John Malone, the company's stock price actually went up. That was not one of Armstrong's favorite days.

Malone Tries to Help

In July 2000, with the stock at an all-time low, Malone thought he could help. When Leslie Cauley of the *Wall Street Journal* made one of her periodic calls "trolling for story ideas," as she put it, Malone agreed to speak on the record. No one would have been surprised if Malone had been upset with AT&T's management. Thanks to the stock's slide, he had lost about $1 billion on paper. He had made no secret of the fact that he thought Somers had allowed too much short-term debt to accumulate and then compounded the error by disposing of assets in transactions with high tax costs. He had also been disappointed when Armstrong decided that he didn't need the complications of tracking stocks, as originally contemplated in the TCI acquisition.

But Malone, who had built his career on rocking the boat, had decided to go along. He had voted with the other directors on every one of the company's major acquisitions and strategic moves. And he wanted to send a clear signal that he supported Armstrong and had no desire to take over. In fact, right after hanging up with Cauley, he called Armstrong and told him what he had done. Armstrong told me to expect a story in the next day's *Journal* that would set the record straight on Malone's support. When Cauley called for comment on a story that had obviously already been written, we declined. I saw nothing to be gained by appearing to argue in print with one of our directors and largest shareowners. Even with hindsight, it's hard to know whether Armstrong was hopelessly naïve about the media or Malone was. My guess is that they both were.

The *Journal* story opened with the following sentence: "Cable-TV pioneer John Malone, one of AT&T Corp.'s biggest individual shareholders, says he is promoting several recommendations to top management—like it or not—that he thinks could provide some significant fixes for the ailing telephone giant."[2] The "fixes" were a mix of ideas that Malone had floated in print before (such as tracking stocks) and ideas that had worked for him in the past (such as getting into programming to leverage AT&T's new status as the nation's largest cable TV operator). But by inserting the parenthetical phrase "like it or not," the reporter put a negative spin on everything that followed. She made nothing up. She quoted Malone accurately. But she also created the impression that Malone and Armstrong were somehow at odds. The ostensible purpose for doing the interview didn't appear until the eighth paragraph: "Mr. Malone also says he supports Mr. Armstrong and believes he is doing a good job under the circumstances."[3]

Now, John Malone is a financial genius of the first order. In the cable industry's early days, when raising money was a challenge, Malone specialized in devising incredibly convoluted deals that allowed his investors to shelter income and avoid taxes, in effect using Uncle Sam as a silent, if unknowing, partner. He created tracking stocks and moved assets in and out of them to suit his purpose or the investment fad of the moment. But he would not have gotten away with any of it—even though it was all perfectly legal—at AT&T. The company was simply too big, too visible, and under too much scrutiny.[4] Even a reporter whom he considered a friend used him for her own purposes. There simply was no story in Malone's supporting Armstrong. It explained nothing. It was certainly inconsistent with what she was hearing from others, including the recently departed Leo Hindery. And boardroom intrigue was simply sexier.

I know from several lengthy conversations with Malone that he doesn't have the first idea of how the media operate and never will because he simply doesn't care. It didn't bother him when then Vice President Al Gore called him "the Darth Vader of the cable industry." And he didn't understand why anyone should have been upset by the *Journal* article. But although nothing in the article said that Malone and Armstrong were at odds, and there were several statements to the exact opposite effect, most journalists interpreted it that way. And that interpretation appeared in stories that ran in everything from *Business-*

Week to the *New York Times,* usually as an aside that was beginning to assume the currency of a truism.

In September 2000, when the *Industry Standard* ran Malone's picture with a caption saying that he was one of Armstrong's critics, Armstrong sent Malone a copy with a handwritten note: "If you can fix, I'd appreciate it (unless you'd make it worse)." Malone called me the next day for advice on "fixing the perception of a feud" between the two men. I couldn't offer much. Most of the reporters who covered the industry not only believed that there was a feud, but had written about it so much that they now had a stake in its outcome. I suggested that Malone fax a handwritten note expressing his support for Mike. (True to form, Malone wrote the letter on ruled paper, with no letterhead, and signed it "John." Armstrong's secretary had to pencil in "Malone.")

The full text of the note gives some insight into the real source of Malone's discomfort—not strategy, but "deal-making execution":

Mike—

I really appreciated the presentations at the Board retreat, especially Chuck's obvious involvement. Clearly, the deal-making execution of the basic strategy will be critical in building long-term shareholder value in each of the businesses.

I don't know why the media keep trying to create a rift between us—I think AT&T couldn't have a better CEO than Mike Armstrong during this difficult period. If I can help in any way, please let me know.

John [Malone]

I gave copies of the note to several reporters, but I don't think it affected their writing in any obvious way. I guess it was just hard to believe that someone who had lost a billion dollars in a company could have anything but hard feelings about its management. The only technique that seemed to work was one that I had used before. The next time Leslie Cauley ventured to write about Armstrong and Malone, I arranged for them to be interviewed together, even though it meant that Malone had to rush back to Denver from a charity event in New York and Armstrong had to delay his departure from a meeting in Denver by several hours. They did the interview from a small room at

Liberty Media's airplane hangar, hunched over a speakerphone. It wasn't much of a story—which was the whole idea.

Board Retreat

The board retreat mentioned in Malone's note was the climactic meeting in September 2000 at which Noski laid out the company's precarious financial position, and Armstrong first raised the possibility of breaking up the company.

While the company was not yet in a liquidity crisis, the sound of bouncing checks was not far off. No one was sure how long the company's deteriorating operating results would support its debt rating. The consequences of failing to deal with that situation were disastrous on every level.

Cash on hand seldom matches outgoing cash to the penny at any company. With its current credit rating, AT&T could borrow money overnight if it needed cash to cover the checks it wrote. When it had more cash in its bank accounts than it needed, it lent that cash to other creditworthy companies that temporarily needed it. This was how the so-called commercial paper market worked. But if the company's debt rating were lowered, not only would its borrowing costs significantly increase, but the commercial paper market could eventually be closed to it.

AT&T had debt of $32 billion coming due within a year, and in the fall of 2000, the company had a standby line of credit, or a "bank facility," of only $10 billion. (In one of his last acts as CFO, Somers had reduced the bank facility to save on the associated fees.) The company would have to line up a consortium of banks that were willing to increase its backup facility by about $25 billion. Meanwhile, its growth businesses had a seemingly insatiable appetite for capital.

Ironically, if each business were a separate company, each would have its own credit rating, and (thanks to the vagaries of the debt markets) their combined borrowing capacity would be greater than that of a single, integrated AT&T. Furthermore, at least two of the divisions (AT&T Broadband and AT&T Wireless) had growth rates that were attractive enough to support their own equity offerings, which would have given them another potential source of cash.

Finally, it really bugged Armstrong that investors saw the sum of AT&T's businesses as an enterprise with only modest growth and declining earnings. There was a huge gap between the value of the company's individual parts and the consolidated "T" stock. "If they won't value the company on the sum of the parts," he said, "we'll give them the parts."

Zeglis, eager to finally run his own company, jumped on the breakup bandwagon and fed Armstrong's new strategy back to him. Noski had always suspected Zeglis of inflating his unit's capital needs to force the break-up discussion. Now, he watched Zeglis eagerly grab a felt-tip marker. He drew four columns on an easel and labeled each with the name of one of the business units. Then he drew a horizontal box across the columns. "We've been spending 90 percent of our energy trying to build bundles across these businesses," he told the directors. "But 90 percent of the value of bundles is within each business." His best example was AT&T Wireless's Digital One Rate calling plan, which treated long distance as just another wireless call. It attracted far more customers and was far "stickier" than trying to put wired and wireless accounts on a single bill.

On top of that, all four business units had come up with potential merger partners or investors if they were spun off from AT&T. The board had plenty to chew on.

Before Armstrong's arrival, AT&T's annual board retreats were held at genteel resorts such as the Greenbrier in West Virginia. Spouses were usually invited, and afternoons were free for golf, tennis, or organized sightseeing and shopping. Evenings featured gourmet dinners, sometimes with entertainment. Under Armstrong, board retreats were held at the company's Basking Ridge, New Jersey, conference center. They started on Thursday or Friday evening and ran through Saturday or Sunday lunch. One dinner was at a local restaurant; all the other meals were taken at the conference center. There were no sports, no entertainment, and no spouses. But even though the board members had plenty of time to discuss the ramifications of the situation being outlined for them, as well as the proposed solutions, there were so many moving parts and open questions that no one had any illusion that a decision would be reached over the weekend.

The board asked Armstrong to continue exploring strategic alternatives, but since the members had already talked themselves into somehow segregating the declining consumer long-distance business from the rest of AT&T, it was only a short step to breaking up the whole company.

The company's deteriorating financial position left few practical alternatives. If AT&T spun off only its consumer long-distance business, its credit rating would drop because of all the cash flow it would lose. Similarly, AT&T's credit rating might suffer if it spun off AT&T Wireless because it would lose the ability to raise cash by selling additional wireless tracking stock. There was no industrial logic to leaving business long distance and cable together, and, as a separate company, the cable unit could float its own initial public offering to raise capital.

Any one of these moves without the others would endanger the company's credit rating just as it needed to refinance more than $30 billion worth of short-term debt. It was like being caught in a braided finger cuff—the harder you pull, the tighter it becomes.

Armstrong knew that as these various scenarios began to jell, the company was approaching a disclosure cliff. Once again, he did not have the luxury of time, and making piecemeal announcements would simply extend the period of pain, so he proposed bringing a full recommendation to the board at its next regular meeting on Monday, October 23.

As AT&T's board members left the conference center on Saturday to catch their limousines and jets, they had each crossed an invisible line. Imperceptibly, they had moved from discussing *whether* to throw in the towel and break up AT&T to discussing *how*.

On Monday morning, Armstrong met with his senior team. Most of us had been at the board meeting, so he didn't have to describe what had happened, but it was clear that in the single day since we had said good-bye, he had gone from imagining the company's new structure to living in it. The October board meeting was no longer a progress report in his mind; it was the deadline for getting approval for whatever we were going to do, and we would then announce it immediately. Armstrong said it was time to tackle "the really tough stuff": how to explain the company's breakup to employees, customers, shareowners, regulators, the media, and anyone else who had a penchant for backseat driving.

There was also another critical audience that was now even more important than the sell-side analysts—the three debt-rating agencies: Moody's, Standard & Poor's, and, to a lesser extent, Fitch. The big question was when to brief them on the company's plan so that they could issue credit ratings that reflected what we were learning about the industry and the business, as well as how we intended to cope with it. Noski didn't want to get ahead of the board, although both he and Armstrong had been keeping the rating agencies apprised of new developments as they occurred. In the end, we decided to brief the rating agencies the morning after the full board meeting.

The announcement itself, which would come on Wednesday, October 25, would have three major elements. The company would be broken into four investment vehicles—wireless, cable, business, and consumer—that would ultimately be spun off to current shareowners. AT&T shareowners would also have an opportunity, but no obligation, to exchange their shares of AT&T for shares of AT&T Wireless with an equivalent value.

For the first time in 473 consecutive quarters, the company would lower its dividend beginning in the fourth quarter of 2000, although the size of the reduction would not be announced until discussions with the rating agencies had been completed. The size of the dividend reduction was the last cushion the company had if the rating agencies were still uncomfortable.[5]

Restructuring

AT&T's restructuring was one of the biggest business news stories of 2000. Between October 23 and November 9, we tracked and analyzed 1,006 articles and news broadcasts about the company's decision "to divide itself into four parts." Ironically, *more than half* of everything that was written about the company's restructuring during this period actually appeared *before* we made the announcement. An independent research firm, Delahaye Medialink, characterized 52 percent of the coverage as "negative," with 38 percent "neutral" and 10 percent "positive." Its analysis, however, showed that the neutral tone of the coverage was skewed by brief and factual television reports when the news first broke. Discounting television, fully 69 percent of the coverage had a negative tone. Looking back, it was naïve to have expected otherwise.

Early in the planning for the announcement—before I even knew its major elements—I had consulted some of the best minds in the public relations field. Their prognosis was consistent: The story of Armstrong's "failure" would be our biggest issue. Our only credible alternative was to acknowledge the shift in strategy and quickly change the subject. By early October, I had developed a storyline around three key points:

Storyline: Keeping Promises

1. We laid out the right strategy in 1998 and made *good progress* against it.

   - Competitive costs. Industry-leading margins. Doubled revenue growth in 1998 and 1999. Less dependence on voice—50% of revenue in 2000, down from 79% in 1997. Growth businesses of $40+ billion, growing 11%.

   - Built the largest broadband services footprint in the United States and upgraded network to offer five new categories of service—digital video, telephony, high-speed data, small business, and interactive TV.

   - Capped circuit-switched network and invested $40 billion to accelerate deployment of high-speed packet networks and fiber rings to meet businesses' data needs.

   - Built $4 billion outsourcing and network management business from nearly standing start.

   - Transformed a patchwork of local analog cellular systems into nationwide digital service that redefined wireless industry.

2. But *time was always our enemy* and we ran out of it.

   - Industry-wide decline in long distance voice masks new revenue growth and is accelerating at a faster pace than anyone thought. (Ask WorldCom.)

   - Customers place greater value on bundles within the same facility—e.g., voice, video and data on cable, local and long distance on wireless. Bundling across facilities best done through commercial contracts.

   - Cross-unit management slowed down decision-making.

3. Restructuring combines *power of single vision* with speed and focus of separate companies.

   - Each new AT&T business will have the resources to provide facilities-based, end-to-end broadband services. They will also be able to bundle each other's services on a single bill, if that's what customers want.

   - Investors will be able to buy shares of the company that best meets their financial goals—e.g., income or growth.

Armstrong didn't buy it.

He had no argument with my litany of accomplishments, but to his mind, he had not run out of time and he was not changing his strategy. All he was doing was changing the company's structure; the shareowners would still own the same assets, just in four stocks rather than one. In fact, as he got into his salesman's spiel, it became even clearer to him that his strategy all along had been to build three new networks—wireless, cable, and data. Mission accomplished. Now it was time to turn them loose.

I dutifully developed a communications plan to position the restructuring (never "the breakup") as "the next logical step in AT&T's transformation." By the time I presented it to the AT&T board at the end of a very long day on October 23, the story had already leaked. In fact, before the meeting began, as the directors took their turns at the coffee urn, one of them wondered out loud whether the board even needed to meet, since the *Wall Street Journal* itself had apparently settled any remaining debate on the company's restructuring.

Adding to the day's somber mood was a report that I had received just before Armstrong called the meeting to order—the board of Lucent Technologies had fired its CEO, Rich McGuinn. I passed a copy of Lucent's news release to Armstrong, who read it aloud to the directors, most of whom had known McGuinn when Lucent was part of AT&T. Armstrong tried to lighten the mood by joking that he could step out of the meeting if the directors wanted to consider similar action. Playing along, one of his best friends on the board suggested instead that he do a "Welch," leaving when he's on top. Sadly, that was a position that Armstrong would never see again.

Media Coverage

If anyone wants to put an epitaph on my gravestone, I've asked my children to have "this is the next logical step in his transformation" carved into the granite. Almost all the stories positioned the company's restructuring as a "reversal of strategy" and "caving in to Wall Street." But, while AT&T's stock price was certainly a factor in the company's decision to restructure, the overwhelming reason was the need to recapitalize the company so each unit could fund its growth plans. Incredibly, no reporters or columnists focused on that issue. It doesn't even appear as a factor in the thirty-eight-page Harvard Business School case that was written on the company's restructuring.

Part of the reason was that Armstrong himself focused everyone on whether or not he had changed his strategy. We had arranged for a full-scale analyst meeting at the Sheraton Hotel in mid-Manhattan within hours of the news release's being issued. Because of the stories that had already been written, the analysts were not surprised by the announcement, but they had lots of questions, ranging from how the AT&T brand would be managed across four separate entities to the schedule of the various spin-offs. They were also understandably skeptical. As one of the company's investment banker's put it, "Because of the events of the last six months, no one thinks you're telling them everything when you tell them anything."

Armstrong and Noski were primed to tell them almost everything we knew, but there were still many open issues. In fact, the biggest uncertainty was whether the banks would provide the additional $25 billion facility we needed as a safety net if our credit rating were downgraded while we had $32 billion of short-term debt coming due. But Armstrong had other things on his mind. When he got to the podium, as a preamble to his formal remarks, he told the assembled analysts that he was "personally offended" by accusations that he had changed his strategy. Then he went into the same pitch he had given me earlier in the month.

This was a huge mistake, even though he appeared to sincerely believe it, because he made "changing the strategy" the story instead of what we were announcing. It also damaged his credibility. It would have been far better to say, "We had the right strategy, we made progress against it, but we ran out of time," which would have had the advantage of being not only true, but credible.

For months Armstrong persisted in denying that he had changed his strategy, despite my warnings that he was losing what little credibility he had left. He finally stopped arguing the point, but still had some of the attitude of Galileo, who, after being forced to recant his teachings that the earth revolves around the sun, said quietly under his breath, "but still it moves." The difference, of course, is that Galileo was right.

It wasn't until he read a draft of this book that Armstrong conceded he had "misjudged that keeping the company together was the only strategy people cared about."[6] But then in a May 2004 interview with the *Wall Street Journal*, he remembered that in the fall of 2000, "I lay there night after night . . . what should I do, change the strategy or change the company?"[7]

This isn't sheer obstinacy. Psychologist Daniel Kahneman, who won a Nobel Prize for his study of decision making, says most people are not aware of changing their minds even when they do. "Most people, after they change their minds, reconstruct their past opinion," he says. "They believe they *always* thought that."[8] Tragically, that leaves them vulnerable to making the same mistakes and makes it impossible for others to learn from them.

There is another lesson to be learned here as well. The first leaks were stories in themselves. Bloomberg News, for example, reported, "AT&T will break up once again, according to a story in this morning's *Wall Street Journal*." (I once had the experience of asking Bloomberg to correct a story it had issued based on an earlier *Wall Street Journal* story that was so clearly in error that the *Journal* editors had already agreed to run a correction the next day. Bloomberg refused to correct its story, declaring it was reporting what the *Journal* had written, not the underlying facts the *Journal* had written about. It did, however, offer to report the *Journal*'s correction when it ran.)

When we finally made the official announcement, most of the media picked up on the tenor, and in many cases the thesis, of what had already been written. The *New York Times* declared, the "company revises 3-year effort to consolidate all services." Even *Newsweek*'s Allan Sloan, who may have been one of Armstrong's last fans among financial writers, chided him for "changing directions to cater to Wall Street's whimsical tastes." Ken McGee, of the Gartner Group, set himself up just outside our news conference to do a series of tag-team interviews bemoaning "the sad day in corporate history" and the "surrender to Wall Street."[9]

I don't mean to suggest that all reporters and editors treat what is written in one another's papers as gospel. They don't. But they do use it as a jumping-off point. When the *Journal* reported the restructuring as a reversal of strategy—and Armstrong took the bait—this became the angle from which nearly every other paper played it. For the most part, we failed to give them something else to write about. As CEO, Armstrong was paid to take a long view and to think the unthinkable. Sometimes that means changing your mind as circumstances change. We had not made the media and financial analysts part of that process, so it is not surprising that they were not prepared to make the journey with us.

Furthermore, we had not anticipated that, when reporters reduced our corporate strategy to bumper-sticker dimensions (i.e., "one-stop shopping"), they had developed a stake in it. In reality, putting multiple services on one bill had not been as high a priority for Armstrong as it had been for John Walter. Armstrong's approach was more sophisticated. He knew that, while customers *said* they wanted everything on one bill, they weren't willing to pay for this. On the contrary, they expected a discount for buying multiple services. Bundled bills were an invitation for price cutting. Furthermore, they had very little stickiness. If customers could get a lower price for a service somewhere else, they would take it, even if that meant getting multiple bills.

The best bundles were those that combined services in such a way that they couldn't be pulled apart—for example, a "bucket" of wireless and long-distance minutes. Next in terms of stickiness were services that ran on the same infrastructure—for example, high-speed data service that ran over cable TV lines. Nevertheless, to reporters, "one-stop shopping" became Armstrong's original goal and breaking up the company became its antithesis.

Finally, the breakup of AT&T was an emotional issue for millions of people. We belatedly began addressing this in Armstrong's speeches and in direct communications with key stakeholders. "AT&T, this American icon," Armstrong said, "would have been only a memory if we hadn't taken these steps."[10]

In the aftermath of the restructuring announcement, I kept reminding Armstrong that he and I were the only people on the face of the earth who read everything written about him. No one else did. Despite very heavy media coverage (an estimated 379 million "impressions" or "readership" in three weeks), only 39 percent of the general public and 55 percent of active investors were even aware of AT&T's restructuring. Even though 52 percent of AT&T's media coverage was highly negative, most people (76 percent of the public and 73 percent of investors) said it didn't affect their attitude toward the company.

Employee Reaction

But, as usual, the external media had their most pronounced effect on our internal stakeholders. Our surveys told us that thirty days after the restructuring announcement, less than a third of AT&T's employees thought that it was a "good" idea. On the positive side, most of them had not yet formed an opinion on how it would affect the company, its customers, or the employees themselves. But less than half told us that the communications they had received were "complete." Employees had questions about stock options, movement between units, and other individual issues. But even fewer thought that our communications were "believable" or "helpful." Employees were particularly put off by two things: the contrast between the upbeat internal message and the external media coverage, and the debate about whether or not the company had changed its strategy.

Not surprisingly, the worst scores were within the organizations of "AT&T Classic," i.e., all but the wireless and cable units. And management employees in those units were even less positive than represented employees. Both groups were confused about the company's strategy, uncertain about their unit's viability, and concerned about their personal future. Employees at all levels were still trying to process the restructuring announcement in terms of its personal impact on them. The high-level messages that we were using externally weren't working in the absence of information that addressed employees' more specific questions.

Faced with these data, Armstrong ordered more communications, but we argued that it would be futile to try to address such emotional issues through nonpersonal media. This was something that the company's senior managers had to tackle personally. The only problem was that they felt just as deceived, particularly when word began spreading that, after the various units were spun off, Armstrong planned to go with the broadband company.

So we scheduled a half-day mandatory seminar for all the senior officers in AT&T Classic, about 100 people. And every session started with a presentation by Chuck Noski on the company's debt position. For the first time since the restructuring announcement, and perhaps even for months before that, AT&T officers just one or two levels below those of us who reported to Armstrong understood the situation we faced. And 90 percent said that the seminar not only better equipped them to communicate with their own people, but also increased their personal confidence in the company's direction. If they had one complaint, it was that we had not given them the information sooner.

Postscript

A year and a half later, eight of AT&T's eleven largest competitors had filed for bankruptcy, Qwest's CEO had been replaced amid an SEC investigation, and the telecom industry was in a shambles. The dean of telecom analysts, Howard Anderson, wrote an op-ed for the *Wall Street Journal* entitled "The Last Telecom Standing."[11] Without explicitly recanting his view that AT&T's restructuring was "silly," Anderson said, "If there's a medal for seeing a train wreck coming and getting your shareowners safely out of harm's way, [Armstrong] ought to get one."

Anderson pointed out that each of AT&T's businesses, including the long-distance business, was better positioned than any of its rivals. "During all the wheeling and dealing," Anderson wrote, "Mr. Armstrong made a couple of side bets few people noticed: He invested $35 billion in local and global services for business. Today he has the fastest-growing local operation, the strongest managed-services business, a state-of-the-art data Internet network, and one of the best global networks. . . . Anyone want to offer Mike Armstrong an apology?"

Anderson's op-ed didn't create a groundswell of contrarian commentary on Armstrong's tenure at AT&T. He quietly left the company just six months later and was just as happy that not much was written about it.

14

Credibility Breaks All Ties

The last asset that a company should surrender is its credibility. More precious than anything in its treasury, credibility cannot be bought or leased. It must be earned. It's about behavior— delivering on promises, not simply making them. Credibility is built over time, but can be lost in an instant. Once it is lost, it is even harder to regain. In the court of public opinion, the winner is not the one who spins the best tale or generates the most ink; it's the one whom the public trusts.

Enter Comcast

Armstrong couldn't fathom why so many people didn't get it. Armed to lay out the rationale for AT&T's restructuring one more time, he traveled to the January 2001 media conference and extravaganza mounted by Salomon Smith Barney's star analyst, Jack Grubman. But if restructuring the company addressed a number of thorny financial issues, it also created new ones, and the biggest among them was that it put into play the very cable assets that Armstrong had assembled at such a high financial and psychic cost.

Comcast's Roberts family, father and son, had never really abandoned their lust for the MediaOne properties that AT&T had ripped from their grasp. When, in October 2000, AT&T announced its intention to spin off its cable division as a separate company, they saw an opportunity to get back into the game.

Brian Roberts was also at the Salomon Smith Barney conference, and he asked to meet privately with Armstrong and Noski in his suite at the Scottsdale Princess Resort. He wasted little time in getting to the point, proposing a merger between AT&T's cable division and Comcast. He argued that a merger would be quicker than the path AT&T had proposed, would face less market uncertainty, and would create greater shareowner value. He even had a few simple charts that showed what the combined companies would look like.

Armstrong and Noski listened politely, saying little more than that his proposal was "interesting." Finally, Armstrong explained that AT&T had recently filed the proxy for a $7.5 billion exchange of AT&T stock for shares in its wireless tracker. Under the circumstances, AT&T could not consider Roberts's proposal. In fact, Armstrong wouldn't even commit to talking about a merger when the exchange closed. As far as AT&T was concerned, it had laid out its restructuring plan, and it was sticking to it. Roberts had to be at least a little frustrated when Armstrong and Noski left, but he could be patient—up to a point.

Shortly after the wireless share exchange closed at the end of May, Brian Roberts called again. Armstrong dispatched Noski to meet with him. Brian Roberts had once described Somers as "a cowboy who comes into the room with both six shooters blazing," but Noski was clearly cast from a different movie genre. In fact, he was a lot like Brian Roberts himself—quiet, thoughtful, and measured unless provoked.

Their first meeting was to be in a private dining room in one of New York City's better hotels. It turned out to be a small ballroom. The two men ate alone at a small table in the center of the room, under a crystal chandelier, with a single waiter hovering nearby.

Their second meeting, on Father's Day, was in a suite in a Philadelphia hotel, and again they met alone, armed with nothing but pads of paper on which they both jotted notes.

Noski briefed the board on his conversations with Roberts at the end of its regular meeting in June, but not before Armstrong excused John Malone. When Armstrong had returned to New Jersey following the Salomon Smith Barney conference, I told him that one of the cable industry magazines had called to chase down a rumor that he was talking to Comcast about a merger. It ultimately got lost in the flurry of gossip issuing from the Scottsdale Princess Hotel that month, but Armstrong was clearly agitated, and he thought he knew the source of the rumor—John Malone must have heard about it from one of the

Robertses. Armstrong himself hadn't told anyone but the company's general counsel, Jim Cicconi.

I think that was when Armstrong decided that if Roberts ever brought the proposal up again, he would excuse Malone when he briefed the directors. He didn't need an excuse—many of the other board members had been warning Armstrong for months that Malone was the source of many leaks. But, in fact, the Comcast discussions would create conflicts for Malone because of his holdings in Comcast's QVC shopping network, as well as the programming that Liberty Media provided to Comcast. When the moment came, Armstrong told Malone (in a "What can I do?" tone), "Counsel has advised me you should leave the meeting," and he let him believe it was because the board was going to discuss the spin-off of Liberty Media as part of the corporate restructuring.

When Malone learned the real reason just one month later, he resigned from the board, expressing frustration that he had been excluded from discussions of such a significant transaction and calling Comcast's bid "inadequate." But Armstrong was determined to avoid leaks that could throw the entire restructuring scheme into disarray.

In any case, after Noski's briefing, some board members were skeptical, but they authorized him to continue the discussions on two conditions. First, Roberts had to understand that the board wanted voting control to follow economic interests in any merger agreement. In other words, AT&T would not agree to different classes of stock such as those at Comcast, which gave the Robertses control of the company. That had been one of the reasons that board member Amos Hostetter had objected to Comcast's original offer to buy MediaOne. Second, Comcast had to sign a standstill agreement that would bar it from launching an unfriendly bid if the talks foundered.

When Noski called Brian Roberts two days later to give him the board's conditions, Roberts said, "You've really ruined my weekend. I'll call you back later."

Reenter Comcast

No one called until the July Fourth weekend. On Sunday, July 8, the fax machine at Armstrong's home in Connecticut spit out a letter from Ralph and Brian Roberts; at about the same time, the letter appeared on the fax machines of newspapers around the country. The Robertses were making what is technically known as a subsidiary bear hug for AT&T Broadband. The financial terms were straightforward enough: Comcast stock worth about $44.5 billion and the assumption of $13.5 billion in debt for the core cable assets, with the value of other properties, such as the company's interests in Time Warner Entertainment and Cablevision, to be negotiated separately.

But the way Comcast positioned the deal was brilliant. It announced the deal late on the Sunday afternoon of a holiday weekend, when most reporters—and the experts they would consult—were away from the office, helping to ensure that the first reports would be based primarily on its news release and that AT&T's response would necessarily be vague. Comcast had also hired the investment bankers with the most widely followed cable analysts, Morgan Stanley and Merrill Lynch, to eliminate any commentary that those analysts might otherwise make. Then it added AT&T's traditional lead banker, J. P. Morgan, to the list to help finance the deal.

But the real punch line came the next day at an analyst meeting Comcast staged at the St. Regis Hotel in New York City. The company's president, a former Disney executive named Steve Burke, laid out the most compelling reason for approving the merger: Comcast could do a better job of running the cable business.

Burke compared Comcast's 41 percent margins to AT&T Broadband's, which were running at about 18 percent. Function by function, service by service, he showed how Comcast could wring savings out of AT&T's cable systems. He even showed how Comcast had already brought its telephone operations to breakeven, while AT&T wasn't predicting that for several quarters. In fact, he said, Comcast had improved the profit margins of systems it had previously acquired from AT&T by six percentage points in just six months.

Comcast made its offer a referendum on AT&T's management of its cable systems. It also exploited another common suspicion when it hinted that "certain social issues" got in the way of the informal discussions Comcast had had with the company. In other words, Armstrong wanted to run the merged companies, and Comcast couldn't agree to that. There was no truth to that insinuation, of course; the talks had never gone that far, breaking down at the first hint the AT&T board was uncomfortable ceding control of the merged company to the Roberts family. But most observers were quite willing to believe it.

When Noski met with one of the largest institutional holders of AT&T stock, he was not surprised to find that it was quite willing to take the money and run. While the board considered governance a big deal, it was of little concern to professional money managers; on the contrary, they considered it an excuse for management stonewalling.

Among AT&T's directors, there were as many who thought that Comcast's offer was "stupid" as there were who felt that the company should take a closer look at it. AT&T's bankers, noting that Comcast's financial projections assumed that it would get only 50 percent of the synergies identified, believed that Comcast was poised to increase its offer. Meanwhile, both Robertses winged around the country with Steve Burke, calling on large institutions that owned AT&T shares to convince them to lobby management to accept the Comcast bid. Behind the scenes, the company's bankers and public relations firms planted stories about AT&T Broadband's ineptness.

In a hostile takeover, the advantage goes to the raider, who controls the timing and the initial message. While the target is still getting organized, the raider is wooing the media and putting four-color presentations under the noses of the target's largest shareowners. The target generally has no choice but to pledge that the raider's offer will receive "serious consideration." From then on, it's all about money unless the target can raise other concerns that matter to shareowners.[1] In AT&T's case, we had two issues to flog: corporate governance, which was not yet much of an issue in mid-2001, and telephony, which had been the primary rationale for our cable purchases but didn't figure much in Comcast's plans.

Comcast was a family-run company. Although the Robertses owned less than 3 percent of the economic interest in the company, they had about 80 percent of the voting power, appointed all the members of the board, and controlled every aspect of the business. This was not uncommon in the cable industry. The Rigas family exercised similar control over Adelphia; heirs of company founder James M. Cox controlled Cox Communications; and the father-and-son team of Charles and James Dolan controlled Cablevision. But the AT&T board of directors was extremely uncomfortable with the concept. "It might be great when things are going well," said Amos Hostetter, "but what happens when markets turn south? Brian's a capable executive, but what if he wants to make his dumb nephew his successor?"

The bankers, who had sold the properties to AT&T in the first place, claimed that the Robertses' offer came when AT&T's cable operations were at their low point. While they appeared to be offering a good premium to the operations' current value, their bid reflected none of the venture's future value. "They're bidding for a traditional cable company," went the argument. "But AT&T Broadband is more than that. It's the first multiservice broadband company, offering high-speed data and telephony as well as digital entertainment that go far beyond CNN and HBO."

Broadband in Play

At the July 19, 2001, board meeting, which took place in Denver, where the directors could get a firsthand briefing on the cable business from the people running it, the board decided to reject the Comcast offer as "inadequate." But the board also had to concede that Comcast had effectively put AT&T Broadband into play. For example, two days after the Robertses' offer was made public, Armstrong received a call from AOL Time Warner's co-chief operating officer, Dick Parsons, who suggested that a merger of the two companies' cable properties would not only trump Comcast's offer but resolve their long-running dispute concerning Time Warner Entertainment (TWE).

By the end of the week, Armstrong and Noski had dinner with AOL Time Warner CEO Gerry Levin at the New York Athletic Club. Joined by Parsons, co-chief operating officer Bob Pittman, and chief financial officer Mike Kelly, Levin pulled out all the stops. He spun a scheme under which AT&T would combine its cable systems with Time Warner Entertainment's to form a new company, to be called AT&T Time Warner. The new company would embrace Armstrong's vision of a broadband services company providing communications, data, and entertainment services. The TWE problem would go away. AOL Time Warner would own the majority of the company, but AT&T's shareowners would have a significant minority position. Mike would be its chairman and Noski the CFO.

Jim Robbins, the CEO of Cox Communications, also called Armstrong and asked if they could do a deal. He offered to match Comcast's offer, promised a greater commitment than Comcast to cable telephony, and left open such issues as the new company's name and management. But he also said that the Cox family needed to retain its supermajority voting stock, giving it effective control.

Disney's CEO, Michael Eisner, wanted to talk about ways in which the two companies might work together and, not incidentally, expand the Mouse's programming on AT&T's cable systems. Bill Gates offered to increase Microsoft's existing $5 billion investment in AT&T if that would help its cable division stay independent or combine with anyone but AOL Time Warner. Vivendi's Jean-Paul Messier called to stick his toes in the water, suggesting that he was willing to make a substantial investment in order to gain access to the company's cable distribution. Armstrong even received a three-page e-mail from a dot-com in Alabama, proposing a merger and reverse spin-off of AT&T's noncable assets.

By the end of July 2001, AT&T Broadband was ready to update investors on its performance and its prospects. Its presentation showed that telephony penetration was improving and would break even in nine months. High-speed data service had already reached breakeven. And the unit planned to achieve industry-average margins within three years. We arranged a Webcast of the presentation from New York on Tuesday, July 24, followed by a dinner at the Four Seasons for invited analysts and a similar luncheon the next day in Boston.

Then Armstrong and Noski took the AT&T corporate jet out to the West Coast for a series of meetings with Disney, Microsoft, and others. As they moved between Seattle and Hollywood, both men were struck by the fact that companies in the high-tech and entertainment worlds shared a common characteristic: They had few friends but many common enemies. And preeminent among the latter was AOL Time Warner. To keep AT&T's cable systems out of its clutches, Armstrong and Noski knew that Disney and Microsoft were making the same offers of assistance to Comcast, Cox, and who knew who else.

Comcast heard about the meetings almost as soon as they were scheduled, leading some of us to wonder how serious the West Coast bidders were. Steve Rattner, one of the partners at Quadrangle Investments, which was advising Comcast, had been a reporter for the *New York Times* earlier in his career. He still had many friends in the media. But, more significantly, he knew how a well-timed leak could tilt a story's center of gravity. What might have been reported as lively interest in AT&T Broadband became a mad coast-to-coast scramble to generate interest. In hindsight, we should have leaked word of the calls that came in after Comcast's bid had first been announced.

But our more fundamental mistake was not doing anything about the forces unleashed by our October 2000 restructuring. The restructuring put AT&T Broadband in play, but we didn't take that possibility seriously enough, even after Comcast's initial probes in January. Remembering Comcast's deep resentment when AT&T swooped onto the scene and stole MediaOne from its grasp, many of us thought that the company might try to interfere with the spin-off of the Broadband unit. But we thought it would make its move toward the end of the year, when we launched the initial public offering for the AT&T Broadband tracking stock.

None of us realized that we would force the Robertses' hand when we scheduled the "beauty contest" for the tracking stock's underwriters on July 9. Comcast's own investment banks, which had been invited to bid for the work, would have had to give AT&T their estimate of the broadband unit's value, seriously compromising Comcast's negotiating position. In fact, after Comcast launched its unsolicited offer on July 8, the beauty contest went forward as scheduled, but none of Comcast's banks showed up.

No one can anticipate every eventuality, but we should have shored up AT&T Broadband's story much earlier, including making an earlier change in management. The latter was not for lack of trying, however. After Hindery left at the end of 1999, Armstrong had interviewed and wooed practically everyone who was running a large U.S. cable system, including Steve Burke, but it was mid-October of 2001 before he landed a cable industry veteran. Bill Schleyer, who was a close associate of Amos Hostetter's and had run Continental Cable for him, gave the business instant credibility within the industry and among the people who followed it.

Instead, whether through arrogance or naïveté, we acted as if we were still in complete command of our destiny. Once Comcast disproved that by launching its hostile bid, we should have portrayed it as a small, family-run, regional company with an insular board made up of the founder's cronies. Instead, we allowed Comcast to gain momentum and present itself as an equal to AT&T, one of the most widely held stocks in the world. Once Comcast attacked, our response should have been immediate and devastating.

Comcast Reaches Out

In mid-August 2001, perhaps feeling that the momentum of its preemptive offer was slowly ebbing, Comcast reached out to AT&T once more. This time the feeler took the form of a phone conversation between Comcast's outside lawyer, Dennis Hersch of Davis Polk & Wardwell, and AT&T's outside counsel, Dick Katcher of Wachtell Lipton.

Hersch said that he had been picking up signals that there was some kind of animosity towards Comcast. That was unfortunate, Hersch said, because if Armstrong wanted to do a "wow" deal, Comcast was ready. Maybe the Robertses and Armstrong should sit down and talk. Katcher said that was all very interesting, but what would they talk about? Hersch said that they could talk about the price of the acquisition, how to value the noncore assets, and even governance. While Comcast wanted the Roberts family to maintain what he called "blocking rights" and Brian Roberts would not relinquish the CEO position, everything else was open for discussion. Katcher said he'd pass the word along.

In fact, Katcher knew that we had little choice but to talk, even though it would stick in Armstrong's craw. It would look bad if this ever turned into a proxy fight and management had refused to even discuss the deal that was first put on the table, especially after the board had instructed it to explore all alternatives. After discussing it with Armstrong and Noski, Katcher called Hersch and said AT&T would be happy to talk if Comcast would commit to keeping the discussions confidential. We wanted no more leaks that would make us look desperate.

Armstrong and the Robertses, father and son, eventually met for dinner in a private room at the Bernards Inn, not far from AT&T headquarters. It was the first time they had met in person since the previous January. Brian Roberts began by clearing the air. "Mike," he said, "making an unsolicited offer for Broadband may have been the dumbest thing I've done in my business career." Armstrong complained about the stream of negative leaks from the Comcast side, and Roberts promised to end them. Then they both agreed to let bygones be bygones and see if they could reach agreement on a deal.

When lawyers from the two sides followed up in an August 22 meeting in Wachtell Lipton's office, it was apparent that they were far apart on price. Katcher, representing AT&T, said that Comcast's offer was far too low, but he would not say by how much. The Comcast lawyers vacillated between asking for more data to justify a higher price and insisting that they didn't need confidential information, which would also have restricted their ability to partner with other companies in constructing their bid.

For its part, Comcast wanted AT&T to agree not to talk to other bidders. "Everyone is trying to pick our pocket in return for agreeing to stand down," Comcast's lawyers complained. On the other hand, they also expressed the conviction that there was no one else in the wings. AOL Time Warner, they said, would have regulatory problems. Disney wasn't really interested in owning cable. And Cox was too small. In the end, while acknowledging that they "had identified more synergies," Comcast's people said that they couldn't increase their offer much without hurting their own stock price, which wouldn't help anyone. As they left, Hersch again expressed the hope that there wasn't so much animosity between the two companies that they couldn't reach an agreement.

They could, and ultimately would, but not until Noski and Armstrong had wrung every last nickel and governance concession out of Comcast. The elder Roberts, Ralph, had shown his cards when he pulled Noski aside after a Saturday lunch meeting in New York City. Saying that he knew that there was still bad blood between Armstrong and Brian and that AT&T's board was going to consider multiple offers before making a final decision, Roberts asked Noski a personal favor: "When it comes down to the wire, will you give us a chance to top the best bid?" Noski replied, "You know I can't do that" and said that he would have to follow the bidding process. But Ralph Roberts had shown him how desperately he wanted to win.

The bidding for AT&T Broadband went through three cycles, with the same three companies—Comcast, AOL Time Warner, and Cox—submitting their final bids at 6 p.m. on Sunday, December 16, 2001. Teams of bankers worked through the night at Wachtell Lipton to force the competing bids into side-by-side analyses. On Monday, the AT&T team met to compare the bids and to identify areas that needed clarification. The next day, Noski called all three bidders to tell them that the bids were roughly the same.

Brian Roberts was in the middle of Comcast's Christmas party at the QVC studios outside Philadelphia when Noski reached him on his cell phone. "Brian," Noski said over the din of the revelers, "it's close." "Do we have to improve our bid?" Roberts asked. "I can't say that," Noski said. "I can only tell you it's close." Then, remembering Ralph Roberts's plea and noting how many times the elder man had said he encouraged Brian to "go for it," Noski added, "Listen to your father." There was silence for a moment, then Roberts said, "Let me talk to my father. I'll get back to you."

Ultimately, all three bidders revised their offers but when Brian

Roberts called Noski early on Wednesday morning, he raised Comcast's bid so much that it was no longer even close. But Roberts had a final request. "If we have the best bid, do we have your endorsement?" he asked Noski. "Brian," Noski said, "if it's the best bid, you might have Armstrong's endorsement, but not mine."

"Jesus," Roberts said with some exacerbation, "how much more do you want?"

"It's not money, Brian," Noski said. "To get my endorsement, you have to promise me that when this is over, if you win, we're not going to read that you won and Mike lost. Call off your PR dogs."

After a long pause, Roberts quietly said, "You have my word."

Noski and Armstrong recommended that the board accept Comcast's offer, which was now 26 percent better than its original July 8 proposal despite a $3 per share decline in its stock price. While Comcast retained its two-tier voting structure, the Roberts family reduced its voting power to 33 percent.[2] For seven hours—two hours longer than it had allocated—the board compared all three bids against the possibility of staying independent. Meanwhile, the Robertses moved between Davis Polk's offices and their suite at the St. Regis Hotel. Dick Parsons went about his business at AOL Time Warner's offices near Rockefeller Center. And Cox Communications's negotiators flew up from Atlanta and sat in their corporate jet on the tarmac at Teterboro airport. One of the Cox executives sent a steady stream of e-mail messages, pleading for crumbs of information, to the Blackberry of one of AT&T's deal makers, who was sitting in on the board meeting. As the December sun began to set, his e-mails became desperate. "It's getting cold out here," he tapped.

At around 5 P.M., the board voted to accept Comcast's offer. Armstrong called the Robertses, who, along with their negotiating team, were just blocks away in Davis Polk's offices. "Are you doing anything?" he said. "Come on over." When Armstrong and Brian Roberts had signed the agreements, Armstrong called the Cox executives at Teterboro airport and AOL Time Warner's co-chief operating officer, Dick Parsons, who was still in his office. By 7 P.M., champagne was flowing in the hallways of Wachtell Lipton, and we issued a news release announcing the board's decision.

Comcast had won an agreement that would make it a media and communications powerhouse, with 29 percent of Americans who subscribed to cable TV, 33 percent of those taking digital cable, 31 percent of those with high-speed Internet access, and 67 percent of those with cable telephony.

From that moment until the deal closed nearly a year later, Brian Roberts called Noski every few weeks and asked, "How am I doing?" He had kept his word.

Credibility Breaks All Ties

One should not interpret the length of the board meeting as suggesting that the directors were struggling with a decision. In fact, most of them had made up their minds on one issue (selling) weeks before.

At the September 2001 meeting that kicked off the official bidding process for AT&T Broadband, Armstrong had made one last pitch to stay the course and spin off the cable business intact. Standing at an easel pad, he drew columns of numbers showing how a sale could be avoided if some smaller cable systems were sold off and minority interests were turned into cash.

Among those minority holdings, the biggest was Time Warner Entertainment. But some of the directors had come to the conclusion that as long as AOL Time Warner thought AT&T needed a deal, it would press for terms that no one could agree to. A former Time Warner insider once warned one of AT&T's negotiators, "The old Time Warner entered every negotiation intending to come out on top, but AOL goes into negotiations intending to come out with their foot on your throat." (In fact, it was only after AOL Time Warner suffered its own reversals, culminating in Levin's resignation, that Comcast was able to negotiate its exit from TWE.)

Thinking that Armstrong's assumptions were a little optimistic, Noski picked up a marker and added another, less upbeat column of numbers to the easel pad. Months after I left AT&T, one of its directors told me that this was a turning point for the board. He said that when the board went into executive session, one of the directors told the others, "Noski looks worried."

Saving AT&T

To Noski, AT&T's restructuring was not simply about "enhancing shareowner value." It was about saving the company. And while it wasn't his first choice, he had come to believe that selling AT&T Broadband at the right price would give the rest of the company its best shot at surviving. By December, Armstrong and the board had come to agree with him. AT&T's directors had met no less than seventeen times, either in person or by telephone, in the four months since Comcast had launched its unsolicited offer. Noski had conducted the auction to wring the most value out of the interested bidders in the shortest period of time. And Comcast's offer, valued at $73.3 billion on the day the board considered it, was truly breathtaking.

As personally unappealing as it may have been, the AT&T directors took the path that they believed presented the least risk to the overall company's survival. They weren't swayed by pundits, editorialists, or popular opinion. But even if at that point the directors thought that Gerry Levin would wake up one morning aching to buy out AT&T's interest in Time Warner Entertainment, allowing AT&T Broadband to go it alone, the board simply did not have the credibility to do anything but sell.[3]

In the court of public opinion, the winner is not the one who spins the best tale or generates the most ink or even is on the side of all that's righteous and pure; it's the one whom the public trusts.

Comcast made its offer a referendum on AT&T's management of the cable business. Its argument came down to "look at their margins, look at ours, and decide which of us you want running the company." The numbers were astounding: Comcast had profit margins of more than 40 percent, whereas AT&T Broadband's were barely 20 percent. Comcast had convinced everyone that AT&T's cable properties were badly managed.

That conventional wisdom soon began appearing in commentaries and even editorials. As early in the process as July 16, before the AT&T board had even formally considered Comcast's proposal, *Barron's* ran an editorial entitled "Armstrong's Folly" saying that the company's directors should give Armstrong clear marching orders: "Sell the cable operations to Comcast or leave the company." The *New York Times* editorialized that there was "a rocky road for AT&T" and predicted Armstrong's "obsolescence."[4] Since all the major investment banks were working for AT&T or one of the bidding companies, the newspapers had to turn to second- and third-tier analysts for usable quotes. Some of these "experts" simply parroted what they were reading in the same media that were interviewing them. Others had a knack for colorful quotes. Jeff Kagan, a sole practitioner operating out of his home in the Atlanta suburbs, became the single most widely quoted analyst in the telecommunications industry on the strength of his ability to turn a phrase, as in "AT&T has the ball and they appear to be positioning themselves as a real catch."

Credibility is earned. It cannot be bought. It's about behavior—delivering on promises, not simply making them. To earn credibility in contentious circumstances, such as a long-running battle between industry players, a company must surrender control to a neutral third party. This is not the same thing as paying people to write letters and give speeches on your behalf. As Clark Judge of the White House Writers Group wrote in a piece for the *Wall Street Journal*, that's what the Pentagon did in agreeing to "embed" the media with the troops advancing on Baghdad in the first weeks of the Iraqi war. "The essential strategy for becoming the standard of truth when no one believes you," Judge wrote, "is to open your operations to the kind of risk that no one would take if he were planning to lie."[5]

He was right, and, in fact, I had tried to convince Armstrong and Noski to let me bring a reporter into the process with the understanding that nothing would be written until the auction was completed to avoid compromising the process. They were skeptical but were willing to explore the possibility. The lawyers, on the other hand, were aghast. It would have required the agreement of all three bidders, a complication that they understandably didn't want to add to the mix of issues they were working on around the clock. I couldn't even get permission to bring a reporter into the small conference room at Wachtell Lipton that was stacked ceiling to floor with operational data on AT&T Broadband. I thought it would provide graphic testimony to the rigor with which the bidding process was being run. The lawyers saw it as a monumental security breach.

In the end, bringing a third party over the wall during the bidding process was unnecessary. It all turned out as everyone had assumed it would: AT&T sold its cable properties to the company that had kicked off the auction with its Sunday afternoon fax. But if the board had decided to reject all three bids and go it alone, its motives would have been questioned. Having a third party on the inside, writing about the debate comprehensively, could only have enhanced our credibility. Since such a rejection would have been only one more round in corporate battles that almost certainly would have included a proxy fight, the public's trust would have been an essential asset.

15

Reimagine Your Company's Mission

The corporate raiders of the 1980s and 1990s were a new class of corporate samurai dedicated to slashing costs and wringing value out of underutilized assets. But financial engineering often begs fundamental issues of business definition, and serial divestitures and acquisitions can leave employees wondering what their mission really is. One of a CEO's most fundamental responsibilities is to identify and communicate the ingredients of long-term value creation.

What's Next, What's Left?

Announcing Comcast's winning bid, of course, was only the beginning of a nearly year-long effort to win regulatory approval.

As Armstrong, Brian Roberts, and I rode to a round of television interviews following a December 20 analyst meeting and news conference, both men called public officials to reiterate our key message that the merger would be pro-competitive and good for consumers. John Dingell, the irascible congressman from Michigan who had tried to pass a bill deregulating the Bell companies, warned Roberts not to throw in with AT&T on that issue. As he stepped out of the car, Roberts appeared surprised by the intensity of the congressman's feelings about AT&T.

"Boy, he doesn't like you guys at all," he said.

It occurred to me, if it didn't to Armstrong, that Roberts was mentally dividing the world into "me" and "them," and we were definitely on the "them" side—even though he had just signed a contract that would eventually make Armstrong chairman of the Comcast board of directors.

Armstrong believed that a company could have only one CEO, and he had already resigned himself to giving up that role in Roberts's favor. But he also thought that he could help Roberts manage what would be a significantly larger company. Roberts dodged Armstrong whenever he suggested that they get together to discuss their respective roles and responsibilities.

Meanwhile, the rest of the world assumed that Armstrong was going to play a role similar to Steve Case's at AOL Time Warner: focusing on long-range strategy. I assumed that Comcast would want to use Armstrong as a roving ambassador, making speeches and glad-handing politicians. In fact, by June 2002, I had a long list of speaking invitations for Armstrong well into 2003, by which time the merger was expected to have closed. I had introduced Brian to Jesse Jackson, whose Wall Street Project AT&T had supported, and urged him to accept an invitation to speak at his Rainbow/PUSH Coalition's annual meeting in July 2002. When Brian accepted, I made it a point to be there myself.

While we were waiting in a small room offstage, I asked who on his staff I should pass Armstrong's speaking invitations to. I mentioned it more to make conversation than anything else, but Brian put a finger in my face and said, "I don't want Armstrong speaking anywhere on anything when he comes to Comcast."

As he backed me deeper into a corner of the room, I suggested that he might be making a mistake in not capitalizing on Armstrong's stature in the industry.

"I don't want him doing to me what Steve Case did to Gerry Levin," he said. "People can't be confused about who's running Comcast. And it isn't Mike."

I was taken aback. Brian Roberts and I were not close, although at the moment our belt buckles were touching. If he was saying things like this to me, who else was he telling?

"Have you had this conversation with Mike?" I asked.

"Not yet, but I have to do it soon," he said.

When I returned to New Jersey, I told Noski about my conversation with Roberts, and he told me that he had indeed heard the same thing from him. Armstrong, however, was still confident that he could work things out. To this day, he claims he did. But Comcast dropped any notion that it would carry the AT&T name. (By then, no one at AT&T wanted it to use the name, anyway.) Armstrong was given an office in New York City overlooking Bryant Park. The only other Comcast people on the floor sold advertising. And, while the Robertses initially said they would try to divvy up the operating jobs equally between their people and AT&T's, none of the company's division presidents and only four of its regional senior vice presidents were former AT&T employees at the end of 2004. Of the five AT&T directors who initially joined Comcast's board, only three were left, including Armstrong, who stepped down as chairman after just a year and a half.

AT&T Leadership

The December 19, 2001, announcement that Armstrong would leave AT&T to become chairman of what was then called AT&T Comcast was actually anticlimactic. The *Wall Street Journal* and other papers had reported his intention to move with AT&T Broadband as long ago as the previous February, and he himself hadn't made any secret of it in discussions with senior executives until we pointed out how it was affecting employee morale.

In fact, when the company announced its restructuring in October of 2000, Armstrong had brought Dave Dorman in as president of the company to run everything but the cable and wireless businesses. Most people expected Dorman to succeed Armstrong as CEO. But when, at the end of February 2001, the board announced that it had made Noski vice chairman and named both him and Dorman directors, at least some AT&T employees thought that there would be a horserace for CEO. In fact, several directors had approached Noski about throwing his hat into the ring for the job.

But Noski made it clear to Armstrong and the board that he was not interested in being one of the entries in a two-man beauty contest. For one thing, he desperately wanted to go home to his family. Crisscrossing the country twice a week for three years had been emotionally as well as physically exhausting. He had had practically no time with his wife and young daughters. In fact, on one of their house-hunting trips east in April of 2001, they were wandering through a prospective home in Short Hills, New Jersey, when his cell phone rang, summoning him back to the office to deal with a crisis at AtHome. He didn't see his family for the rest of the weekend.

And although AT&T was in far better financial shape than it had been, Noski didn't think the company could handle a competition between two of its most senior executives. He could imagine people picking sides and fighting in the hallways. But most of all, he had signed up to help run a media and communications colossus, not to head a declining long-distance company, wherever that eventually might lead. In fact, Noski had tried to resign in February 2002, but the board had convinced him to stay on the grounds that he was the only person who seemed to be able to deal with Brian Roberts.

Dorman, on the other hand, laid proud claim to being Sprint's fifty-fifth employee and had spent most of his working career in the telecommunications industry. Graduating from Georgia Tech with a degree in industrial management, he had held a series of software and sales jobs until 1981, when he joined a small telecom company that was later absorbed by Sprint. Smart and politically astute, he rose through the ranks and became president of Sprint's business services division in 1990.

Four years later, he became CEO of Pacific Bell, California's dominant local phone company. After selling the company to SBC, Dorman hung around only long enough to discover that he didn't like playing second or third fiddle to an imperious CEO. He joined an Internet start-up called PointCast that was flailing about for a profitable business model. AT&T and BT jointly recruited him to lead Concert in March 1999, agreeing to allow him to establish his headquarters in Atlanta, where he had lived most of his life. After becoming AT&T's president in November 2000, Dorman commuted between Atlanta and New Jersey by corporate jet at a cost of $305,000 in 2003 alone. In mid-2004, when a $96,000 a year "temporary living allowance" expired, he sold his home in Atlanta and moved to Manhattan.

In May, as Noski prepared to participate in yet another investor road show, he worried that it could be misleading if he didn't reveal his decision to leave AT&T when its restructuring was completed. So we issued a news release announcing his decision. Less than two months later, the board named Dorman AT&T's next chairman and CEO.

Armstrong and Dorman

Armstrong and Dorman are two of the most capable executives I ever worked with, but they couldn't be more different if they lived in different dimensions. They're both very smart. They both married well and are dedicated to their families. They share the same mid-American values, including restless ambition. And neither would credit his success to anything but hard work and being in the right place at the right time. But Armstrong, the older of the two men by more than a decade, is more dynamic, more inclined to take risks, to try things and fix them if they don't work. Dorman is more analytical and deliberate, more inclined to hedge his bets.

Of the two, Dorman is the more wary judge of talent, less inclined to be impressed by someone's résumé and press clippings until he has personally taken that person's measure. When he makes a hiring mistake, he can be ruthless in correcting it. And he doesn't hesitate to subtly deflect blame toward subordinates.

Armstrong always seemed to believe that he could personally compensate for any shortcomings in his direct reports. If they failed to measure up, he nagged them until they improved or opted to move on; then he called it a mutual decision. Armstrong expects contention between managers and encourages vigorous debate. Dorman likes consensus and harmony and tends to surround himself with people whom AT&T employees came to call "F.O.D.s" ("Friends of Dave"). Armstrong didn't mind being challenged by people so long as they had their facts straight; Dorman took it as a personal affront.

Armstrong and Dorman have inverse leadership qualities. Armstrong's personal magnetism seems to increase with distance. The commanding stage presence that enables him to move large audiences so effortlessly becomes either intimidating or artificial in sustained one-on-one relationships. Dorman, on the other hand, seems folksy and slightly nerdy in large group settings, but warm and engaging in personal meetings. Handsome and radiating confidence, Armstrong looks as if he stepped out of central casting for CEOs. Dorman is anything but polished, with a slight southern drawl, interrupted by a persistent postnasal drip that requires regular clearing. Armstrong, for all his renown, is a relative loner who formed few deep personal friendships at AT&T. A lifelong salesman, he approaches individual meetings as if each is a separate transaction. He's totally focused on closing the sale. Dorman is more attuned to people's psychological needs.

The CEO Personality

There is no ideal "CEO personality." Introverts and extroverts have been equally successful and disastrous for the companies they led.

Personality types fall in and out of fashion. During the boom years of the 1990s, flashy and visionary business leaders were in vogue; in the recession that followed, quiet, nose-to-the-grindstone executives seemed to be more in style. AT&T had a long history of alternating between the two types: John deButts, an outgoing, garrulous CEO, was followed by the introverted and taciturn Charlie Brown, who in turn was succeeded by the energetic and gregarious Jim Olson, who was followed by the quiet and thoughtful Bob Allen, the charismatic Armstrong, and finally the folksy Dorman.

Depending on your assessment of each CEO's tenure, you could make a case that each either fit or mismatched the particular circumstances in which the company found itself. But I think the real lesson here is the importance of developing and cultivating a public persona for CEOs that reflects their true character.

The price of being a CEO is the loss of anonymity. Like it or not, CEOs have become the public personification of their company. Internal and external stakeholders look to them for clues about the company itself. How people see the CEO in large measure molds their attitudes toward the company. To a company's public relations counsel, the CEO is not only the boss but a corporate asset that needs to be protected and exploited.

While it may strike some as immodest or self-aggrandizing, CEOs should approach the task of managing their public persona as seriously as they would the task of managing any other corporate asset. First, based on a thoughtful and candid analysis of their personal strengths and weaknesses, they should select the core attributes for which they want to be known.

None of the executives I served were introspective enough to do this by themselves. Some, like Bob Allen, recoiled at any hint of "handling." But when we captured their voice in the messages we developed for them, they recognized it. And when we selected communications channels that were suited to their strengths, they felt comfortable and were themselves. That is the key—not to create a facade behind which you can hide the real CEO, but to capture his or her real strengths and present them in self-reinforcing ways that give people confidence and hope.

Bob Allen was not a charismatic public speaker, but his dry wit and self-deprecating humor made audiences comfortable. While his direct reports often found him enigmatic, he had a gentle manner that made rank-and-file employees comfortable. While he was long described as a loner, on his last day at work, AT&T employees formed a line to say good-bye that stretched from his office out the door of the building and a quarter of a mile down the road to the exit for Route 287.

Mike Armstrong, by contrast, was a forceful speaker who often galvanized audiences. He had an outgoing charm and an easy grin that drew people to him. When he left, employees sent him e-mail messages and copies of photos of themselves with him that they had taken on one of his many visits to the field. But he could also appear combative and defensive. Both men had great strengths and real weaknesses. I saw my job not as hiding the latter, but as projecting the former.

Armstrong's decisive leadership shook the company awake. But he never really succeeded in pulling his direct reports together as a team. He never named a chief operating officer, preferring to play the role himself by quizzing his business unit leaders in periodic operational reviews. But a company as large as AT&T cannot be managed by inspection.

One and a half years into Armstrong's tenure, we brought in a consultant who had long experience studying the attitudes of AT&T employees. This time, his assignment was to survey only the 505 highest-level people in the company. He found a group of managers who were nearly unanimous in their belief that the company finally had strong leadership. But there was a pattern he had never seen before: The further managers were from the seniormost ranks, the more decision-making authority they believed they had.

There were many days when Armstrong told me that he should have been a psychiatrist to be the CEO of AT&T. He had never seen so many senior people, he said, who needed hand-holding and reassurance. In fact, they were not unlike most people. Before deciding whether or not to follow someone into battle, we all ask, "Is he one of us?" When Armstrong let it be known that he would be going with the cable business when the company was once again broken apart, he confirmed their worst suspicions.

AT&T 2.0

Even though Armstrong had decided to stay with the cable business as early as the fall of 2001, he also thought AT&T's long-distance business had a better than even chance to prosper on its own. While the consumer division's stand-alone long-distance business was clearly in decline, it still enjoyed margins of about 30 percent, about six times better than MCI WorldCom's at that point. The company was finally beginning to convince state public service commissions to set viable wholesale rates for leasing local lines from the Bell companies. The influential New York commission was leaning toward a wholesale discount of more than 30 percent, which would finally allow AT&T to make a small, but reasonable profit on local service. And once AT&T Consumer was separated from the cash-hungry cable businesses, it would be able to invest more aggressively in the deployment of digital subscriber loop technology, which would allow it to offer high-speed data service along with any-distance communications.

Furthermore, while everyone had focused on Armstrong's multibillion-dollar cable acquisition spree, few had noticed that he had also invested about $46 billion in the company's business service capabilities. The company's data services revenue was once again growing at double-digit rates. When the cable businesses were spun off and merged with Comcast, AT&T would have a smaller debt burden than its major long-distance competitors. Noski would have succeeded in lowering the company's debt by more than $50 billion, from $65 billion following the MediaOne acquisition to $13 billion when the Comcast merger closed. AT&T's debt would be just one and a half times its earnings before interest, taxes, depreciation, and amortization (EBITDA), a coverage ratio that was on a par with that of the Bell companies and much better than that of the likes of MCI WorldCom and Sprint. All in all, Armstrong saw some risk ahead for AT&T, but some real opportunity, too.

However, ever since Dorman had been appointed president in November 2000, the company's rumor mill had him negotiating a merger with BellSouth during weekend golf games. It all seemed so logical. BellSouth was the only Bell company that had shied away from serial acquisitions. Verizon and SBC were now too big to pass regulatory muster in a merger with AT&T; Qwest was too sick. Dorman had been brought up in Atlanta and still maintained his principal residence there. BellSouth's CEO, Dwayne Ackerman, would be within a year or two of retiring by the time a deal closed. The rumor mill graciously decided that he could keep his job; Dorman was still young enough, and confident enough, to take his chances on succeeding him. The company would keep the AT&T name, of course, but would make its headquarters in Atlanta. The rumor mill had figured out everything but the size of the bankers' fees.

A September story in *Fortune* magazine entitled "Say Good-Bye to AT&T" seemed to confirm the rumors. Based on interviews with former executives and industry experts, the article predicted that AT&T would be scooped up by one of the Bell companies as soon as Comcast completed its acquisition of the cable business, which was a foregone conclusion. Armstrong had been interviewed for the piece, and we had primed him to communicate one idea: Thanks to the investments he had made in AT&T's communication services businesses, the company was in control of its own destiny. Armstrong knew how to bridge from the reporter's question to the point he wanted to make. So when she asked how he felt about AT&T's $20 stock price, he said, "I'm far from proud of a $20 stock, but I'm proud that we've given AT&T everything it needs to control its own destiny in an industry undergoing such tumultuous change."

Armstrong said the right words, but he was on a different wavelength from the reporter. She was writing about AT&T the *institution*, the company that people had grown up with, the ubiquitous "Ma Bell" that brought traveling dads home to say goodnight to their kids, that reunited far-flung families for a few minutes on Sunday evenings, and that was always there when you needed her. Perhaps revealing a mindset that got him into this fix in the first place, Armstrong was talking about AT&T the *investment*, and when the *Fortune* reporter mentioned "industry consolidation," he didn't hesitate to say, "Some people talk about consolidation as failure, but it can be good for shareowner value." Internally, it was like putting a "For Sale" sign on the company.

Then, on September 26, a *BusinessWeek* reporter asked for comment on a story he was writing that AT&T and BellSouth were in "advanced merger discussions." He said that Dorman had been seen in BellSouth's headquarters, code names had been assigned, bankers had been hired, and a deal was "imminent." When the story appeared on *BusinessWeek*'s Web site,[1] editors at other publications put their reporters into the chase.

By the weekend, the story was everywhere. As often happens, the same rumor mill that ignited the story quashed it just a week later when word spread that BellSouth had been spooked by the "leaks." Neither company has ever officially acknowledged talking.[2] But the damage that I had been afraid of had been done.

Reimagining a Company's Mission

Rumors of merger discussions contributed to a sense that AT&T was not only under siege but probably destined for the dustbin of business history. There was an atmosphere of futility around the company as people waited for AT&T Broadband to be spun off and the vultures to descend on the rest of the company. Meanwhile, the AT&T board had not taken steps to clarify the leadership of AT&T after Armstrong. The period between December 2001 and July 2002, when Dorman was officially named Armstrong's successor, represented a leadership vacuum that we should never have allowed. When my arguments that Armstrong shouldn't move to Comcast fell on deaf ears, I urged him to prod the board to name a successor as quickly as possible. However, Armstrong didn't want to be a lame duck if the Comcast merger ran into regulatory problems.

As it turned out, that's exactly how he was seen almost from the day of the merger announcement.

He lost so much credibility with AT&T employees that Dorman often refused to be seen with him in front of large gatherings, even canceling his participation in a meeting with retired senior officers because Armstrong would be there. Senior managers began to question the allocation of debt between AT&T Broadband and the rest of the company, fearing that the long-distance businesses would be burdened with obligations that should be going to Comcast. Operating managers began sniping about the terms of inter-unit contracts for using each other's facilities.

By January 2002, the board of directors acknowledged that the interests of the long-distance and broadband businesses would diverge over the coming months. It passed a resolution requiring the full board to review any changes in operating budgets, capital plans, asset allocations, interentity agreements, or anything else that could represent a conflict between the units' interests.

But the board's action didn't set people's minds at ease. The basic problem was that the people in AT&T's core businesses had lost their sense of mission. For months, they had been told that their businesses were either "unsustainable" in the new digital age or "uncompetitive" compared to MCI WorldCom. The solution they had been given was to diversify into adjacent industries, such as wireless and cable. But now those adjacencies were gone, and they were left with the same mix of unsustainable, uncompetitive businesses. Plus, the guy at the top was bugging out.

An employee survey that we fielded in March and April of 2002 showed that only 20 percent of the employees in AT&T Classic believed that the company was "headed in the right direction" or had any "confidence in the senior management of AT&T."

I had participated in previous efforts to launch a "new AT&T," first after the company's manufacturing subsidiaries were spun off in 1996, then when John Walter joined in 1997, and again when Armstrong took over in 1998. I did not have the heart to launch the new, new, new, new AT&T. Besides, the previous efforts had been resoundingly unsuccessful, particularly as a means of compensating for more negative news coverage about downsizing, CEO greed, and bungled executive succession. But that was the wrong lesson to draw from those abortive efforts. Their focus had been external. They were designed to convince the outside world that it had underestimated the company. Unless it is preceded by an effective internal effort, any such positioning program is built on sand. No one outside the company will believe a message that is not reflected in her day-to-day experiences with the company. And no one inside the company will believe a message that does not comport with what he sees on the job every day.

What AT&T needed in early 2002 was an internal effort to reimagine the company's mission. For four years, AT&T's focus had been on financial issues, from cutting costs, to divesting assets, to acquiring companies, and finally to spinning off those companies in a massive restructuring that seemed to bring most of the company's employees back to the starting point. In the meanwhile, AT&T's people had forgotten why we were in business. The sense of mission that had animated the company's workforce for the first century of its existence—universal service, giving as many people as possible access to a telephone—had never been replaced with a new mission when it was essentially accomplished in the late 1960s.

To his credit, John Walter sensed this and brought in Jim Collins, who had written the business best-seller *Built to Last*,[3] to help his senior team articulate a "higher purpose" for the company. What they came up with was not poetry, but it had an element of nobility and decency worthy of AT&T's employees who still believed in a "spirit of service." It was "to improve the quality of people's lives around the world through communications." Unfortunately, few employees ever saw it, and when Walter left, it was forgotten.

Horizontal Communications

The task of preparing AT&T's employees for life without AT&T Broadband and C. Michael Armstrong was too important to delay until the board had appointed a successor. In fact, while the CEO is, for many employees, the personification of the company, it's their immediate boss that people listen to for evidence that things will really change. But in most corporations, first-line supervisors are often the forgotten managers. Every survey identifies them as employees' preferred channel of communication. But in most companies, they know as little as the people they are paid to supervise.

AT&T actually had a good story to tell in 2001: While revenue was declining across the industry, customer satisfaction was improving; there were signs that growth was returning to our data and professional services businesses; our consumer local business was finally gaining traction in several states; and our network reliability had never been better.

Grand statements of direction echoing off marble walls would have to await the appointment of a new CEO, but there was a crying need for a simple baselining of AT&T's strengths after the Broadband spin-off. Ironically, Noski was taking this story to the investment community in a series of analyst meetings, but because the ever-politically attuned Dorman was afraid of appearing presumptuous, we failed to rally our internal audience.

We should have taken those facts directly to first-line supervisors and equipped those supervisors to communicate the facts to their people.

This horizontal or lateral approach puts public relations in the role of facilitating communications, not dictating them. It means identifying influential rank-and-file employees and engaging them in an open-ended discussion about the company's performance: where we're winning, where we're losing, and what it all means. Supervisors needed to be trained to communicate with their work groups effectively, and they needed answers to the questions that their people were asking. The whole process needed to be monitored so that it could be adjusted and fine-tuned based on front-line experience.

Instead, AT&T's employees spent 2001 and 2002 under the dark clouds that hovered over the entire communication services industry, which was caught in a spiral of declining revenue and downbeat news. Companies that were once the darlings of the new economy, including

Global Crossing, Teligent, and Macleod USA, were filing for bankruptcy. At least five of the largest communications companies revised their earnings guidance. Regulators accused some telephone companies of artificially inflating their revenue and subpoenaed their records. Qwest fired its CEO, former AT&T executive Joe Nacchio.

Even MCI WorldCom, which *Fortune* magazine once described as "the poster child for amazing growth," began to falter.[4]

Following the release of MCI Worldcom's first-quarter 2001 financial results, some analysts questioned the quality of its earnings. In reaction, its stock price began a long slide. By summer, rumors began to fly that its chairman, Bernie Ebbers, might have to declare personal bankruptcy to get out from under margin calls on loans he had taken to purchase his company's stock. In February 2002, in the wake of the dot-com bust, MCI WorldCom had to schedule a conference call to fight off rumors that it was in danger of going under because so many of its data customers had closed their doors. By mid-March, the Securities and Exchange Commission began an inquiry into MCI WorldCom's accounting practices.

On April 30, Ebbers resigned as CEO. And on June 26, the company announced that it would be reducing its reported 2001 and 2002 year-to-date earnings before interest, taxes, depreciation, and amortization by more than a third because of inappropriate capitalization of network operating expenses. The company also announced that its CFO had been fired and its controller had resigned. On July 21, 2002, MCI WorldCom, which had once had a market value of $180 billion, declared bankruptcy.

MCI WorldCom's admission cast a pall of suspicion over the entire industry. Investors, tired of dealing with complexity, fled in the face of all the uncertainty. Our public stance was relatively muted as we took the high road, careful not to look as if we were exploiting another company's misfortune. And frankly, some of us worried that people who live in glass houses shouldn't throw rocks. Who knew what honest mistakes lurked in the thousands of financial records we had filed during our serial acquisitions, divestitures, and bond and share offerings?[5]

Fallout of Fraud

As the full extent of MCI WorldCom's fraud was uncovered, we began to realize just how devastating it had been to Armstrong's strategy. Put simply, between 1999 and 2002, MCI WorldCom had cut its prices by about $10.6 billion to maintain the revenue growth rate on which its stock price depended, and it inflated its earnings by the same amount to maintain the illusion of dramatically greater efficiency than the industry leader, AT&T. MCI WorldCom's competitors had no choice but to match the new prices it had introduced. Consumers can change long-distance carriers with one phone call, and about two million AT&T customers switched every month. On the business side, a small army of independent consultants pores over the contracts that AT&T must file with the FCC. The new pricing that these consultants find is immediately reflected in the one-third of contracts that are renegotiated every year. Pricing information zips around the communication services industry as freely as the bids in a cattle auction.

MCI WorldCom's fraud had distorted industry pricing, lowering AT&T's sales by about $5 billion a year. Without it, the proximate cause of the company's restructuring—rapidly declining industry revenue—would not have occurred, or, at worst, would have occurred much later. Since the company's profit margins before interest, taxes, depreciation, and amortization averaged 33 percent during this period, AT&T would have had about $1.7 billion a year in additional profits, all else being equal. AT&T would have been able to service its debt while divesting itself of noncore assets. It would not have broken itself apart. And it could have taken one more run at managing its voice, data, wireless, and cable businesses as a single enterprise, rather than as a loose confederation of affiliated companies.

In the real world, of course, you play the cards you're dealt, even if the other player is pulling cards out of his sleeve.

We'll never know if Armstrong's strategy would have worked in the long run, because he didn't get a long enough run to find out. AT&T's largest competitor engaged in serial fraud for at least three and a half years, distorting the principal market from which the company derived most of the cash to fund its strategy. AT&T in the Armstrong years did not represent a failure of strategy. It did not represent a failure of execution. The company was mugged.

Coda

AT&T Broadband was spun off from AT&T on November 18, 2002. Dave Dorman became AT&T's chairman and CEO on that day. Two years later, he had still been unable to reverse the company's inexorable slide or to merge it with a stronger partner.

Chuck Noski, who at least one analyst credited with "saving the company,"[6] retired to rejoin his family in California. He left with a special grant of about $3 million from a grateful board for seeing the company's restructuring through to completion. Noski was asked to join several boards, including Microsoft's, he became a special adviser to the Blackstone Group, and he gave a few lectures at the University of Southern California, but he jokes that he "failed at retirement." In late 2003, Northrop Grumman, which is headquartered about an hour from his home near Los Angeles, recruited him to become its chief financial officer.

Mike Armstrong became the chairman of Comcast Corporation and held that position from the day the merger closed until May 2004, when he stepped down in favor of Brian Roberts. During that period, he drew annual compensation of about $2.7 million. Whether he works or not, he will continue to receive that compensation until his contract expires in 2005, and because he stepped down as chairman early, he will also receive an additional $900,000 annual consulting fee until the spring of 2006. Armstrong is a director of Citigroup, the Hospital Corporation of America, and Johns Hopkins University. He is a visiting professor at MIT and Chairman of the Business Round-table's Homeland Security Task Force. When he's in town, he commutes by Metro-North Railroad to offices Comcast maintains for him in Manhattan.

16

Practice Ambidextrous Leadership

Companies exist to create wealth, but not solely for shareowners. Other groups contribute resources to a company's process of wealth creation and accept the associated risks. All these "stakeholders"—employees, customers, investors, and communities— should share the rewards. That requires a degree of ambidextrous leadership that does not come naturally to many business leaders.

"Terrible PR"

I was once introduced to Mel Karmazin, then CEO of CBS, as "the guy who runs AT&T's PR shop." "Oh," Karmazin joked, "AT&T has *terr*ible PR." "But imagine how bad it would be," I countered, "if I weren't there." We both laughed.

Looking back, I realize that Karmazin might not have been joking. And I sometimes wonder whether my rejoinder was more clever than accurate. Of course, we'll never know, just as we'll never know whether Armstrong's strategy would have worked had he not been competing with a company that was perpetrating the most extensive fraud in business history.

But at the end of a thirty-two-year career, let alone in a book that purports to draw lessons from that career, it's natural to ask, "How did I do?"

An editor who covered AT&T during the Allen and Armstrong years tried to give me safe passage by that question in an e-mail after I retired from the company: "att's press wasn't bad because the media are bad—-it was bad cuz the company was in terrible shape. nothing you or bob allen or c.michael armstrong cud have done would have changed that. in other words: it wasn't your fault."

While I appreciate the consideration behind the note (from a man not known for idle sentiment), I think it gives the media too much credit and us too little. We were sometimes our own worst enemy, not only in what we said, but in what we did. Whether anyone else would have fared better is one of those unanswerable questions that business cases are built around. And I can't grade myself separately from the CEO I worked for. To say that I succeeded while he did not is like saying that the operation was a success but the patient died.

In terms of AT&T's trading value, the jury is still out. Before Armstrong arrived, an AT&T investor owned shares in a company that essentially provided a single service (long-distance) that was soon to be made obsolete by changing technology and regulation. Armstrong used the company's strong balance sheet and the cash thrown off by its consumer long-distance business to upgrade its data networks, expand its wireless footprint, and buy cable television companies. When he left, AT&T investors owned shares in the original long-distance company, the largest independent wireless services company, and the largest broadband services company.

In October 1997, 100 AT&T shares were worth about $4,487. By December 2002, when Armstrong left the company, they had become 30 shares of AT&T, worth about $600; 48 shares of Comcast, worth about $1,575; and 48 shares of AT&T Wireless, worth about $405. That represents an annual decline of about 8.8 percent, not taking dividends into account. Fidelity's Select Telecom Fund, by contrast, decreased 9.4 percent a year. Of course, someone who traded in and out of the stock during these years might have done far better (or woefully worse), and no one knows how that basket of stocks will fare in the future. In fact, part of the basket will be cashed out at $720 (pretax) when Cingular Wireless completes its acquisition of AT&T Wireless. And stock of the long-distance company, which was dropped from the closely watched Dow Jones average in April 2004, continued to slide toward the low to mid-teens in the months that followed.

But all that assumes that a company's primary purpose is to optimize its share price. If Armstrong's mandate was to "give AT&T a future," we probably deserve no more than an "incomplete with an explanation." Many people expected Armstrong to transform AT&T into something bigger and more powerful. But whether AT&T will survive as an independent company is at best an even proposition. Its consumer division continues to shrink in size and profitability, although at a slower rate. From around $26 billion in revenue in 1997, it ended 2003 with sales of about $9.5 billion. When the consumer long-distance business finally stabilizes, AT&T will probably be little more than a niche player in residential communications services.

AT&T's corporate services division is better positioned, thanks to extensive investments during Armstrong's tenure that went largely unnoticed, and unreported, by most observers. But in the long term it will be an attractive acquisition target for the Bell companies, whose own traditional businesses are declining. With revenue of more than $25 billion in 2003, it is by far the largest, most profitable company serving businesses' communications needs in the United States.

According to the *New York Times,* at least one of AT&T's directors believed that "[Armstrong] did the best he could with the cards he was dealt."[1] In many ways he did, but I fear we all misunderstood the meaning of corporations in general and this one in particular. While we liked to say that AT&T traced its roots to Alexander Graham Bell's invention of the telephone, in reality the company was the creation of a man named Theodore Vail, and his view of a company's purpose was far more comprehensive than is currently fashionable.

Theodore Vail

Vail was a senior executive with the company that is now known as AT&T at two of the most critical moments in its history: from 1878 to 1887, when the telephone began its voyage from fledgling invention to ubiquitous home and office appliance, and from 1907 to 1919, when the company, beset by competitors and despised by its customers, moved from the brink of financial ruin to a de facto monopoly affectionately known as "Ma Bell."[2]

Vail was hired away from the U.S. Post Office for his experience in managing complex operations when the Bell Telephone Company was less than one year old and controlled by a small group of Boston-based investors. He almost immediately began building the Bell System, with regional companies providing local service, a long-distance company interconnecting them, and a captive supplier manufacturing all the necessary equipment.

But within nine years, Bell's Boston investors, impatient to see a return on their capital, refused to fund more expansion. Vail resigned, writing in an unusual parting shot: "We have a duty to the public at large to make our service as good as possible and as universal as possible, and [our] earnings should be used not only to reward investors for their investment but also to accomplish these objectives."[3]

In the following years, the new managers milked the business that Vail had built, raising rates and allowing service quality to slip. When the Bell patents expired in 1894, its disaffected customers couldn't wait to give their business to competitors. By 1907, Bell was in sorry financial condition. Financier J. P. Morgan agreed to bail the company out only if it would agree to bring Vail back as president. Vail was sixty-two years old, his wife and only son had recently died, and he had made a fortune in South American transit development. No one would have blamed him if he had wanted to stay on his farm in Lyndonville, Vermont. But he got back in the saddle and served as president of AT&T until June of 1919, when he retired at the age of seventy-four. He died less than a year later.

The company's earnings per share trended steadily downward during Vail's years and didn't recover until he had been dead for six years. The company's share price declined from about $123 a share in May of 1907, when he took over for the second time, to $106 a share when he left in 1919. But few would argue that he didn't serve the company and its stakeholders well.

As John Brooks put it in his history of the Bell System, *Telephone*, Vail's failure to increase earnings or the stock price was really his triumph, "the measure of his stature as a builder rather than a moneymaker."[4] Under Vail, the number of phones in service more than doubled, from fewer than 6 million to more than 12 million; nationwide service was inaugurated; local service was improved; and the predecessor to Bell Laboratories was formed.

The business system he built survived for another sixty-five years, paying dividends through world wars and depression until it had become the most valuable company in the world by the time of its centennial in 1976. The principles on which Vail conducted business—high quality, friendly service, and managing for the long pull—had survived in AT&T's DNA.

As a monopoly trying to justify its profits, the Bell System's motto was: "We earn to serve." But when its monopoly was broken—in fact, if not yet by court decree, in the mid-1970s—someone suggested reversing the order to "we serve to earn" to justify eliminating some of the "gold plating" that made the company less competitive. It was more than a semantic difference; it was a confusion of means and ends. When "we earn to serve" was the corporate motto, earnings were a necessary by-product of serving customers. We can provide phone service, the company said, perhaps a bit defensively, only if we can earn a fair return on the investment required to keep this whole thing running. Under "we serve to earn," customers are a means of generating profits, a sometimes inconvenient, troublesome path to what we're really in business to produce: fat returns for our shareowners.

But business philosopher Charles Handy sees it differently. "The principal purpose of a corporation," he writes in *The Age of Paradox*, "is not to make a profit. Full stop. It is to make a profit in order to do things or make things and to do so ever better and more abundantly."[5] Handy suggests that this confusion of means and ends is, by definition, self-defeating. Someone who lives to eat, rather than eats to live, he reminds us, will be distorted in more ways than one.

When a shareowner's greatest return comes from a rising share price that bears no relation to the performance of the underlying business, things really get perverse. But as my friend Ed Block says, great CEOs keep their eye on the store, not just the ticker. And truly great companies operate in the public interest, manage for the long run, and make customer satisfaction their top priority.

PR Misconceived

Serious scholars, like Columbia University's Louis Lowenstein, have suggested that the "Voice of the paparazzi" has become a powerful new factor in corporate governance, "transforming how boards and managers [see] themselves."[6] And that brings us to the role of public relations in corporate governance.

Many business executives, understanding the power of the paparazzi, define public relations largely in terms of *media* relations. In fact, one senior PR counselor I know was frank in describing the job as ensuring that the CEO could read the *Wall Street Journal* at breakfast without developing indigestion. And AT&T's first foray into public relations, way back in 1903, was to hire the Publicity Bureau of Boston to "place nice little stories about the telephone" in the nation's media. The Publicity Bureau account executive, who later moved onto the company's payroll, was a former newspaperman who was not above paying editors to run his stories verbatim in their news columns. Nor was he unwilling to sabotage a competitor's news conference by salting the audience with shills who would ask embarrassing questions and generally disrupt the proceedings.

But in 1926, the chairman of AT&T, perhaps motivated by the still fresh memory of a bomb exploding outside the offices of J. P. Morgan a few blocks down the street, asked Arthur W. Page to take over the company's public relations department. Page had been the editor of *The World's Work*—that era's version of *BusinessWeek*—and he told AT&T's chairman that if he was looking for a press agent, he could keep looking.

Somehow, AT&T's chairman convinced Page that he needed someone who could help the company navigate the crosscurrents of public opinion in an era of doubt and skepticism about big business. Not only did he hire Page and make him an officer of the company, he put him on the board of directors.

Page's basic advice at the time rings just as true today: "All business lives by public approval and, roughly speaking, the more approval you have, the better you live." Of course, he also pointed out that "the fundamental way to get approval is to deserve it."[7]

You can advertise and publicize a "personality" or "image" for your company, but character arises from what a company does, not just what it says. Corporations have a moral obligation to serve their customers honestly, to give their employees an opportunity to develop and grow so that they can care for their families, to give their shareowners a fair return on their investment, and to help build a civil society. Running a business isn't about creating short-term trading value, it's about building a long-lasting institution. Corporations are such a relatively new institution—only a few hundred years old in their current form—that we tend to forget this.

Many people think that the primary reason to incorporate is to limit liability, and, in our litigious society, that is indeed an advantage. But *Blackstone's Commentaries on the Laws of England*, which codified English common law for the first time in 1758, explained that corporations were devised because "personal rights die with the person" and "investing a series of individuals, one after another, with the same identical rights, would be very inconvenient, if not impractical." Corporations are "artificial persons" who enjoy "a kind of legal immortality." Indeed, Blackstone listed "to have perpetual succession" as the very first of a corporation's "rights and capacities" and "the very end of its incorporation."[8]

Not every company is worthy of such immortality. The average life cycle for a public company is only forty years. Those that endure are those that have found a way to balance the legitimate interests of all their stakeholders: employees, customers, investors, and the communities in which they live and work. But that requires a standard of ambidextrous leadership that not many managers have mastered. It means addressing the legitimate interests of multiple stakeholders, not sequentially, but simultaneously.

F. Scott Fitzgerald said, "The test of a first-rate intelligence is the ability to hold two opposed ideas in the mind at the same time and still be able to function." Great companies demonstrate that kind of intelligence by treating profit and stakeholder goals as complementary, not contradictory. AT&T was once such a company.

Lessons of the Past

There are two reasons to remember the past. As the Spanish poet and philosopher George Santayana suggested, one reason is to avoid repeating its mistakes. Another is because the past is always with us. "The past is not dead," William Faulkner once wrote. "The past is not even past." AT&T's past stretches back more than one hundred years. It can be ignored, denied, and belittled, but it cannot be escaped.

In the calm following the storms of my last six years at AT&T, I've played an endless game of "what if," replaying major events in my mind, rethinking choices, and anticipating the consequences of each with the crystal clarity of hindsight. In the process, I relearned some old lessons and discovered new ones. Running through them are three principles that appear to have universal application. They concern the exercise of power, not in the financial, political, or technological realms, but in a moral sense. Following the corporate scandals of recent years, talk of moral decisions naturally implies choosing between right and wrong, good and bad. But that's a minimum bet. Real moral power taps three interrelated resources deep within a company's soul.

The Power of Common Purpose

At the end of his masterful history of the Bell System's last days, *Heritage and Destiny*, Alvin von Auw makes a case for the importance of words. That may not be surprising coming from someone who spent much of his forty-two-year career writing speeches for AT&T executives, the last twelve for three successive chairmen and CEOs. But he had more than rhetoric in mind. "For it is words that embody an institution's idea of itself," he wrote. "It is words, even more than numbers, that provide the motive power of business."[9] Great companies, like countries, need a "sustaining myth" that binds their people together in a worthwhile undertaking. That sustaining myth may be expressed in anecdotes, iconic symbols, or heroic tales, but it always expresses the higher purpose to which the company was dedicated.

This is not simply an exercise in corporate poetry. While a mission is necessarily articulated in words, even stirring words, that can be printed on cards with laminations thick enough to read in the shower, its real communication depends on taking actions to realize it.

To von Auw, it mattered deeply whether the leaders of an enterprise saw themselves as stewards of a public trust or simply as "the managers of a portfolio whose first responsibility is to position the business in whatever markets will profit it most."[10]

In reviewing my calendars, I was surprised to see that the most significant announcements during the Armstrong years were made at, and sometimes for, a meeting with financial analysts. Wall Street was ever on our minds. With 20/20 hindsight, I now see that this skewed not only the form, but the substance of our messages. We were positioning AT&T as the answer to the question, "How do I make quick money in the stock market?" as if that were our mission.

But AT&T's heritage—and the "future" that Armstrong had promised its board of directors—demanded much more. Von Auw had foreseen the day when future leaders of AT&T would have to decide whether they were stewards of a "business" or of an "enterprise of historical significance." The choice they made would spring from a sense of their own heritage, obliging them to seek what von Auw called the company's "highest and best use."

Some argue that AT&T essentially accomplished its original mission—making affordable phone service universally available—in the 1960s, and that its history since then has been a chaotic flailing about for a new mission. That may be. What seems certain to me is that in recent years, through happenstance and errors of judgment, AT&T lost any meaningful link to its heritage, despite moving Golden Boy across the Hudson River and up and down New Jersey highways, as the company's chairman moved his office.

We belittled the era of the "Bellheads," appropriately discarding the vestiges of their rigidly hierarchical culture. But we failed to articulate a mission that was worthy of our past and capable of driving our future. In fact, in many ways, we suggested that AT&T's past had come to a dead end in an "unsustainable business." The company's consumer business, for example, was left in that cul de sac while we used its earnings to blaze new paths elsewhere.

Ironically, it was the challenge of renewing a company of historical significance that drew Armstrong away from his new home in California. And many of the actions he took could have animated a new sense of corporate purpose. But that purpose was lost in a flurry of deal making. And without the framework of such a mission, the deals hung on a scaffolding of financial engineering that ultimately fell in the gales of capricious markets.

The Power of Promise

A "promise" is either something you make to others or what others make of you. Anyone can make loud promises, and, if these promises are grand enough, they will stir people's imaginations. Over time, they become inflated, and when they bump up against reality, they have a tendency to burst. Overpromising is a slippery slope, but it's one that can easily be avoided. The promise that others have invested in you, however, is equally volatile. On the one hand, it provides the energy you need to conquer the challenges ahead, but unless it is tempered, it can be explosive.

If I could do one thing over again, I would counsel resetting and lowering the expectations that piled up around Armstrong like a high wall from the very beginning. He was right in anticipating that the media and analysts would allow him only ninety days of silence. But the roots of the company's problems extended back fifteen years, to 1982, when the company agreed to break up the Bell System.

Ironically, at that time, both AT&T and IBM had correctly foreseen that digital technologies would erase the boundary between the communications and computing industries, and both companies had made acquisitions based on that conviction. AT&T famously tried to use the Unix operating system software, developed at Bell Labs, as a wedge into the computer business, and when that failed, it bought the NCR Corporation in 1991. For its part, IBM had acquired the Rolm Corporation, a maker of office telephone systems, and established a satellite communications business that it later exchanged for an interest in MCI Corporation.

IBM was quicker to realize that the machinery of the digital age was less important than its application. It unloaded Rolm and not only divested its interest in MCI but sold its global data network (in one further irony, to Armstrong's AT&T) so that it could concentrate on business applications and services. AT&T didn't finally throw in the towel on the computer business until 1996.

When Armstrong arrived in 1997, AT&T's remaining long-distance businesses were declining, and the company did not have a workable strategy to extricate itself from fifteen years of blind alleys and ever-deepening ruts. The company had spent billions trying to break into local markets by reselling the Bells' service and had nothing but losses to show for it. Its global strategy was a patchwork of loose alliances and inconsistent services. After a fast start, its Internet service was an underfunded also-ran. Its corporate services were largely analog in a world that was going digital.

When Armstrong broke his silence on January 26, 1998, it should not have been to announce a solution to these problems, or even a partial solution or anything that sounded like a solution. It should have been to begin describing the problem.

One of the lessons I learned in AT&T's October 2000 restructuring announcement is the futility of trying to sell a solution to people who don't really understand the problem. To a lesser but still significant degree, that was also our situation in early 1998. Few people really appreciated AT&T's underlying problem.

The issues that were making the papers—bungled succession, ineffective marketing, bloated costs, high prices, and a slow-moving culture—were important but secondary. The real issue was one of fundamental business definition. It was not going to be solved in year one and possibly not even during Armstrong's tenure. But if we had succeeded in defining our goals in those terms, with clear milestones against which to measure progress, we might have had a fighting chance.

The Power of a Company's People

The word *company* comes from "companion"—people who are on a journey, or a mission, together. It was fashionable for a while at AT&T to avoid referring to its workers as "employees." Rather, they were "associates." I never got comfortable with the idea because it seemed artificial and a distinction without a difference. I don't propose calling employees "companions," but I do believe that they should be treated as such. Everyone who works for a company is on a journey that draws its meaning not from the salary we all draw along the way, but from the mission we share.

Such a mission cannot be described in terms of cost cutting, submitting bills, or even stringing the most sophisticated fiber-optic wires. It must serve a higher purpose that gives dignity to our journey together. A well-considered mission can reconcile apparently unrelated actions, if those actions are indeed directed at accomplishing that mission. Such a mission gives context and meaning to the daily administrivia of corporate life, as well as to the grand strategies. It addresses the emotional, as well as the intellectual, needs of a company's first public: its employees.

That's why I wish I had focused even more on internal communication. On the one hand, we were very successful in communicating the company's business goals in a way that employees could relate to.

About one year into Armstrong's tenure, we fielded a survey of top and mid-level managers that showed a startling level of agreement that Armstrong and his senior team had communicated the company's long-range goals and strategic direction effectively. Fully 96 percent agreed, 31 points above the norm. A similar survey of lower-level employees reflected the same attitude—64 percent said that they understood how their job related to the company's overall strategy.

These surveys were taken when the company's press clippings were mostly positive and the stock price was climbing. But when the media turned and the stock price began a long slow slide, employee attitudes tumbled too.

I wish we had used the relative calm of Armstrong's early days to build a broad, deep consensus around the company's long-term mission. In the absence of such a shared understanding, people filled in the blanks with what they saw and read in the media—a decidedly transactional view of the world that was at odds with the company's historical values.

This is one idea that John Walter had right—people want to belong to something bigger than themselves. The CEO should be the company's principal storyteller, the keeper of the sustaining myth that nourishes its people on their journey together.

The Final Tally

It may sound curious coming from someone who made his career in public relations, but I believe companies go astray when their leaders become more concerned with perception than with reality. While that was sometimes the case at AT&T, when it mattered most, both Allen and Armstrong put aside concern for their personal reputation in order to do the right thing. Allen allowed himself to reconsider his choice of John Walter as successor, even though he knew it would spell the end of his board's support. Armstrong methodically dismantled the empire he had built in order to preserve the value of its piece parts, even though he knew this would take a toll on his reputation. Both men could have chosen easier paths, papering over the problems until they were snugly in retirement.

In my career, I was lucky to work for decent men and women who, for the most part, shared the same old-fashioned values. They were the values of Theodore Vail, who was hired to sell "electric telephones" to people who weren't sure they needed them and built a business system on the promise of serving the public interest. They were the values of Arthur W. Page, who was a scion of the Eastern Establishment at the turn of the last century, but who believed that all businesses existed only by public approval. They were openness, candor, doing right by the customer, serving the public interest, and managing for the long pull.

That may all sound quaint and old-fashioned in a digital world, but if you think about the business scandals that ushered in the twenty-first century, aren't they what was missing? That, in the final analysis, may be the greatest lesson of all.

Selective Chronology: 1995–2002

SEPTEMBER 20, 1995   Bob Allen announces Trivestiture.

JANUARY 2, 1996   AT&T announces 1995 charge and downsizing of 40,000 jobs.

FEBRUARY 8, 1996   President Clinton signs the Telecommunications Act of 1996.

AUGUST 19, 1996   AT&T president Alex Mandl resigns.

OCTOBER 23, 1996   John Walter joins AT&T.

APRIL 30, 1997   Dan Somers joins AT&T as chief financial officer.

JUNE 19, 1997   John Zeglis is appointed vice chairman of AT&T.

JULY 16, 1997   John Walter resigns. Board begins search for new CEO.

OCTOBER 20, 1997   Mike Armstrong joins AT&T. John Zeglis is named president.

JANUARY 8, 1998   AT&T acquires Teleport Communications, Inc.

JANUARY 26, 1998   Armstrong announces initial cost-cutting and growth plans.

MAY 7, 1998   AT&T launches first national one-rate wireless service plan.

JUNE 24, 1998   AT&T and TeleCommunications, Inc., announce plans to merge. Leo Hindery becomes president of AT&T's cable systems.

JULY 26, 1998   AT&T and BT announce formation of global joint venture.

DECEMBER 8, 1998	AT&T agrees to acquire IBM's global data network for $5 billion.
MARCH 4, 1999	David Dorman named CEO of AT&T/BT global joint venture.
APRIL 6, 1999	AT&T imposes $3 minimum on basic calling plan customers.
APRIL 22, 1999	AT&T tops Comcast's offer for MediaOne Group cable systems.
MAY 4, 1999	Comcast drops MediaOne bid, swaps cable systems with AT&T.
MAY 6, 1999	AT&T and MediaOne reach definitive merger agreement.
OCTOBER 6, 1999	Leo Hindery leaves AT&T and is replaced by Dan Somers as head of AT&T cable systems.
DECEMBER 6, 1999	AT&T says it will establish a tracking stock for AT&T Wireless. John Zeglis will be CEO of AT&T Wireless.
DECEMBER 9, 1999	Charles Noski is named chief financial officer of AT&T.
MARCH 29, 2000	AT&T acquires control of Excite@Home from Comcast and Cox.
APRIL 26, 2000	AT&T Wireless tracking stock begins trading at $29.50 a share.
MAY 2, 2000	AT&T revises earnings guidance for third and fourth quarters.
MAY 31, 2000	AT&T eliminates $3 minimum charge and increases basic rates.
JUNE 7, 2000	Facing intense criticism, AT&T defers basic-rate increases.
JUNE 23, 2000	AT&T redesigns basic calling plan.
OCTOBER 25, 2000	Armstrong announces restructuring plans.
NOVEMBER 28, 2000	David Dorman is named president of AT&T.
DECEMBER 20, 2000	AT&T board cuts quarterly dividend by 83 percent.
JULY 8, 2001	Comcast makes unsolicited bid for AT&T cable business.

JULY 9, 2001	AT&T Wireless completes its separation from AT&T.
JULY 18, 2001	AT&T board unanimously rejects Comcast bid for its cable assets.
SEPTEMBER 28, 2001	Excite@Home files for bankruptcy.
OCTOBER 16, 2001	AT&T and BT agree to dissolve their global joint venture.
DECEMBER 19, 2001	AT&T accepts Comcast's bid for its cable business.
FEBRUARY 21, 2002	Dorman and Noski are named to AT&T board.
MAY 23, 2002	Noski announces that he will leave AT&T following restructuring.
JULY 17, 2002	AT&T board names David Dorman next CEO of AT&T.
NOVEMBER 18, 2002	AT&T Broadband merges with Comcast. Armstrong era ends.

Notes

Introduction

1. Alvin Von Auw, *Heritage and Destiny: Reflections on the Bell System in Transition* (New York: Praeger, 1983), p. 397.
2. The statue's original name was "The Genius of Electricity," but it was dubbed "The Spirit of Communications" when AT&T began putting its picture on the company's phone books. Evelyn Beatrice Longman (1874–1954) won a competition to design the statue, and it was placed atop 195 Broadway in October 1916, when both Western Union and AT&T made their headquarters there. It weighs sixteen tons and is made of gilded bronze.
3. Grasso stepped down as CEO of the New York Stock Exchange following revelations that he had engineered a pay package of about $180 million for himself.
4. Welch was quoted as follows by the Corporate Library (www.the corporatelibrary.com) after the revelation that GE would continue to pay for many of his living expenses during retirement: "One thing I learned during my years as CEO is that perception matters. And in these times when public confidence and trust have been shaken, I've learned the hard way that perception matters more than ever." After the SEC began a probe into the agreement, Welch altered the deal, giving up free access to baseball tickets, corporate jets, and a Manhattan apartment.
5. For a good explanation of the divestiture agreement, see Von Auw, *Heritage and Destiny*. For background on AT&T in its monopoly days, see John Brooks, *Telephone: The First Hundred Years* (New York: Harper and Row, 1975).
6. AT&T's net income from continuing operations in 1996 was a record $5.6 billion. Its debt ratio (excluding its Universal credit

card, which had its own receivables) was 18.7 percent, down from 41.3 percent the year before. (*Source:* Company annual reports.)

7. *New York Daily News* headline, October 24, 1996.
8. Michael Schrage, "Daniel Kahneman: The Thought Leader Interview," *Strategy + Business*, Winter 2003.
9. Daniel Boorstin, *The Image: A Guide to Pseudo-Events in America* (New York: Vintage Books, 1962), p. 43.
10. Charles Handy, "What's a Company For?" *Harvard Business Review*, December 2002.

Chapter 1

1. Michael Meyer, "AT&T's New Operator?" *Newsweek*, October 27, 1997.
2. The foregoing is from a transcript of the telephone conference call held on July 16, 1997.
3. Roger Lowenstein, "And Now, Some Questions for AT&T's Board," *Wall Street Journal*, July 24, 1997.
4. John Keller, "How AT&T Directors Decided It Was Time for a Change at the Top," *Wall Street Journal*, October 20, 1997.
5. Walter Lippmann, *Public Opinion* (New York: Penguin Books, 1946 reprint of original 1922 edition), p. 61.
6. Quoted in, among other places, Frank Rich, "So Much for 'The Front Page,'" *New York Times*, November 2, 2003.
7. "We may live in a modern metropolis, but in many respects, we still harbor a Stone Age mind within our skulls." William Allman, *The Stone Age Present: How Evolution Has Shaped Modern Life—From Sex, Violence and Language to Emotions, Morals and Communities* (New York: Touchstone Books, 1995), p. 35.
8. "Building CEO Capital," Burson-Marsteller Public Relations, www.bm.com, 2001.
9. From an interview with Dennis Kneale on June 5, 2003.
10. From an interview with John Huey on June 5, 2003.
11. See the Third and Final Report of Dick Thornburgh, bankruptcy court examiner, U.S. Bankruptcy Court, Southern District of New York, *In Re WorldCom Inc.*, Case No. 02-15533, January 24, 2004.
12. "Could AT&T Rule the World," *Fortune*, May 17, 1993; "1 800-GUTS: AT&T's Bob Allen Has Transformed His Company Into a World-Class Risk Taker," *BusinessWeek*, August 30, 1993; "Why

AT&T's Latest Plan Won't Work," *Fortune*, June 23, 1997; "AT&T: When Will the Bad News End?" *BusinessWeek*, October 7, 1996.

13. Felicity Barringer, "Enron's Many Strands: Early Scrutiny," *New York Times*, January 28, 2002.

Chapter 2

1. This and other news releases cited can be found at AT&T's Web site, www.att.com/news/.
2. Edmund L. Andrews, "Job Cuts at AT&T Will Total 40,000, 13% of Its Staff," *New York Times*, January 3, 1996.
3. Kristen Downey Grimsley, "AT&T Promises Aid to Laid-Off Workers; Package Reflects New Trends in Downsizing," *Washington Post*, January 3, 1996.
4. Andrews, "Job Cuts at AT&T."
5. John J. Keller, "AT&T Will Eliminate 40,000 Jobs and Take a Charge of $4 Billion," *The Wall Street Journal*, January 3, 1996.
6. Kathleen Kennedy, CNN *World News*, January 3, 1996.
7. NBC *Evening News with Tom Brokaw*, January 3, 1996.
8. The economic data cited were widely available from public sources such as the Bureau of Labor Statistics. The public opinion data are drawn principally from a national poll conducted by the *New York Times* from December 3 to 6 that formed the basis for a seven-part series, "The Downsizing of America" (March 3–10, 1996), and put a human face on the issue of job losses.
9. Robert B. Reich, "How to Avoid These Layoffs?" *New York Times*, January 4, 1996.
10. Buchanan was quoted in Jack Beatty, "Downsizing Days Are Here Again," *The Atlantic Online: Atlantic Unbound*, January 13, 1998.
11. Allan Sloan, "For Whom Bell Tolls," *Newsweek*, January 15, 1996.
12. Ibid.
13. Louis Uchitelle and N. R. Kleinfield, "On the Battlefield of Business, Millions of Casualties," *New York Times*, March 3, 1996.
14. AT&T's 1996 proxy, filed on February 26, 1996, p. 37.
15. Carol Loomis, "AT&T Has No Clothes," *Fortune*, February 1996.
16. Allan Sloan, "Jobs—The Hit Men," *Newsweek*, February 26, 1996.
17. Robert E. Allen, "The Anxiety Epidemic," *Newsweek*, April 8, 1998.
18. *BusinessWeek's* cover story appeared on March 11, 1996.

19. Ellen Neuborne and Susan Page interviewed President Clinton for *USA Today*. The story that resulted ("Clinton Takes Aim at Corporate Decency Issue") ran on May 16, 1996, the day of the White House Conference on Corporate Citizenship.

20. William Safire, "The Great Disconnect," *New York Times*, March 11, 1996; George Will, "Wall Street Is Partners with Main Street," *Los Angeles Times*, March 3, 1996; James K. Glassman, "Jobs: The (Woe Is) Me Generation," *Washington Post*, March 19, 1996; Robert Samuelson, "The Politics of Self-Pity," *Newsweek*, February 26, 1996; Michael Prowse, "Blame Consumers," *Financial Times*, March 18, 1996; Herbert Stein, "Good Times, Bad Vibes," *Wall Street Journal*, March 14, 1996; Michael Hammer, "Who's to Blame for All the Layoffs," Manager's Journal, *Wall Street Journal*, January 22, 1996; James Champy, "Jobs Die so Companies May Live," *New York Times*, January 7, 1996; Marjorie Kelly, "Breakup, Resurgence of AT&T Offer a Lesson About Change," *Minneapolis Star Tribune*, March 4, 1996; Ed Koch, "Is Downsizing a Disaster?" *New York Post*, February 23, 1996. All of which demonstrates that having powerful people on your side is not always enough.

21. Jerry J. Jazinowkski, "In Defense of Big (Not Bad) Business," *Washington Post*, March 17, 1996.

22. Prepared remarks by Robert Eaton, chairman and CEO, Chrysler Corporation, at the Economic Club of Detroit, March 18, 1996.

23. Keith H. Hammonds, "America's Hate Affair with Big Business: What Can Be Done," *BusinessWeek*, March 4, 1996.

24. Walter Lippmann, *Public Opinion* (New York: Penguin Books, 1946 reprint of original 1922 edition), p. 154.

25. John Keller, "AT&T Plans to Slash Work Force—Breakup Will Involve Financial Revamping, Over 20,000 Job Cuts," *Wall Street Journal*, September 27, 1995.

26. Lippmann, p. 157.

27. Sloan, "For Whom Bell Tolls."

28. A twenty-year Pepsi veteran named Larry Smith, who was responsible for bottling franchises in Texas, was the first person to realize that "people were drinking [Coke's] trademark." When he couldn't get the headquarters staff in New York to pay attention to his ideas, he hired a local ad agency, which designed the famous blind taste tests in 1985. The challenge took Pepsi's share

of the Texas soft drink market from 6 percent to 14 percent and ultimately led Coca-Cola to reformulate its soft drink. Despite their marketing prowess, Coke's executives missed the key point of the tests: They were *blind*. When people knew which brown, fizzy liquid was Coke, most said it tasted better. Their taste buds were overwhelmed by the symbology surrounding Coke, the feelings of refreshment it evoked, maybe even the warm memories of small-town parades and patriotism. For an entertaining account of the cola wars, see Thomas Oliver, *The Real Coke, The Real Story* (New York: Random House, 1986).

29. John Keller, "Beleaguered CEO: AT&T's Robert Allen Gets Sharp Criticism Over Layoffs, Losses—Foray Into Computer Field Was a Costly Failure; Aloof Style Irks Many—But He Makes No Apologies," *Wall Street Journal*, February 24, 1996.

30. AT&T's shareowners approved the employee option grant, which at the stock's peak in mid-1999 was worth about $2,000. Before the options could be exercised, however, the stock price declined below the strike price and never recovered. In September of 2002, the company offered to exchange the options for a smaller number of restricted shares, which were to be held for three years before they could be sold.

31. Lesley Stahl, "Easy Money in Hard Times," *60 Minutes*, April 7, 1996.

Chapter 3

1. Mark Landler, "How Snap Analysis Spurred an AT&T Slide," *New York Times*, August 21, 1996.

2. Andrew Kupfer, "What, Me Worry?" *Fortune*, September 30, 1996.

Chapter 4

1. Michael Maccoby, "Narcissistic Leaders: The Incredible Pros, the Inevitable Cons," *Harvard Business Review*, January–February 2000.

Chapter 5

1. John Keller, "Ringing Bell: AT&T's New President Is Wasting No Time in Shaking Things Up—Walter Is Centralizing Power, Challenging Managers, Revising Local Strategy—A Salesman in 'Carpet Land,'" *Wall Street Journal*, December 24, 1996.

2. To this day, Keller swears that John Walter was not his source for the story about the SBC merger discussions. Most of the circumstantial evidence points to AT&T Wireless executives who wanted to talk to Bell company managers about trading wireless systems. When they were told that they could proceed with their discussions in any territory except Southwestern Bell's, they deduced that high-level discussions on a merger might be taking place. Keller spent much of the Memorial Day weekend calling contacts throughout the industry because one of his editors had a hunch that the telecom industry was ripe for consolidation. He claims to have literally stumbled across the AT&T/SBC merger discussions.

3. Reed Hundt, *You Say You Want a Revolution?* (New Haven, Conn.: Yale University Press, 2000), p. 219.

4. Mark Landler, "In Unusual Move, FCC Criticizes a Possible Deal," *New York Times*, June 19, 1997.

5. Mark Landler, "AT&T Is Said to Break Off Merger Talks with SBC," *New York Times*, June 28, 1997.

6. Steve Rosenbush, "AT&T's Allen Rips FCC's Hundt," *USA Today*, July 1, 1997.

7. Kahneman and Tversky, who won a Nobel Prize in behavioral economics, devised many experiments to demonstrate how psychological myopia affects people's attitudes and behavior. For example, they showed two lists to a group of people. One was of nineteen famous women; the second, of twenty unknown men (or vice versa). Asked which list was longer, 80 percent of respondents picked whichever list had the famous names. Another group was asked to memorize a list of words that included many terms of praise (such as clever, handsome, agile, and so on) and then asked to evaluate someone in a news story. They thought much more highly of that person than a similar group who was asked to read the same story after memorizing a list of negative words. For an introduction to Kahneman and Tversky's findings and theories, see *Choices, Values and Frames* (Cambridge University Press, 2000).

8. For an entertaining and informative discussion of these psychological effects, see John Allen Poulos, *A Mathematician Reads the Newspaper* (New York: Doubleday Anchor Books, 1996). Availability error, the halo effect, and the anchoring effect are discussed on pp. 14–18.

9. This is called "confirmation bias" and has been widely validated. For example, basketball fans are familiar with the phenomenon of a "hot hand," a player who shoots baskets in streaks. Once a player is on a such a streak, it can last for several periods or even the remainder of the game. Cornell University social psychologist Tom Gilovich analyzed the hits and misses in the Philadelphia 76ers' 1980–81 season and discovered that, statistically, the players were no more likely to sink a ball after making their previous shot than not. He also examined the Boston Celtics' free-throw records and showed that the outcomes of the two throws were independent. Players made the second shot 75 percent of the time, whether the first ball went in or not. Given a copy of Gilovich's paper, Red Auerbach, the brain behind the Boston Celtics, read it and declared, "It doesn't mean anything." That's how deeply confirmation bias is set. Gilovich is the founding father of "hot hand" research based on a 1985 article on the subject coauthored with Robert Vallone and Amos Tversky. See "The Hot Hand in Basketball: On the Misperception of Random Sequences," *Cognitive Psychology*, 1985, pp. 295–314.

10. John Keller, "Bell's Curve: A Telecom Novice Is Handed Challenge of Remaking AT&T—Company Surprises Everyone by Tapping Printer Chief as Bob Allen's Successor—Found in the Yellow Pages," *Wall Street Journal*, October 24, 1996.

11. Bernard Cohen, *The Press and Foreign Policy* (Princeton, N.J.: Princeton University Press, 1963), p. 13.

12. For example, sociologist Allan Mazur claims, "Increased coverage [of risky technologies] not only makes the risk salient, but also turns public opinion in a negative direction, causing . . . heightened fear of technical hazards. There is by now considerable documentation that public opposition to risky technologies rises and falls with the volume of reporting." See Allan Mazur, "Technical Risk in the Mass Media," *Risk: Health, Safety & Environment*, vol. 5, summer 1996.

13. Hundt, p. 218.

Chapter 6

1. Armstrong presented his approach to corporate transformation in a speech to the "CEO Academy" sponsored by executive search firm Spencer Stuart on November 29, 2001.
2. Peter Elstrom, "New Boss, New Plan," *BusinessWeek*, February 2, 1998.
3. G. William Dauphinais, Grady Means, and Colin Price, *Wisdom of the CEO* (New York, Wiley, 2000), p. 148.
4. In Armstrong's first months at AT&T, a number of writers wanted to document his approach to turning the company around. Some of these approaches led to published works, notably *The Mind of the CEO*, by Yale School of Management Dean Jeffery Garten (New York: Basic Books, 2001); *Lessons from the Top: The Search for America's Best Business Leaders*, by executive recruiters James Citrin and Thomas Neff (New York: Currency, 1999); and *Wisdom of the CEO*, by PricewaterhouseCoopers partners Dauphinais, Means, and Price. This quote is from a "pitch letter" by a consultant who requested anonymity.
5. Ibid.
6. Armstrong speech to the CEO Academy, November 29, 2001.

Chapter 7

1. Leo Hindery provides a colorful rendition of this meeting in his book, coauthored with Leslie Cauley, *The Biggest Game of All* (New York: Simon & Schuster, 2003).
2. It was December 2003 before Time Warner became the first cable company to announce its intention to offer Internet-based telephone service on a broad basis, working with MCI and Sprint. Ironically, AT&T became the first "phone company" to announce similar intentions just days later.
3. Geraldine Fabrikant, "Investing It; Enigmatic Architect of a Cable Resurgence," *New York Times*, June 21, 1998.
4. "AT&T Chief Armstrong Delivers on Expectations," *Chicago Tribune*, June 25, 1998; "A Hookup for the Millennium: AT&T–TCI Merger Means Packaged Services for Sale," *Washington Times*, June 25, 1998; Peter Elstrom, "At Last: Telecom Unbound—AT&T–TCI Could Deliver on the Promise of Melding Telephones, TVs

and Computers," *BusinessWeek*, July 6, 1998; George Taber, *Time*, July 6, 1998; FCC Chairman William Kennard's quote is from a brief statement issued by the agency on June 24, 1998; "The Battle to Wire America," *New York Times* editorial, July 5, 1998.

5. John Higgins, "John Malone Explains It All," *Broadcasting and Cable*, July 13, 1998.
6. From a transcript of the news conference.
7. Elstrom, "At Last: Telecom Unbound."
8. Stephanie Mehta and Jared Sandberg, "AT&T Tries Again to Clarify TCI Deal," *Wall Street Journal*, July 2, 1998.
9. Yankee Group, "AT&T and TCI: Fortune Favors the Bold," *Telecom Report*, Vol. 13, No. 10, July 1998.
10. Higgins, "John Malone Explains It All."
11. Sallie Hofmeister, "AT&T Likely to Restructure TCI Deal to Reduce Shareholder Risk," *Los Angeles Times*, July 3, 1998.
12. Adamik was quoted in Mehta and Sandberg, "AT&T Tries Again To Clarify TCI Deal."

Chapter 8

1. John Higgins, "John Malone Explains It All," *Broadcasting and Cable*, July 13, 1998.
2. Leslie Cauley and Stephanie Mehta, "Leaders of AT&T's Consumer Unit Differ—Will Hindery, Zeglis Be Able to Make Power-Sharing Arrangement Work?" *Wall Street Journal*, June 30, 1998.
3. Sallie Hofmeister, "AT&T Cancels TCI Stock Plan at Last Minute," *Los Angeles Times*, January 9, 1999.
4. Leslie Cauley, "AT&T Plans to Buy More Cable TV Gear," *Wall Street Journal*, September 29, 1999. Cauley's story included the following: "The equipment purchases amount to a strong endorsement of the General Instrument–Motorola combination, which stands to advance consolidation in the cable-TV industry. AT&T has previously indicated it supported Motorola's plans to buy General Instrument. On the day the deal was announced, Leo Hindery, head of AT&T's cable and Internet unit, showed up at Motorola's press conference in Manhattan to make it clear that AT&T endorsed the move."
5. David Faber, *The Faber Report*, CNBC, October 6, 1999.

Chapter 9

1. Leslie Cauley, "AT&T Will Offer Hard-Core Adult Movies in Drive to Lure Digital Cable Subscribers," *Wall Street Journal*, May 31, 2000.
2. "Phone Sex," *Financial Times*, July 19, 2000.
3. Ibid.
4. Peter Drucker, *The New Realities* (New York: Harper and Row, 1989), p. 99.
5. "Alumni Facts, Feats, Phenomena," *Rutgers Magazine*, Summer 1993, p. 41.

Chapter 10

1. In October 2003, a federal appeals court reversed the FCC's decision not to regulate broadband access, sending the issue back for another round of rule making. By then, AT&T was out of the cable business.
2. "Cut the Telecom Tax Now," *Wall Street Journal*, February 2, 1999.
3. The Bell companies appealed the FCC's decision to delegate the setting of wholesale rates to the states and won. In March 2004, the U.S. Court of Appeals for the District of Columbia said that the FCC had delegated too much authority to the states. In June 2004, the FCC decided not to appeal the ruling and began drafting new rules after extracting a pledge from the Bell companies not to increase rates for a while.
4. Gene Kimmelman, codirector of Consumers Union's Washington office, was widely quoted praising the plan. This quote is taken from the Associated Press story filed by Kalpana Srinivasan on February 25, 2000.
5. Steve Labaton, "AT&T Move Means Millions Will Face Higher Phone Bill," *New York Times*, June 7, 2000.
6. From a presentation Hanson made to the annual meeting of the Arthur Page Society, in September 2003. Hanson is executive director of the Markula Center for Applied Ethics at Santa Clara University.
7. In January of 2004, after MCI and Sprint increased prices on many of their most popular calling plans, AT&T reimposed a

monthly charge of $3.95 on all its basic-rate customers. This time, the company sent postcards announcing the charge to all 10 million customers affected and also told them about calling plans that could lower their costs. The public reaction was relatively muted.

8. Allan Sloan, "Can't Anyone Here Play This Game?" *Newsweek,* June 19, 2000; "Wrong Number," editorial in the *Denver Post,* June 11, 2000; Cal Thomas, "AT&T Goes From Ma Bell to Call Girl," *Los Angeles Times* Syndicate, June 8, 2000.

Chapter 11

1. Leslie Cauley, Rebecca Blumenstein, and Stephanie Mehta, "AT&T Makes $54 Billion Bid for MediaOne," *The Wall Street Journal,* April 23, 1999. Ken McGee was quoted in the *Los Angeles Times* on April 23, 1999, in a story entitled "CEO's Vision Is to Be Much More Than Ma Bell." Paul Farhi, "AT&T: Too Big Again?" *The Washington Post,* April 27, 1999.

2. Brendan Intendola, "AT&T CEO Turns Bargaining Table Into Round Table," Reuters Business Report, May 6, 1999.

3. All the stories appeared on October 5, following an October 4 story in the *Wall Street Journal* reporting on rumors that AT&T's consumer unit might be spun off.

Chapter 12

1. From a motion filed by bondholders of AtHome Corporation in U.S. Bankruptcy Court, Northern District of California, San Francisco Division, Case No. 01-32495-TC (Chapter 11), October 2001.

2. Louis Lowenstein, "Corporate Governance and the Voice of the Paparazzi," Working Paper No. 131, The Center for Law and Economic Studies, February 22, 1999.

Chapter 13

1. Peter Elstrom, "Mike Armstrong's Strong Showing," *BusinessWeek,* January 25, 1999; Steve Rosenbush, "AT&T Can't Buy It's Way Out of This Mess," *BusinessWeek,* September 4, 2000.

2. Leslie Cauley, "John Malone's Prescription for AT&T: New Tracking Stock, Focus on Content," *Wall Street Journal,* July 12, 2000.

3. Ibid.

4. When the TCI acquisition closed, *Newsweek*'s Wall Street editor, Allan Sloan, had a lot of fun explaining how Malone arranged to give some of his TCI shares $170 million more value than other shareowners. "Pretty tacky," wrote Sloan. "I'm not saying any of this is illegal . . . I'm just saying it's not right." Allan Sloan, "John Malone's $170 Million Prize," *Washington Post,* June 30, 1998.

5. While the delay in announcing the size of the dividend cut was probably necessary, it reaffirmed a basic lesson: When you have bad news, get it all out at once. By announcing our intention to cut the dividend in October, but delaying the announcement of its actual size, 83 percent, until December, the board guaranteed that there would be two separate stories. If it had all been announced together—along with the larger restructuring story—the dividend cut would have been an interesting sidebar instead of another round of stories focusing on the depth of AT&T's failures.

6. From conversation with the author, April 18, 2004.

7. Rebecca Blumenstein and Peter Grant, "Former Chief Tries to Redeem the Calls He Made at AT&T," *Wall Street Journal,* May 26, 2004.

8. Schrage, "Daniel Kahneman: The Thought Leader Interview."

9. Seth Schisel, "AT&T in Pullback Will Break Itself Into 4 Businesses," *New York Times,* October 26, 2000; Allan Sloan, "AT&T's Magic Act," *Newsweek,* November 6, 2000. The ubiquitous Ken McGee did interviews on CNN, CNBC, and Bloomberg television and was quoted in many national newspapers.

10. C. Michael Armstrong, "Adapting to Change," speech to the San Francisco Chamber of Commerce, November 1, 2000.

11. Howard Anderson, "The Last Telecom Standing," *Wall Street Journal,* July 23, 2002.

Chapter 14

1. In one famous case, McGraw-Hill fended off a takeover attempt by American Express by suggesting that *BusinessWeek*'s editorial independence would be compromised were the publishing giant to become part of the financial services company. It was a risky gambit, but it worked. American Express walked away from the deal.

2. Brian Roberts told Noski that he couldn't go lower because he

wanted to retain the flexibility to do "one more big deal." In February 2004, Comcast made an unsolicited offer for Disney, which it withdrew in April 2004, when its own shareowners showed little enthusiasm for the deal and Disney's board strongly opposed it.

3. At the time, one might have constructed a reasonable argument that the more attractive long-term option for AT&T shareowners might be to stay the course and spin AT&T Broadband off as a separate company. J. P. Morgan had recently published a paper endorsing AT&T Broadband's telephony strategy, and Sanford Bernstein had recently completed research that showed a very high level of customer satisfaction among subscribers to its phone service. A new management team was making steady progress in improving margins and had filed suit against John Malone's Starz Encore pay-movie company to get out from under an onerous contract that alone accounted for several points of marginal costs. (Comcast eventually forced Starz Encore to revise the terms dramatically.) The company's cable upgrades were back on track after a period of neglect; in fact, when Comcast took over, it was surprised to find the physical plant in far better shape than it had anticipated. A November 2001 survey of AT&T's individual shareholders showed a dramatic shift in attitude; 55 percent, up from 24 percent, now believed that they would benefit more from a spin-off of AT&T Broadband than from a sale. An early December assessment of institutional investors showed views shifting toward going it alone, whereas a solid majority had wanted the unit to be sold just a month earlier. However, in the end, the board judged the risks to the rest of the company if the spin-off of AT&T Broadband somehow failed or was seriously delayed to be too great.

4. "A Rocky Road for AT&T," editorial, *New York Times*, July 16, 2001.

5. Clark Judge, "Management Journal: PR Lessons from the Pentagon," *Wall Street Journal*, April 1, 2003.

Chapter 15

1. Steve Rosenbush, "AT&T and BellSouth Talk Merger," *BusinessWeek*, October 6, 2001.

2. Serious merger discussions between AT&T and BellSouth reportedly began again in mid-2003 and continued until they eventually cratered in the fall over valuation and "social issues," i.e., Bell-

South refused to make a firm commitment that Dorman would
succeed Ackerman as CEO.

3. James Collins and Jerry Porras, *Built to Last: Successful Habits of Visionary Companies* (New York: Harper Business, 1994).

4. Stephanie Mehta, "WorldCom's Bad Trip," *Fortune*, February 19, 2002.

5. In mid-2003, AT&T discovered that two low-level managers had manipulated the company's accounting for access charges to cover up earlier errors that they had made. Both managers and their supervisors, who should have noticed the charges, were fired. The impact on the company's financial results was less than a penny a share.

6. Adam Quinton, Merrill Lynch & Co., quoted by Edward Teah in "Deconstructing AT&T," *CFO Magazine*, July 2002.

Chapter 16

1. Seth Schisel, "The AT&T Chief's Report Card," *New York Times*, December 22, 2001.

2. There is only one book-length biography of Vail. *In One Man's Life* was written by a contemporary, Albert Bigelow Paine, and offers little insight into Vail's business philosophy. John Brooks's *Telephone: The First Hundred Years* (New York: Harper and Row, 1975) has several very informative chapters on Vail's business philosophy. See, for example, pp. 131–132 and 143–144.

3. J. Edward Hyde, *The Phone Book: What the Telephone Company Would Rather You Not Know*, (Chicago: Henry Regency, 1976), p. 23.

4. Brooks, *Telephone*, p. 154.

5. Charles Handy, *The Age of Paradox* (Cambridge, Mass.: Harvard Business School Press, 1994), p. 159.

6. Louis Lowenstein, "Corporate Governance and the Voice of the Paparazzi," Working Paper No. 131, The Center for Law and Economic Studies, Columbia University, February 22, 1999.

7. Arthur W. Page, *The Bell Telephone System* (New York: Harper & Brothers, 1941), p. 154.

8. William Blackstone, *Blackstone's Commentaries on the Laws of England* (Oxford: Clarendon Press, 1765), vol. 1, p. 455.

9. Alvin Von Auw, *Heritage and Destiny: Reflections on the Bell System in Transition* (New York: Praeger, 1983), p. 395.

10. Ibid.

Index